BUSINESS GUIDE TO COMPETITION LAW

BUSINESS GUIDE TO COMPETITION LAW
The Essential Facts

Cameron Markby Hewitt

John Wiley & Sons
Chichester, New York, Brisbane, Toronto, Singapore

Published in the United Kingdom in 1995 by
Chancery Law Publishing Ltd
Baffins Lane
Chichester
West Sussex PO19 1UD

National (01243) 779777
International (+44) 1243 779777

Published in North America by
Wiley Law Publications
7222 Commerce Center Drive
Colorado Springs
CO 80919 USA

International (+1) 719 548 1900

Typeset in 11/13 pt Times by York House Typographic Ltd, London
Printed and bound in Great Britain by Biddles ltd. Guildford and King's Lynn

ISBN 0 471 95704 6

British Library Cataloguing Data

A copy of the CIP entry for this book is available from the British Library.

CONTENTS

PREFACE

The competition law of the EC and its Member States can be complex and confusing. It is easy for businessmen to become frustrated when they find their freedom of action restricted by the rules. Too much time can be spent getting to grips with the system, finding out how the different laws work and interrelate, how the regulators operate and what information they may require. Business people sometimes feel that the available textbooks are too full of legislative minutiae, detailed case law and jargon to be really useful to them.

We have found that clients faced with competition problems often appreciate a practical layman's guide. This was the idea behind our book.

We have concentrated on the competition law procedures which most commonly affect businesses. *Business Guide to Competition Law* highlights the circumstances in which the authorities will be interested in your distribution, licensing, joint venture or merger plans, when they will look closely at your discussions with competitors, what information they will want and the procedures they will follow. Our aim has been to give concrete examples and to provide checklists and flow charts to illustrate how the regulations operate. We consider the EC rules and those of the European Economic Area, move on to the very different UK domestic law, and conclude with a brief look at the systems in France and Germany.

Business Guide to Competition Law has been written by members of the European and Competition Law Group, and the French Law team at Cameron Markby Hewitt. We are grateful to Dr Karl-Maria Walter of Schurmann and Partners in Frankfurt for the chapter on the domestic rules in Germany. Our thanks are also due to Alison Bradford, Monica Townsend and Hideo Takigawa for their help. The preparation of the text has been cheerfully carried out by Martine Descy.

We have endeavoured to state the law at 1 January 1995.

Susan Hankey, Nick Paul, Elisabeth Ruiz,
Cameron Markby Hewitt,
London and Brussels

CONTENTS OF CHAPTER 1

European
Community Law

1. EUROPEAN COMMUNITY LAW

Introduction

The law

Articles 85 and 86 of the Treaty of Rome control at Community level anti-competitive practices such as agreements which restrict or distort competition (Article 85) and the abuse of a dominant position (Article 86).

Certain other Articles of the Treaty, such as competition in the public sector (Article 90) and provisions dealing with the anti-competitive effects of "dumping" and state aid, are also relevant to competition law. Both of these may impact on a business but their separate systems and procedures are outside the scope of this book. There is various "delegated legislation" in the form of European Commission regulations, for example the series of block exemptions for typical types of agreement, as well as important guidance notices.

One of the most important developments of recent years was the adoption of the Merger Regulation (Council Regulation 4064/89) which, very broadly speaking, introduced "one-stop shopping" for the control of large mergers, regulated by the European Commission and not by the national authorities.

The provisions of EC competition law are directly applicable in Member States and are invoked by both plaintiffs and defendants before national courts and the European Court of First Instance (CFI) as well as being enforced by the Commission itself. The European Court of Justice (ECJ) hears appeals from decisions of the Commission and the CFI and decides points of law referred to it by domestic courts. The Courts' decisions are important in determining the application of the relevant Articles of the Treaty which are themselves expressed in very general terms.

Annex 1 explains the functions of these various bodies, the types of legislation and terminology. In this book we refer to EC competition law and reserve the term EU for the Member States. The texts of Articles 85 and 86 are at Annex 2.

For the conversion of ECU into £ sterling we have adopted the figure of ECU 1 = £0.79 (marginally above the rate for January 1995).

What sort of agreements are caught by EC law?

The answer is practically any sort of commercial agreement of reasonable size. For example, a company structure might resemble that shown on the following page, or at least incorporate some of these elements:

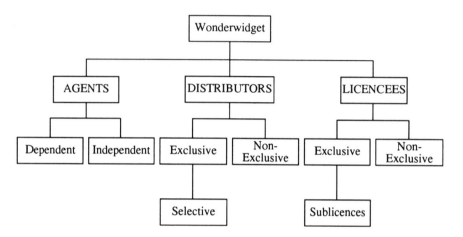

Competition law questions arise in relation to all these elements. They may also be relevant to the formation of Wonderwidget itself.

The role of the national courts

Articles 85 and 86 have direct effect in all Member States; they grant rights to, and impose obligations on, Community residents. The national courts are responsible for the application of Articles 85 and 86 in the domestic forum. The Commission, which has been overrun with notifications and complaints, announced that it now concerns itself only with matters which have particular political, economic or legal significance for the Community. Complaints received by the Commission (see below) must receive a response, but that response may often be an indication that the complainant should address his complaint to his national court. Guidance notes to this effect were published in February 1993.

In theory at least, complaints about breaches of Articles 85 and 86 should therefore generally be handled by national courts, which can award damages (not available from the Commission) and act more quickly than the Commission to adopt interim measures and end infringements. National courts are not, however, empowered to make decisions under Article 85(3), so applications/notifications for negative clearance/individual exemption must still be made to the Commission, where they will as a rule be dealt with by way of comfort letter. (See 32 below.)

Complaints

Undertakings which have a "legitimate interest" may request the Commission to initiate a procedure to establish the existence of an infringement of Articles 85 or 86 (and/or Articles 53 or 54 of the European Economic Area Agreement). Thus a company which believes it is being damaged by the restrictive practices of other companies or by the abuse by another company of its dominant position, may make a formal complaint on Form C. This form requires details of the alleged infringement and the ground on which the complainant claims his interest, together with documentary evidence and names of persons, especially those affected by the alleged infringement, able to testify to the facts.

Complaints relating to transport must be made on separate Forms.

The Commission is obliged to consider the complaint, but may, in cases which do not have particular political, economic or legal significance for the Community, tell the complainant that he would be better served in his national court.

Enforcement by the Commission

If a complaint is made to the European Commission, then infringements are punishable by fines. Fines may be imposed:

(i) to punish a breach of EC competition rules

(ii) in connection with notification and discovery procedures (for example, for the supply of misleading information)

There is no tariff of fines, but there are lower and upper limits.

The lower limit is ECU 1,000 (approximately £790). The upper limit is ECU 1m (approximately £790,000) *or* up to 10% of the turnover in the preceding year of each of the undertakings participating in the infringement. Where the rules talk about the "undertakings" here, they mean not just the subsidiary company which was involved in the guilty agreement, but the whole of the group to which that company belongs.

National competition authorities

In some Member States of the EU, Article 85/86 competition cases are taken to specific competition authorities. In the United Kingdom, the Office of Fair Trading does not have any jurisdiction as regards Articles 85 and 86 and cases are taken straight to the national courts. The case law is not yet very well developed, but, following the European Commission's decision in February 1993 that most routine breaches of the competition rules must be dealt with at the local level, the United Kingdom can expect a growth in case law. The UK courts can grant an injunction – to prevent or stop a breach of Articles 85 or 86 – or award damages.

Commission investigations

The European Commission's officials can carry out investigations with or without prior notice to undertakings involved – they may telephone in advance or carry out an unannounced dawn raid; they may be on their own or with Member State competition authority officials. In some circumstances, fines will be imposed for refusal to submit to an investigation, and certainly for intentional or negligent failure to produce the requested materials.

There is legal professional privilege for lawyer/client communications that have been made for the purpose and in the interest of the client's right of defence, and that either come into existence after the proceedings have started or were made earlier but have a relationship to the subject matter of these particular proceedings. Everything else will be open to inspection.

An individual can refuse to answer Commission questions in a competition case if to answer would incriminate him and his company, but a November 1993 judgment of the ECJ states that this rule does not apply in civil cases in domestic courts. In national courts, national law defines the extent of the rules necessary to the rights of defence and these do not have to be the same as at EU level.

Transactions outside Europe

Companies outside the EU can be caught by the competition rules. Parent companies located outside the Community have been held responsible for the anti-competitive conduct of their subsidiaries located inside the EU. This is sometimes called the "economic unity theory" and can involve the whole of a group in violation and fines. Companies which have no permanent EU presence at all can also be caught; the decisive factor is where their agreements are implemented or have their effect, rather than the place where they are made.

Thus if third country undertakings agree to apply a common pricing policy within the single market, whether they have subsidiaries or branch offices within the EU is irrelevant. Their actions have an effect on supplies of goods in the EU. Nor does it matter where the contract is signed. An arrangement made between a Japanese and an American businessman sitting side by side in a plane over India may affect the way their respective companies distribute goods in the EU.

Similar principles apply to the European Economic Area (EEA) (see Chapter 4).

Other chapters to read

The competition system of the EEA: Chapter 4.

How to enforce your EC rights in commercial disputes – practical hints on whether to take an action to the European Commission or your national court: Chapter 3.

What the national authorities can do:

– France:	Chapter 6
– Germany:	Chapter 7
– UK:	Chapter 5

Article 85

Article 85 regulates business agreements and arrangements which may be anti-competitive and affect trade at EU level.

The prohibition

Article 85 contains a blanket prohibition on:

- agreements, arrangements, concerted practices
- between undertakings
- which may affect trade between Member States.
- which have as their object or effect the prevention, restriction or distortion of competition within the common market, and in particular where they
    - directly or indirectly fix purchase or selling prices or any other trading conditions
    - limit or control production, markets, technical development or investment
    - share markets or sources of supply
    - apply dissimilar conditions to equivalent transactions with other trading parties, thereby placing them at a competitive disadvantage
    - make the conclusion of contracts subject to tie-in of supplementary obligations unconnected with the subject matter of the contract.

The text of Article 85 is at Annex 2.

Article 85(2) states that any agreement prohibited pursuant to Article 85(1) is automatically void.

Article 85(2) has both prospective and retroactive effect. It is clear, however, that it is not the whole agreement which is automatically void, but only those clauses which infringe Article 85(1). The whole agreement becomes void only if the offending clauses cannot be separated from the contract.

The question of severability is determined by the national court dealing with the dispute by reference to the law applicable to the contract. This will usually be the law chosen by the parties and in the absence of express choice the judge will look at the Rome Convention or the law applicable to contractual obligations.

Agreements which may not be prohibited

Some agreements which are caught by the prohibitions in Article 85(1) may in fact be assumed to be harmless because the parties and their market shares are simply too small to have any real effect on trade between Member States and on competition. Such agreements may be of "minor importance" – see below.

Further, the prohibitions in Article 85(1) may be inapplicable because the agreement in question qualifies for exemption under the criteria in Article 85(3). In some cases such exemptions are automatic because the agreement in question falls within one of the "block exemption" regulations. In other cases, an individual application to the Commission will be necessary. These steps are explained below.

Article 85

- Article 85(1) prohibits agreements

    - which may affect trade between Member States and

    - which prevent, restrict or distort competition within the Common Market

- Article 85(2) makes such agreements void

- Article 85(3) can clear agreements which

    - improve production/distribution or promote technical/economic progress, and

    - give consumers a fair share, and

    - contain only indispensable restrictions, and

    - do not lead to substantial elimination of competition

- Only the Commission can give individual 85(3) clearance

- Automatic clearance under block exemptions

Definitions

An undertaking

The concept of an "undertaking" is a European one, and is designed to mean an "economic operator", or "any entity engaged in economic or commercial activities". This is difficult to define precisely. The undertaking could be involved in production or manufacture, distribution or sales agency, retail or wholesale exchange of goods and services. It could be an individual with a newly developed invention or patent, but also extends to multi-national companies. It is irrelevant whether the undertaking is privately or publicly owned, civil or commercial.

An undertaking comprises everything in the same economic unit; thus the undertaking ICI includes both the main company and all subsidiaries under its control. Control is determined on a *de facto* basis. The group would be counted as one undertaking. It is important to remember this because undertakings in breach of Articles 85 or 86 are susceptible to fines of up to 10% of their whole worldwide turnover.

Article 85 does not apply to intra-group relationships (parent/subsidiary) unless the subsidiary can be shown in practice to act independently, which would be unusual.

An agreement

It is important to understand that in following the Community's policy of promoting inter-Member State trade, an "agreement" is defined very widely and encompasses not only the documentation for a sophisticated joint venture but also agreements reached in an exchange of correspondence, an unminuted meeting, or a confirmatory fax or letter.

Decisions by associations of undertakings

An association of undertakings may be a trade association, a federation or syndicate. For instance, a trade association representing producers, distillers and dealers in Armagnac and the group of banks belonging to the Eurocheque System have each been considered an association of undertakings.

Concerted practices

A concerted practice is an informal co-operation between under-takings which replaces their independent action on the market. This co-operation is achieved through direct or indirect contact, *e.g.* a "meeting of minds" will suffice.

So undertakings may be caught by Article 85 even though their action leaves no trace of a written agreement.

For instance, there may be a concerted practice:

(i) where producers co-operate with their competitors, in any man-ner whatsoever, in order to arrive at a co-ordinated line of action for a price increase;

(ii) where a producer and its distributors informally agree that none of the distributors will sell the producer's goods outside his given territory (even though this ban on parallel imports is not em-bodied in any form of agreement); or

(iii) where banks co-operate and co-ordinate their efforts to apply a uniform charge to money transfers by banks located in different Member States.

A concerted practice may have the effect of producing cartels between a number of economic producers or suppliers. A cartel is evidently in operation where companies formally set up a discussion group which has no other object than a desire to control pricing. But what about the consequences which arise as a result of there being only a small number of suppliers in the market who, without any formal agreement, may act "as if" there were a cartel merely by responding quickly to any market changes caused by acts of their competitors? A real response to market forces is not a concerted practice. But any hint of a formal, or indeed informal, deliberate arrangement between undertakings in a market would call for in-vestigation under Article 85.

Does the agreement distort, restrict or prevent competition?

An agreement may be caught by Article 85 if either its *effect* or *object* (or both) result in a change to the market.

There is no need to show intent. Actual or potential effect is considered. It is not necessary to offer proof that an agreement has in fact affected trade; it is sufficient to show that the concerted action is capable of having a restrictive effect.

Examples of practices caught by Article 85

Practices which can lead to trouble under Article 85(1)

- Price fixing
- Bid rigging
- Market sharing
- Limitation on control of production
- Information exchanges
- "English clauses"
- Technical development limitations
- Joint selling/joint purchasing
- Boycotts
- Resale price maintenance
- Tie-ins
- Requirements contracts

Price fixing

Article 85 expressly forbids agreements which directly or indirectly fix purchase or selling prices or any other trading conditions.

The following would therefore be caught:

- a straightforward agreement between suppliers to set prices;
- simultaneous and uniform price increases made by competing suppliers;
- agreements on particular elements of a pricing strategy, for example rebates, discounts, margins;
- agreements on recommended prices (although the individual re-commending of a price by a supplier to his own distributors is not caught by Article 85 unless the supplier uses duress to ensure the distributor sticks to that recommendation);

- agreement on prices set by a trade association;

- price agreements on imports into or exports out of the EU insofar as they affect trade within the common market; and

- collective resale price maintenance.

The concepts relevant to price fixing are also relevant to the fixing of any other trading conditions, such as the terms on which goods are supplied or the types of customers to whom they may be sold.

Bid rigging

Agreements or schemes to allocate successful bids among competitors, for example by agreements to refrain from bidding for particular contracts so that a competitor will get "his turn", would amount to the sharing out or control of markets or sources of supply.

Market sharing

It will be seen that Article 85 explicitly forbids agreements which would allocate business among competitors on either a geographical or a customer basis, through distribution or licensing or other arrangements. Markets can be divided by (*inter alia*):

- class of customer;

- geographical region;

- manipulation of intellectual property rights for territorial reasons; or

- quota setting.

Such divisions need not be between inter-brand competitors, but may also result from vertical arrangements.

Limitation or control of production

Agreements which:

- limit total output;

- restrict investment levels;

- set production or sales quotas; or

- prevent some parties from manufacturing certain products

will often form part of a more complex arrangement which has as its aim or effect the sharing of markets or fixing of prices.

Exchange of information

Companies should be careful about swapping price or other commercially sensitive information since this can lead to co-ordination of pricing policies contrary to Article 85(1). The European Commission has clearly stated that "it is contrary to the provisions of Article 85(1) ... for a producer to communicate to its competitors the essential elements of his pricing policy, such as price lists, the discounts and terms of trade he applies, the rates and dates of any change to them and the special exceptions he grants to specific customers".

English clauses

Another aspect which causes difficulties in this area is the "English clause". This is where the supplier says that if the purchaser can show that he has been offered better terms by a third party, then the supplier will meet those terms, failing which the purchaser is free to go and get his supplies elsewhere. The Commission's view is that this is an objectionable practice, not because of its effect on exclusivity, but because it allows competitors access to each others' pricing policy information and other commercial terms. So price fixing/market sharing might result.

Technical development limitations

Agreements between potential competitors to use only a particular type of technology or technical standards may, in some circumstances, benefit the end user in that he has a greater choice of compatible products, but generally this will be overridden by the fact that no competing technologies can develop.

The use of only agreed standards will also be restrictive of competition if it prevents imports reaching a market or divides the market geographically or by customer.

Joint selling/joint purchasing

Agreements between groups of suppliers to deal exclusively through certain approved dealers, agreements on prices or methods of purchase to be observed by groups of competitors, and operating a joint sales subsidiary or agency through which all sales in a particular jurisdiction are carried out, may each be contrary to Article 85. The underlying question would be whether the ability of each competitor or potential competitor to act independently *vis-à-vis* third parties had been removed.

Boycotts

Collective use of blacklisting – refusal to sell to particular customers or to buy from particular suppliers – can be a serious offence. There is not much reported EC case law on this point, but the Commission has found a boycott organised by a trade association under an agreement between competing suppliers to be "a particularly severe violation of the rules of competition, since its aim was to eliminate a troublesome competitor".

Resale prices

Collective and individual resale price maintenance agreements are generally contrary to the competition rules. If a supplier introduces minimum resale prices into his distribution agreement, the reseller may regard these as an indication of what the supplier would like ("recommended resale prices") but can in fact ignore them. Distributors must be free to set their own prices according to their own reading of the market. Attempts by the supplier to enforce his r.r.p. will be contrary to Article 85. In addition, such practices are often contrary to national law. (See Chapter 5 for UK law on resale prices.)

Tying in

An arrangement where the supply of one type of goods is "tied" to the supply of another which is not in a related field, will generally get you into trouble. Withholding supplies or refusing to enter into an agreement unless the customer takes additional goods of a different genre restrict that customer's freedom to obtain what he wants where he wants. This may be contrary to Article 85 (*e.g.* it would prevent your being able to take advantage of the "block exemption" for standard exclusive purchasing agreements – see page 23) but it will be especially vilified if the supplier is in a dominant position in his market.

Requirements contracts

The European Commission has often objected to long-term industrial supply agreements where the purchaser must agree to take the whole of his requirements from one source. Again, this can be especially difficult where the purchaser or supplier (or both) is/are in a position of strength on their market. An alternative may be to set fixed quantity requirements, but not if these are agreed so as effectively to equal all or a very high proportion of the purchaser's requirements over the period. The Commission takes the view that a long-term all-requirements contract freezes the relationship with potential suppliers, and the role of offer and demand is eliminated to the disadvantage of new competitors, who cannot get near this customer, and old competitors who, in the meantime, may have become more competitive than the actual supplier.

Agreements of "minor importance"

Arrangements only come within the scope of Article 85 if their effect on competition and on inter-state trade is appreciable.

The *de minimis* argument was established in a case about washing-machines, where the amount of trade between the two Member States (in this case 800 machines) was so small in relation to the market that it was not considered to affect trade between the two countries.

The Commission has issued a "Notice concerning Agreements of Minor Importance" which sets out some guidelines on what is meant by "appreciable effect". This notice is not binding on the courts and the thresholds are only a guide.

Broadly speaking, the Commission takes the view that an agreement will not have an appreciable effect unless:

- the aggregate turnover of all participating undertakings is more than ECU 300m (currently about £237m); *and*
- the goods or services which are the subject of the agreement, together with the participating undertakings' other goods or services which are considered by users to be equivalent, in view of their characteristics, price and intended use, do not represent more than 5% of the total market for such goods or services in the area of the common market affected by the agreement.

The phrase "participating undertakings" includes not only the companies which sign any agreement, but also the whole of any groups to which they may belong.

So the parties involved have to be comfortably below *both* thresholds to be sure that Article 85 does not apply.

How the minor importance guidelines work

XCo, a subsidiary of XYZ Ltd (the XYZ Group), makes garden gnomes. It enters into an exclusive licensing agreement with ABC (a small private company) so that ABC can make the gnomes and sell them in a particular geographical area. Is the agreement *de minimis*? Both tests must be passed.

The turnover test

- ABC annual turnover   ECU 3m

- XCo annual turnover   ECU 15m

    But XCo is a member of the XYZ Group, so the turnover of the whole group must be taken into account.

- XYZ Group consolidated annual turnover   ECU 175m

- Turnover of all participating undertakings   ECU 178m

    The parties are under the turnover threshold. To benefit from the *de minimis* guidelines, they must *also* be under the market share threshold.

The market share test

What are the products concerned? They include garden gnomes and any other product made by the companies which consumers would regard as equivalent in purpose and price. This is very often a difficult question. In this case, the parties also make garden furniture (not substitutable for gnomes), bird-tables and bird-baths (considered to have a different purpose, not just decoration), and small stone garden ornaments, mainly animals (considered substitutable for gnomes). The companies decide that the relevant product is small garden ornaments including gnomes.

How the minor importance guidelines work (*continued*)

- What geographical area is concerned? This will be the area of the common market "affected by the agreement", that is, in which the companies make and sell the gnomes and ornaments. ABC will make and sell the products in the Netherlands. XCo and other XYZ Group companies make and sell the products throughout the UK and in Belgium and Germany.

- The companies estimate their market shares as:

UK	12%
Germany	7%
Belgium	4%
Netherlands	new market

The 5% guideline is exceeded.

Is the agreement of minor importance?

The companies' combined turnover is under ECU 300m *but* their market share is over 5%. The agreement cannot be considered to be of minor importance. An Article 85 analysis must be carried out.

Parallel trading

Where a distributor or a licensee has sole occupation, as it were, of a particular territory, then it is possible for him to act in an anti-competitive manner, for instance by charging higher prices than he would be able to if there were half a dozen distributors competing in that territory. A distributor may enjoy absolute territorial protection where the contractual restraints on the supplier and other distributors prevent anyone else selling into his territory. He is then said to be protected from "parallel imports".

Parallel imports are generally those bought in a low priced area of the Community and exported to higher priced areas, where they can be sold at reasonably low prices, thus preventing traders in the higher priced areas maintaining excessively high prices. The concept of parallel trading thus reflects the principle that the free movement of goods throughout the Community should ensure that significant differences in prices in different areas of the market cannot be maintained. Ideally, prices should settle down at broadly similar levels throughout the Community. It has to be said, however, that this is a counsel of perfection which depends on effective competition also being maintained.

Active and passive sales

It is important to make a distinction between "active" and "passive" sales. Active selling is where, for example, a distributor or licensee in one territory sets out to market products outside his territory, advertising or distributing into other territories. Passive selling, on the other hand, is where a distributor simply fulfils unsolicited orders from users or resellers from outside his territory.

A distribution agreement, for example, may grant exclusivity to the distributor in the contractual territory. The distributor will need to concentrate on sales in his territory and will generally be banned from actively seeking customers outside his territory. Reciprocally he will be protected from active sales in his territory by other distributors appointed in other territories. The distributor, however, cannot be prohibited from selling to customers based outside his territory who place unsolicited orders. In addition, he cannot stop distributors appointed in other territories from selling to his customers based in his territory who place unsolicited orders with them. Exclusivity cannot, therefore, amount to absolute territorial protection and must leave scope for parallel trading or parallel imports.

The relationship between Article 85 and industrial property rights

Patents and other industrial property rights are commonly used to assert "ownership" of, for example, a new design or technical innovation. Other parties are thereby restrained from taking advantage of such innovations without the consent of the patent holder. The

ECJ has distinguished the existence or ownership of such a right under national law (which is not in principle affected by EC law) from its exercise (which may be).

Owners of intellectual property rights are restrained in their exploitation of such rights by the operation of Article 30, which prohibits not only quantitative restrictions on imports but also all measures having "equivalent effect". The potential justification for restrictions on grounds of the protection of industrial and commercial property in Article 36 has been narrowly construed. Thus, as a general rule under Articles 30–36, ownership of a right confers the power to exploit the intellectual property, for example to manufacture and sell a product and to prevent unauthorised use of the right, but those rights cannot be exercised to prevent or restrict parallel imports.

Articles 30–36 are addressed to Member States. Articles 85 and 86, on the other hand, apply to undertakings where a concerted practice or a dominant position can be identified. The correlation between these two sets of rules can be complicated. The Commission's analysis of the potential effects of the exercise of intellectual property rights on competition is reflected in the drafting of the various block exemption regulations governing intellectual property licences.

Analysing the application of Article 85(1)

There are three distinct elements in analysing the application of Article 85(1).

(i) Does the agreement have an anti-competitive effect?
    First, one has to consider whether the agreement will have, or is intended to have, an anti-competitive effect. This will depend on whether it affects competition between the parties or restricts their freedom of action in dealing with customers or suppliers. This can involve market collusion, as well as expressly restrictive agreements, such as standardised contract terms, and exchanges of market information.

(ii) Will the arrangements affect trade between Member States?
    Second, there is the question of whether the agreement is

capable of having a direct, or indirect, effect on trade between Member States. If not, EC competition law will not apply. The question here is whether the arrangement will cause the pattern of trade within the Community to change. Both the Commission and the ECJ have given increasingly wide definitions to the concept of what constitutes an effect on trade between Member States. It does not have to be a prejudicial effect. It may be actual or potential, related to future patterns of trade. Article 85 can apply to an agreement between parties in the same Member State which only concerns business in that State. For instance, exclusive distribution agreements may make it more difficult for undertakings in other Member States to find an outlet for their products, or one of the parties may be a branch or subsidiary of a company in another Member State whose position may be affected by the agreement.

Partitioning the market through distribution arrangements which give the distributor complete territorial insulation is an obvious culprit. But what about a joint venture between three companies to design and develop new apparatus? This might affect trade because, if they had not entered into the agreement, the companies might each have developed new apparatus independently and marketed it across the Community. The consumer would have had three choices instead of one. So one has to look beyond the terms of the agreement and ask what the consequences might be. What competition is there now and what will there be after this agreement is implemented?

(iii) Is the effect appreciable?

Finally the effect on competition and inter-state trade must be "appreciable", so agreements between small and medium sized enterprises with a combined market share of less than 5% may fall outside the scope of Article 85(1) in accordance with the principles set out in the Commission's 1986 Notice on Agreements of Minor Importance (see above).

If the agreement appears to be caught by Article 85 (1) and the companies' turnover and/or market shares are too great for the arrangement to be of minor importance, an exemption from the prohibition might still be available.

Six questions vital for the application of Article 85

- Is there an agreement or concerted practice?

YES   NO
                             Stop here

- Could it restrict, distort or prevent competition?

YES   NO
                             Stop here

- Could it affect trade between EC countries?

YES   NO
                             Stop here

- Is it of minor importance as regards turnover *and* market shares?

YES   NO
Stop here

- Is there a block exemption available?

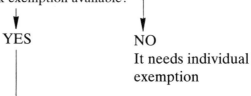

YES   NO
                             It needs individual
                             exemption

- Can you bring your agreement within the block exemption?

YES   NO
Use it

- It needs individual exemption

Exemptions

There are two ways in which an agreement may be exempted from the provisions of Article 85(1):

(i) under the terms of a "block exemption"; or

(ii) by individual notification to the Commission.

An exemption (either individual or block) does not mean that the agreement falls outside Article 85(1); rather, it *does* fall within Article 85(1) but is exempt for the reasons in Article 85(3).

Individual applications by way of Form A/B are considered below under "Notifications to the European Commission" (see page 28).

The aim of block exemptions is primarily to ease the burden on the Commission by removing the need to file individual notifications. Where suppliers and dealers can bring their agreements exactly within the terms of the relevant block exemption regulation, the Commission considers that the agreement is acceptable and does not need to be individually notified.

Block exemptions have been granted for agreements which satisfy the detailed requirements of the relevant regulation. There are block exemptions relating, for example, to:

(i)   exclusive purchase agreements;

(ii)   exclusive distribution agreements;

(iii)   motor vehicle distribution agreements;

(iv)   specialisation agreements;

(v)   research and development agreements;

(vi)   franchise agreements;

(vii)   know-how licensing agreements;

(viii) patent licence agreements; and

(ix)   certain types of insurance agreement.

A new block exemption on technology transfers was originally intended to come into force on 1 January 1995. It will replace the existing patent licence and know-how regulations with a more flexible category of exemption. It is now expected to come into force on 1 July 1995.

How a block exemption works

The workings of the block exemption regulations can be demonstrated through the example of exclusive distribution agreements. These have since 1983 been subject to Regulation 1983/83.

The Commission's view is that exclusive distribution agreements lead in general to an improvement in distribution, facilitate marketing, help new manufacturers enter and compete in a market and generally result in benefit to the consumer. The regulation contains a "white list" of acceptable clauses and a "black list" of prohibited terms. The inclusion in an agreement of any blacklisted terms means that it cannot benefit from the block exemption. The Commission has in addition the power to withdraw the benefit of exemption where it finds that any agreement satisfies the requirements of the regulation but is nonetheless incompatible with Article 85(1). The regulation cannot apply if the agreement is between competing manufacturers. The major factor when considering whether exclusive distribution agreements are exempted under the regulation is that the agreement must not try to create complete marketing insulation for such products. In particular, there must be a "parallel" route by which another trader can import contract goods into the contract territory, otherwise the block exemption will not be applicable.

How the Exclusive Distribution Block Exemption works

The regulation applies to agreements between only two parties

- where A appoints B as his only distributor for his goods within the whole or a defined area of the common market; and

- where no restrictions on competition are imposed on A other than the obligation not to supply the contract goods to users in the contract territory; and

- where no restrictions on competition are imposed on B other than obligations

  (i) not to manufacture or distribute goods which compete with the contract goods

  (ii) to obtain the contract goods for resale only from A

(iii)to refrain, outside the agreed territory and in relation to the contract goods, from seeking customers, from establishing any branch and from maintaining any distribution depot.

The supplier may require the distributor to take the complete range of goods or minimum quantities, to use specified trade marks or packaging, to advertise, provide customer and guarantee services and employ specialised staff or otherwise promote the product.

No other restrictions on competition may be imposed on either supplier or distributor.

Distributor restrictions which fit in the block exemption

Yes it will fit	*No it will not fit*
Contains non-compete clause	Specifies resale prices
Bans active sales outside territory	Bans passive sales outside territory
Specifies minimum quantities	Contains export bans
Requires an after sales guarantee	Places customer restrictions
Specifies staff should be well trained	

The benefits of the regulation can be withdrawn if the agreement has the effect of restricting parallel imports, or where the distributor refuses to supply certain categories of customer without good reason, or if the prices charged by him are excessive.

Where agreements do not comply with a block exemption regulation, the Commission has power to grant individual exemptions (see page 28). It is always helpful to draft agreements as close as possible to block exemption requirements.

Exclusive purchasing agreements

There is a block exemption for exclusive purchasing agreements (Regulation 1994/83) which runs in parallel with the exclusive distribution agreements regulation.

Exclusive purchasing agreements provide for one party (the re-seller) to purchase certain goods for resale only from the supplier. Such agreements can clearly be anti-competitive, particularly where a supplier has succeeded in "tying in" a large number of sales outlets in a given area. In such circumstances other undertakings may find it very difficult to find an outlet for competing goods. The longer the duration of such exclusive purchasing agreements, and the wider the range of products involved, the more serious is the barrier to market entry for competitors.

The exclusive purchasing regulation is very similar to the regula-tion covering exclusive distribution agreements in that it exempts only two party agreements and that the permitted restrictions are the same. However, unlike the exemption for exclusive distribution agreements, the reseller is not allotted an exclusive territory.

To take advantage of the regulation the exclusive purchasing agreement must be limited to five years (this period is renewable) and the range of products covered by the agreement must be limited. The reseller can be prohibited from manufacturing or distributing competing goods. The reseller may also be required to purchase complete ranges or minimum quantities of goods, to sell goods under trade mark or packaged in a certain way, and to take steps to promote the product.

The only obligation which may be placed on the supplier is not to distribute the contract goods or competing goods in the reseller's principal sales area.

Agency contracts

Agent or distributor, what is the difference?

- An agent has the authority to negotiate and possibly to conclude sales or purchases on behalf of the principal. He is usually paid by way of commissions on his sales. Unlike a distributor, an agent does not buy the goods from the supplier to resell them.

- The distributor buys the goods to resell them at his own risk.

The choice is a purely commercial decision. The descriptions used in the agreement are not important; what counts is the substance of the relationship.

EC rules on agents

An EC Directive adopted in 1986 (which has been extended to the EEA countries) has harmonised the contractual rules applicable to commercial agency agreements relating to sales of goods. That Directive has left some options to Member States, for instance in relation to the compensation/indemnity to be given to the agents upon termination of the contract. The choice of law applicable to the contract is still an issue.

Competition law is not covered by the Directive – the normal rules apply.

An agency contract may be an exclusive agency contract. It may also contain other restrictions such as a non-compete clause or a ban on active sales outside the agent's territory. Such a ban means that the agent would not be able to advertise or solicit customers outside his territory.

Does Article 85 apply to agency contracts?

Is Article 85 applicable to agency contracts? This is not an easy issue. Article 85 only applies to agreements between two independent undertakings. This will therefore depend on which type of agent a company chooses. The current case law and the Commission's Notice of 1962 on Commercial Agents makes a broad distinction between independent agents and dependent agents. The Commission has been trying for years and so far without success to review its 1962 Notice. This shows one thing: having an agent is not always the easy solution.

Independent agents

An independent agent is an agent who is required to keep a substantial stock of products at his own risk and who is often required to organise a substantial service to the customers free of charge. He will be able to fix prices or conditions of sales and so forth at his own discretion. Such an agent will be regarded as an independent undertaking and therefore the contract with him may fall within the scope of Article 85.

Dependent agents

An agent who is entirely dependent on a particular company is in a different situation: he will generally not be required to hold any stock nor accept any financial liability. A contract with this agent will not be covered by Article 85. However, when dealing with "dependent agents" companies must still look at the relevant national rules on competition which may limit the sort of clauses and restrictions which they want to put into the agency contract.

Notification of agreements to the European Commission for individual exemption

Many commercial agreements contain restrictions on the parties which will, to a greater or lesser extent, affect competition. Some of these agreements will be acceptable, indeed desirable, from the overall economic point of view, but not of the sort which fall easily into block exemption formats.

For example, whereas an exclusive distribution agreement will often fit into the block exemption, other forms of distribution arrangements will not. A supplier may prefer to have a "non-exclusive" or "selective" distribution system.

- Non-exclusive distribution agreements.
  These may fall foul of Article 85(1) if they restrict the distributor's freedom to deal with the product, for example, if a supplier wishes to recommend or fix retail prices, to restrict the distributor's dealings with the consumer, to prevent his carrying competing lines, to restrict his choice of market including any ban on exporting the product.

- Selective distribution agreements.
  Where the supply of goods is limited to a certain class of approved dealers chosen according to the manufacturer's criteria because of their particular technical or other specific qualifications, an agreement will not be contrary to Article 85 if it fulfils certain conditions.

  (i) The product must be one which justifies the qualitative criteria.

  (ii) The criteria must be qualitative, not quantitative, and based on the technical suitability of the dealers; all dealers meeting the technical criteria must be allowed to act for the supplier.

If, however, a manufacturer tries to exclude a dealer from the network because he thinks a particular market is already saturated with distributors, his criteria are quantitative, not qualitative and the agreement contrary to Article 85(1). He will need to consider notification for exemption.

What to put in a selective distribution agreement

Can include	Cannot include	Should notify
Technical criteria	Resale price maintenance	Minimum annual purchase
Qualifications of staff	Export bans	A system of waiting lists
Suitability of the premises	Quantitative restrictions	

Article 85(3) therefore provides for the individual exemption of certain agreements which contravene Article 85(1). This is obtained by individual notification to the European Commission.

The grounds for individual exemption

There are four main criteria for exemption. These are, broadly, that:

(i) the agreement contributes to improving the production or distribution of goods or providing technical or economic progress;

(ii) the end consumer is allowed a fair share of the resulting benefits;

(iii) the restrictions on the parties are the minimum necessary to achieve these objectives; and

(iv) competition is not eliminated in respect of a substantial part of the products covered by the agreement.

In an application for exemption, the parties have to show that all four of these requirements are satisfied.

How to notify: Form A/B

A notification/application on Form A/B may be filed to obtain:

- an exemption under Article 85(3);
- a negative clearance whereby the Commission states that there are no grounds for action on its part against the agreement; or
- a comfort letter.

Form A/B is a lengthy document, revised in 1994. The parties must include extensive market share and economic data together with details of the proposed arrangements.

Parties who notify an agreement for exemption frequently in the alternative seek what the Commission terms "negative clearance", where they fear a possible infringement of competition rules. The Commission gives formal clearance by issuing a decision stating that on the basis of what it has been told there is no evidence that the agreement will breach Articles 85 or 86. Applications for negative clearance and notification for exemption under Article 85(3) are made on the same Form A/B.

Notifications in connection with maritime transport and air transport must be made on special forms MAR and AER respectively.

Notification itself does have other advantages, the most significant being that it gives immunity from the prospect of fines once the agreement has been notified. It does not guarantee immunity from third-party actions in national courts.

There is no time limit for notifications – an agreement may be notified to the Commission at any time. But it is wise to do this sooner rather than later, the better to get the full benefit of exemption and immunity from fines (see above).

See Annex 8 for Form A/B.

Advantages and disadvantages of notification

Advantages:

- A notification is a prerequisite to an exemption from the Commission. No notification means no possible exemption under Article 85(3), *even if* the agreement were to meet the conditions laid down by Article 85(3).

- Notification will lead to immunity from fines otherwise applicable for breach of Article 85(1) from the date the notification is received by the Commission, provided strict conditions are met.

- Companies should take this advantage seriously. Community competition officials have expressly stated that fines are currently not acting as sufficient deterrent and will be raised.

Disadvantages:

- Notification involves a substantial disclosure of information to the Commission.

- The filing of Form A/B can be difficult, costly and time-consuming.

- The Commission may require substantial amendments to the agreement as a condition to exemption.

Notification and risk

Questions to ask

- *De minimis?*

- Available block exemption?

- Effect on competition in
  the market
    - parties' competitors?
    - economic analysis   - market and market shares/
    - effects of collaboration   dominance
    - co-ordination of policies   - on existing/potential
    - foreclosure?   competition
    - spillover?

Notification and risk (*continued*)

- Attitude of competitors

- Big players, high profile, substantial effect on market?

Decisions to be made

● Notify European Commission	● Take the risk
– Form A/B	– Important provisions may be vulnerable
– Protects from fines (not court actions)	– Investment may depend on these provisions
– Commission may investigate/require amendment	– Disgruntled third parties may complain
– Formal clearance/ comfort letter	– Commission fines
	– Court actions

Comfort Letters

Very few arrangements will receive an individual decision by the Commission, which is continually dealing with a backlog of work. Instead of a decision, the parties may have to be content with a "comfort letter". Whilst giving the parties an idea of the Commission's attitude to the agreements, this is not a formal decision. Where a national court is asked to apply Article 85, the contents of a comfort letter, although persuasive, will not safeguard the addressee against the national court's declaring the agreement void under Article 85(2).

There are differing types of comfort letter. The first is a statement that, on the information received, the Commission would probably take the view that the notified agreement does not infringe Article 85(1). Companies may also receive a letter indicating that the Commission's file is closed, or a letter indicating that although it seems that the agreement notified appears caught by Article 85(1), DG IV does not propose to do anything about it. The latter is potentially dangerous as it has no binding force on the Courts and, although of some comfort, it is tangible evidence of a "bad" agreement.

Checklist of information required to determine whether a transaction is caught by Article 85: What your lawyer will ask you

1. *Questions related to the undertakings involved in the arrangements*

   Do the undertakings form part of groups of companies?

   List main parent companies and subsidiaries, giving place of registration and main type of business.

   Provide copies of latest reports and accounts together with relevant company publications such as catalogues

2. *Questions related to the products or services involved in the arrangements*

   What exactly are the products or services involved?

   Are they new, where are they already marketed, do they involve a great deal of research and development ...?

   What products are generally considered interchangeable with the products which are the subject of the arrangements?

3. *Defining the arrangement*

   What is the object of the arrangement?

   What is or will be its effect (actual or potential) on the market?

   What is the impact of the arrangement:

   –   on the parties involved

   –   as regards third parties (competitors, consumers)?

**Checklist of information required to determine whether a
transaction is caught by Article 85:
What your lawyer will ask you (continued)**

4. *The market related to these products or services*

   What is its geographical extent?

   How competitive is it:

   – identify the main existing competitors – their size (turnover,
   market shares, location . . .);

   – how difficult is it for new suppliers to enter the market
   ("barriers to entry": start-up costs; financial and technological lead of the parties over their competitors)?

   Who are the consumers (individuals, corporations, wholesalers
   . . .) and where are they located?

   What is the chain of supply?

5. *Turnover*

   What is the turnover in the goods or services affected by the
   arrangements:

   – of the undertakings involved and their groups

     (a) nationally

     (b) in the Community; and

     (c) world-wide.

6. *Market shares*

   What is the share or services of the product/market affected by the
   arrangement:

   (i) of the undertakings involved and their groups

     (a) nationally

     (b) in the Community; and

     (c) world-wide?

The most recently available figures must be provided, with, if possible,
any available supporting documents (such as market surveys, financial
analysis . . .).

Article 86

Article 86 governs the abuse by an undertaking of a possible dominant position in the market and is therefore concerned both with monopolies and oligopolies (the control of a market by a small number of suppliers/dealers etc).

Article 86 applies where:

- one (or more) undertakings which
- have a dominant position
- on a relevant product and geographical market
- abuse that dominant position; and
- the abuse may affect trade between Member States.

Article 86 concerns the unilateral conduct of undertakings in their dealings with third parties.

As with Article 85, the Commission and national courts will be concerned with the Article 86 abuse where it may affect trade between Member States. The second paragraph of Article 86 gives examples of the kind of behaviour which will be considered to be abusive. The list of examples given in Article 86 is not exhaustive; the Commission and the ECJ and CFI reserve the right to consider a far broader range of activities than those exemplified. It can be seen that the examples given closely correspond to the examples of offensive agreements discussed in Article 85(1).

Dominant position

The concept of a dominant position, although not defined in Article 86, is usually taken to mean the degree of market control which enables an undertaking to behave to an appreciable extent independently of its competitors and customers. First you have to establish what products constitute the relevant market and what its geographical boundaries are. Substitutability and the definition of the relevant geographical area are considered separately below.

The question of market dominance should be considered when a company has a substantial market share. There is no precise threshold above which dominance is presumed and the level will vary from market to market depending on its particular characteristics. As a very rough guide, a 40% market share is sometimes taken as a benchmark above which it may be difficult to dispute dominance, although in some circumstances it is possible also to have a dominant position below that level.

A company does not necessarily have to be big in terms of turnover to be dominant. One important question is what sort of competition there is in a particular product market – how many players and on what do they compete? The more fragmented the competition, the lower the percentage share which may enable the market leader to dominate the sector.

The ease with which new competitors can enter the market and existing players get out – the barriers to entry and exit in terms of cost, regulation, availability of raw materials, attitude of other players and so forth – are also important.

None of these characteristics is enough on its own to prove or negate the existence of market power. When the Commission (or for that matter the relevant national authorities under their domestic legislation) comes to investigate the existence of dominance and its possible abuse, it will undertake research and put together detailed evidence of what the market is really like.

Article 86

- Article 86 prohibits conduct

    – by one (or more) undertakings

    – in a dominant position, which

    – abuses that dominance, and

    – where the conduct may affect EC trade.

- Dominance

    – in a product and geographical market

    – can act independently of competitors and customers

- No exemption available

Joint dominance

It is only fairly recently that the ECJ has confirmed that Article 86 can be infringed by a collective dominant position. This was in the Italian flat glass case, a Commission Decision which went to the ECJ.

The Court said that collective dominance can arise where two or more independent entities are united by such economic links in a specific market that together they hold a dominant position *vis-à-vis* other operators. This may occur, for example, where such undertakings jointly have, through agreements or licences, a technological lead over their competitors. Parallel behaviour, structural links, organisational links, common methods of dealing, may all be indicators of collectivity. Whether a group of undertakings which is acting in a collective manner also has dominance will depend on the normal tests for dominance, cited above.

If collective dominance is established, then behaviour which seeks to exclude a competitor, for example by boycott, by refusal to deal, by putting him at a competitive disadvantage through the application of trading terms not applied to other customers, by tie-in arrangements aimed only at that competitor, or by other predatory actions, would be contrary to Article 86.

Definition of the market

One of the most difficult, and yet one of the most critical, questions will be the definition of the relevant market. This is true for both European and domestic situations. Whether a dominant position may exist will often depend on how the market is defined. For this reason, those under investigation often argue for the largest possible definition of the market thereby reducing their market share and the effect of their allegedly anti-competitive practices. On the other hand, those complaining will frequently argue the reverse. In one sense the arguments can be circular because if there is actual evidence that, for instance, a practice has had an anti-competitive effect, this will tend to show that the firm concerned must have had sufficient market power within its markets.

The market where the undertaking may have a dominant position must be defined by product and by geographical area.

The relevant product market

It is first necessary to identify the relevant products (or services) concerned by the dominant position. A product market will include:

- the products directly concerned; and
- substitutable products (see below).

There may be separate markets for:

- products having specific uses;
- raw materials;
- spare parts;
- groups of products within a potentially very large market.

When the product market has been identified, it is necessary also to look at the conditions for competition prevailing on that market. This chapter now looks in more detail at substitutability and geographical issues.

Substitutability

In one case it was suggested that a particular firm had a large market share in relation to the supply of bananas. The firm argued that the relevant market was not the one for bananas, but the whole of the fruit market, on which basis they enjoyed a relatively small market share. This argument was based on the proposition that one fruit was an effective substitute for another (that a customer who found bananas to be too expensive would be satisfied with buying another type of fruit as a substitute).

It may well be the case that some fruits are "substitutable" or "interchangeable" in this way and therefore form part of a larger market. However, in this case it was decided that bananas constituted a separate and distinct market because of the particular qualities of a banana which were not found in other fruits, namely their appeal to the elderly and the young as an easily digestible food.

This question can also be of particular importance in relation to spare parts. For instance, the manufacturer of a typewriter may have a very small market share in the typewriter market as a whole. However, if he is able to maintain a monopoly or near monopoly on the supply of compatible spare parts, there may be a separate market in spare parts for his type of typewriter.

In assessing competition one may also need to consider the ease with which manufacturers or suppliers can switch from one product market to another.

Geographical markets

The other aspect is the question of the geographical size of the market to be considered. This may, according to the wording of Article 86, be the EU as a whole or a "substantial part of it". The relevant geographical area must be one in which the "objective conditions of competition applying to the product in question must be the same for all traders" and where the dominant undertaking "may be able to engage in abuses which hinder effective competition". This will be a question of fact in each case. In some sectors, an undertaking may not have a large market share across the Community but may nonetheless be dominant in one region or Member State.

The abuse of a dominant position

The mere existence of a dominant position is not a breach of Article 86. There must be an abuse.

Abuse is always a question of fact:

- is the conduct obviously unfair or restricting competition?

- is the conduct obviously different from normal industry practice?

- does the dominant undertaking intend to act in an exclusionary manner or is it legitimately responding to competition?

- what is the effect of the conduct on competitors and customers?

A dominant undertaking can operate on a market without being restrained by effective competition. The unilateral conduct of such companies is, therefore, subject to control under Article 86.

Undertakings may abuse their strength by altering the normal conditions of competition which should apply in their market.

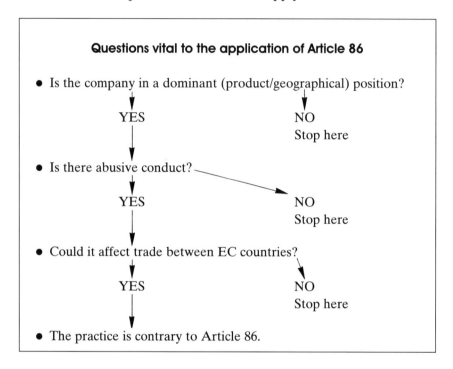

Questions vital to the application of Article 86

- Is the company in a dominant (product/geographical) position?

    YES   NO
                                 Stop here

- Is there abusive conduct?

    YES   NO
                                 Stop here

- Could it affect trade between EC countries?

    YES   NO
                                 Stop here

- The practice is contrary to Article 86.

Examples of abusive behaviour

Fidelity/loyalty rebate schemes

Rebates based on quantities purchased should be applied objectively to all comers. You cannot offer rebates – or other inducements – on the basis that your customer will take all or a large percentage of his supplies from you. The Commission will regard this as another way of trying to gain exclusivity and prevent the customer having a free choice elsewhere, without actually imposing a total requirements obligation.

Refusal to deal

An objectively unjustifiable refusal to supply by an undertaking which has a dominant position on a market will always be contrary to

Article 86. The same problem is encountered when a dominant company makes the supply of its products conditional on its having control of the further processing or marketing of those products. How to prove an "objective justification" will always be a difficult question.

An agreement or understanding with your competitors about behaviour towards a particular customer could also lead to a "collective dominant position". This may be because of structural or organisational links, or because of common methods of dealing, or parallel behaviour within a market. This might in other terms be called "concerted exclusionary conduct".

Predatory pricing

If you are dominant on your market and you set up any arrangements by which you trade at unprofitable prices (selling below cost price or at a barely profitable level), or you address price cuts selectively with a view to "encouraging" a competitor out of the market, or if, because of your position on the market, you can offer special discriminatory prices to your competitors' customers but keep higher prices for your own equivalent customers, you will be abusing the competition rules.

It is sometimes difficult to establish the dividing line between keen but legitimate competition and real predatory or abusive action.

Trade associations

Mostly, of course, the aims of a trade association will be legitimately to enhance the business of its members. But note that a trade association is, for the purposes of the EC competition rules, an "association of undertakings" and thus any of its members' activities may come to be scrutinised in all the ways noted above.

Tying-in

Article 86 prohibits a company in a dominant position making the conclusion of contracts subject to the acceptance by the other parties of supplementary obligations which have no commercial connection with the product or service in question. The sale of product A must not be conditional upon the purchaser's also agreeing to pay for unrelated service B.

Discriminatory pricing

A dominant company must also be careful about its pricing policy towards resellers based in different Member States, to ensure that this does not lead to partitioning of markets.

What is abusive behaviour?

Example A

Company X specialising in equipment for the packaging of liquid and semi-liquid food products in cartons

- enforced standard clauses requiring only X's own cartons to be used on the machines X manufactured

- demanded that supplies of cartons be obtained only from X, with the intention of making customers totally dependent on X for the life of the machine

- sold at prices below average variable costs in certain countries (predatory pricing)

The ECJ said that X's behaviour formed part of a deliberate and coherent group strategy seeking to eliminate competitors.

Fine: ECU 75m (approx. 2.2% of group turnover)

Example B

Company Y applied a system of loyalty rebates and discounts to its major customers by reference to marginal tonnage. It also required its customers to enter into long-term contracts aimed at ensuring effective exclusivity of supply for Company Y, including "evergreen" contracts terminable on 24 months' notice.

The Commission said that Company Y's activities were designed to exclude competitors from the market.

Fine: ECU 20m

What is abusive behaviour? (*continued*)

Example C

Company Z, a computer manufacturer dominant in the market for the supply of certain key products

- refused to supply central processing units without main memory ("memory bundling")

- refused to supply central processing units without software included in the price ("software bundling")

- refused to supply certain software installation services to users of non-Company Z central processing units (discrimination between users)

- failed to give other manufacturers timely information needed to permit them to make competitive products ("interface information")

Company Z did not admit either the existence of a dominant position or abuse *but*, after a Commission investigation, it undertook to amend its practices.

No exemption from the prohibition

Unlike Article 85, Article 86 does not allow any exemption from the prohibition.

In theory, the legislation provides for notification of an activity falling within the ambit of Article 86 to seek a negative clearance, that is, a declaration by the Commission that Article 86 does not apply to the action described. In practice, there must be few cases where this would be appropriate.

The Form A/B used to make a notification for negative clearance under Article 86 is the same as described in the previous section for Article 85 and at Annex 8.

Joint ventures

Joint ventures are as various as the companies which create them. Different structures will be evolved for different projects and these can call for various types of EC competition law control, with or without the need for notification.

They may include:

- joint buying/joint selling arrangements;

- joint after sales/services repairs;

- research and development projects with or without joint production/marketing;

- setting up a jointly owned company to undertake research and development/manufacturing certain products/provide services to parents and/or third parties;

- contractual agreements/a new joint venture company/a partnership/a European Economic Interest Grouping; or

- consortium arrangements to facilitate a joint bid.

What sort of EC competition law implications arise?

At one end of the spectrum, major companies which rationalise their investments in one particular sector through joint ownership might find themselves caught by the concentrative joint venture provisions of the Merger Regulation with its obligatory requirements of rapid notification, without which the validity of the transaction itself is at risk. (See Chapter 2.)

At the other end of the spectrum is, for example, a project where the lead contractor sub-contracts to non-competitors certain aspects of a project which the lead contractor cannot itself fulfil. This would in all likelihood be free from any EC anti-trust complications at all.

In the middle, however, lie the majority of collaborations or co-operative joint venture arrangements to which Article 85 applies and for which notification to the European Commission may be advisable depending on the circumstances.

Where one of the collaborators is dominant in a particular service market (or two are jointly dominant) then Article 86 may also apply.

Joint venture Eurospeak

- Two types of joint venture

    - concentrative

    - co-operative

- Concentrative

    - performs on a lasting basis all the functions of an autonomous economic entity

    - activities do not give rise to co-ordination between parents

- Co-operative

    - has as its object or effect the co-ordination of competitive behaviour of independent undertakings

    - is not a concentration (everything else)

Co-operative joint ventures: definitions

A "co-operative joint venture" is defined by the Commission as one which has "as its object or effect the co-ordination of the competitive behaviour of undertakings which remain independent". It may be one limited in time (not performing a function on a lasting basis), or a partial-function joint venture set up to carry out particular projects, or a full function autonomous entity which yet gives rise to co-ordination between its parents or between the parents and the joint venture (although the latter is less crucial).

The Commission takes the view that co-operative joint ventures are versatile instruments which help companies to pursue different procompetitive goals such as research and development, provision of services, specialisation and penetration of new geographic or product markets, and if used for such objectives they generally deserve favourable treatment under Articles 85(1) and (3).

A common analytical approach should determine whether a co-operative joint venture is caught by Articles 85 and/or 86.

Concentrative/Co-operative: How do you know?	
• Lasting change in structure	• Co-ordination of independent undertakings
• Different business	• Same or related business
	• Parent keeps activities in JV market
• Flies free of parents	• Co-ordination between parents reinforced
– own resources	– prices
– autonomous	– markets
	– output
	– innovation
• No (or minor) parent co-ordination	• Co-ordination in neighbouring/ related markets

In December 1992 the Commission produced a Notice on the assessment of co-operative joint ventures under Article 85.

Co-operation agreements

Certain limited forms of joint venture may have no anti-competitive aspects at all. The Commission recognised this in 1968 and issued a Notice setting out an annotated list of those forms of co-operation which it believes may not restrict competition. It includes agreements which have as their sole object:

- joint market research, the carrying out of comparative statistical and market information studies;

- joint preparation of statistics and calculation models;

- joint placing and/or interpretation of research and development projects and the sharing out of research and development projects between participating companies, providing there are no additional restrictions on what the companies can do individually;

- joint use of facilities;

- joint selling arrangements;

- joint aftersales and repair services, but not where the participants are competitors with regard to the services covered by the agreement.

The arrangements must have one of the above as their *sole* objective. The categories are very narrow. Further, the development of case law since 1968 needs to be considered. So the message is that the Notice is helpful, but that all the facts need to be considered in each case.

Are the parties actual or potential competitors?

Joint ventures between competitors are much more likely to have competition implications than those between non-competitors. Both existing and potential competition needs to be taken into account. Certain questions are especially relevant in establishing whether companies might be considered competitors.

The test is, very broadly speaking, whether each party could have done the job on its own. In the case of a joint venture company set up to perform a particular project for its parents, the main issues will be the effect on the parents' business and on that of third parties. In the case of a joint bid to carry out a project for a third party, the question is whether each parent has the resources to provide the whole service package independently.

Taking as a guide the Commission's Notice on the assessment of co-operative joint ventures, the relevant questions are:

- does each collaborator (joint venture parent company) have sufficient financial resources, managerial qualifications, access to the necessary input products/services?

- does each collaborator know the production/service techniques, itself make necessary upstream/downstream products, and have access to necessary facilities?

- could each collaborator separately bear the technical and financial risks?

- can each collaborator overcome any barriers to entry in the relevant market without great difficulties in time/effort/cost?

Collaboration between non-competitors is rarely problematic. The main point to bear in mind is the effect on market access for third parties.

Where the collaborating parties are competitors – either across the whole or some parts of their respective business areas – the effects of their collaboration must be assessed.

What are the effects of collaboration?

The second big issue is the effects on the market of the proposed co-operation.

Does the arrangement reduce existing competition in the relevant market or prevent potential competition being realised? Article 85(1) will not apply if, even though the arrangements are between competitors, they neither limit the parties' competitive behaviour nor affect the market position of third parties. The following are illustrations of danger points.

Information exchange

If the collaboration requires to a certain extent any "open book" arrangement which could lead to information exchange between the collaborators, then they must beware of such exchange leading to potential market co-ordination (real or imagined).

Spillover effects

What is the effect of the collaboration on competition between the parties outside the joint venture itself? Is there any "spillover" into related areas? For example, does the collaboration encourage co-ordination in other areas where the parties compete – market sharing etc.

Foreclosure

Is there "foreclosure"? Are third parties prevented from competing in the particular market? This can be a particular risk in an oligopolistic market.

Network effect

Is there a "network effect"? If the parties (or one of them) set up a series of collaborations in complementary areas, the Commission may be suspicious that a network of joint ventures is being established which will lead to market sharing.

Notification of joint ventures caught by Articles 85 and/or 86

The parties can notify the Commission for negative clearance or an individual exemption under Article 85 on Form A/B. The arrangements are the same as for any other notification.

In general there are no time-limits within which the Commission has to deal with Form A/B notifications. For structural joint ventures (which are joint ventures involving an important change in the structure and organisation of the business assets of the parents), however, the Commission has adopted some internal administrative rules. These mean that, in the case of structural co-operative joint ventures, the Commission undertakes to give a written analysis and an estimate of how long any full examination is likely to take, within two months of receiving the notification. Form A/B has been amended so that questions asked of parties claiming this accelerated procedure are different from those asked of other applicants.

Joint ventures and the block exemptions

Co-operative joint ventures involving specialisation and/or research and development may take advantage of Regulation 417/85 on specialisation agreements or Regulation 418/85 on research and development.

The Commission even envisages that more complex arrangements, for example a research and development agreement extending to specialisation in manufacture or particular provisions on exclusive distribution or exclusive purchase, may take advantage of provisions contained in more than one block exemption regulation. How to combine and structure those elements in order to take advantage of this view will depend on the individual facts of any case.

Specialisation agreements

This block exemption applies to agreements on specialisation where, for the duration of the agreement, undertakings accept reciprocal obligations to have certain products manufactured only jointly. The Commission believes that agreements on specialisation in production generally contribute to improving the production and distribution of goods, and that undertakings concerned can concentrate on the manufacturing of certain products and thus operate more efficiently and supply products more cheaply.

Specialisation agreements covered

The Regulation applies to various sorts of specialisation agreements. There is a list of white clauses, so that, for example, the parties can include in their agreements an obligation not to conclude with third parties specialisation agreements relating to identical or equivalent products, and certain obligations as to exclusive licensing and distribution of the specialisation products.

If the parties wish, they may also insert into the specialisation agreement provisions covering an obligation to supply other parties with a specialisation product and to observe minimum standards of quality, to maintain minimum stocks and the replacement parts, and an obligation to provide customer guarantee services.

As to black clauses, this block exemption has a blanket prohibition on the inclusion in the agreement of any restrictions of competition other than those listed in the block exemption.

Market share and turnover restrictions

Parties can only take advantage of this block exemption if their market share of the specialisation products (which will include any equivalent products also manufactured or distributed by the parties) does not represent more than 20% of the relevant market in the EU or a substantial part of it, and the aggregate turnover of all the participating undertakings does not exceed ECU 1,000m (approx. £790m). Where joint distribution is involved, the block exemption is only available where the market share does not exceed 10%. Some leeway is allowed, in that the block exemption remains available to the parties if the market share and turnover thresholds are exceeded, during any period of two consecutive years, by no more than one tenth.

Opposition procedure

Where the market share thresholds are not exceeded but the turn-over limits are, then there is a procedure called the "opposition procedure" which may be used. This means that the parties notify their agreement to the Commission and simply wait. If the Commission does not "oppose" the agreement within six months, then it is automatically exempted.

Withdrawal of block exemption benefit

The Commission can withdraw the benefit of the block exemption where in any particular case the parties have made use of the block exemption, but their agreement does not in fact yield any significant results in terms of rationalisation or give consumers a fair share of the resulting benefit, or where there is simply not effective competition for the specialisation products in the EU.

Research and development agreements

A similar format applies in the case of the block exemption covering research and development agreements. It covers arrangements for the purpose of:

(i) joint research and development of products or processes and joint exploitation of the results of that research and development;

(ii) joint exploitation of the results of research and development of products or processes jointly carried out pursuant to a prior agreement between the same undertakings; or

(iii) joint research and development of products or processes excluding joint exploitation of the results, insofar as such agreements fall within the scope of Article 85(1).

The terms are all defined in the Regulation. Research and development or exploitation of the results are carried out "jointly" where:

(i) the work involved is

- carried out by a joint team, organisation or undertaking

- jointly entrusted to a third party, or

- allocated between the parties by way of specialisation in research, development or production;

(ii) the parties collaborate in any way in the assignment or the licensing of intellectual property rights or the communication of know-how to third parties.

Criteria for application

In order for the Regulation to apply, there must be a programme defining the objectives of the work and the field in which it is to be carried out, and all the parties to the agreement must have access to the results of that work.

Where the agreement provides only for joint research and development, each party must be free to exploit the results of that joint research and development and any pre-existing technical knowledge necessary for it, independently.

The joint exploitation must relate only to results protected by intellectual property rights or which constitute know-how which substantially contributes to technical or economic progress, and those results must be decisive for the manufacture of the contract product or the application of the contract processes.

If there are companies which are charged with manufacture by way of specialisation in production, they must be required to fulfil orders for supplies from all the parties.

The block exemption has limited application in time (the duration of the research and development programme and, where there is joint exploitation, five years from the time the contract products are first put on the EU market) and there are market share limits.

There is a white list of acceptable clauses and a black list of conditions which would make the block exemption inapplicable.

How the R&D block exemption works

- Defined type/purpose/programme of work exists

Agreement within block exemption	*Agreement outside block exemption*
No competing R&D	No other independent R&D
Limited technical fields	Quantity made limits
Exclusive manufacture territories	Sales quantity/price
No active cross marketing	Customer restrictions
Exclusive distributors/non-compete	Stopping parallel imports

- Maximum time: duration of R&D programme + 5 years for marketing

---

Opposition procedure and withdrawal of block exemption benefit

Agreements which vary slightly from the block exemption may take advantage of an opposition procedure. The Commission can also remove the benefits of the Regulation in certain cases. The opposition procedure and the circumstances in which the Commission would act are described above in relation to specialisation agreements.

Concentrative joint ventures and the Merger Regulation

A concentrative joint venture will perform on a lasting basis all the functions of an autonomous economic entity, but its activities will not give rise to co-ordination between its parents or between the parents and the joint venture.

A concentrative joint venture which is above the Community dimension thresholds will be treated as a merger under the Merger Regulation and therefore subject to obligatory pre-notification on Form CO within the time limit. To the extent that restrictions accepted by the parties to a concentrative joint venture are ancillary to it (see definition in Chapter 2 below), they also will be assessed under the Merger Regulation.

The thresholds are in most cases applied to the combined parent groups, and the size of the joint venture vehicle itself may be immaterial. If the parent company groups have large turnover both world-wide and in the EU/EEA, the structure of any joint ventures they set up should be analysed carefully.

See Chapter 2 for a discussion of the Merger Regulation.

How to approach joint ventures

The competition law aspects of joint ventures are as varied as the joint venture structures themselves. What is important is to identify at an early stage whether there are any competition law aspects and how to deal with them. A checklist of steps to be taken – a joint venture action plan – will be very useful.

The joint venture competition law action plan

- At the outset of a joint venture, the parties need a checklist:
  - what competition rules are likely to apply?
  - are any notifications mandatory or voluntary?
  - are there *de minimis* exemptions which may apply?
  - is there a block exemption available?

- Having assessed the most likely application:
  - what points will be useful in negotiation?
  - can the legislation help with drafting?
  - are we going to notify?

- If a notification is to be made:
  - who co-ordinates, drafts, gets the relevant information out of subsidiaries/the other parties, liaises with the authorities?
  - organise the timetable (and fit it into the overall plan):
    - what meetings are needed internally/with the authorities?
    - how long will it take to get the necessary information, check it, write/negotiate the submission?
    - when does it have to be submitted?
    - when will we get clearance?

- If you conclude that Article 85 and/or other rules do not apply:
  - make sure you have a record of the reasons for your conclusion.

- Arrangements need to be made to continue monitoring the competition angle:
  - are there particular plans for development which will/may need competition reviews:
    - setting up a Newco
    - organising/reorganising agents, distributors, licensees?
  - will a compliance programme help?

CONTENTS OF CHAPTER 2

EC Merger Regulation

2. EC MERGER REGULATION

Regulation 4064/89 (the "Merger Regulation") came into force in September 1990 and introduced a comprehensive merger control system which covers "concentrations" between businesses which have "a Community dimension".

There is a parallel control in the EEA Agreement for large-scale concentrations which have an "EFTA dimension" (see page 101).

Warnings

- The Merger Regulation has some unexpected applications – it catches various types of transaction which you might not expect to be regarded as an "EC merger".

- It is a mandatory requirement that all transactions covered by the Merger Regulation are notified in advance to the Commission in Brussels. This applies even to the most innocuous transaction where there is no effect on competition.

- Failure to notify not only renders the parties liable to fines but also affects "the validity" of the transaction itself.

- It is important to approach the Commission as early as possible where the Merger Regulation applies, or may apply, to a proposed transaction. The obtaining of clearance (whether on a formal or informal basis) from Brussels frequently has a significant effect on the timetable of the transaction concerned.

Field of application

The Merger Regulation applies to concentrations having a Community dimension. There is therefore a twofold test of structure and size to determine whether a transaction is caught by the Merger Regulation and thus needs to be notified to the European Commission (Merger Task Force (MTF)). This Chapter deals first with the structural issues and goes on to the threshold tests. It then looks at how a notification is made.

Merger Regulation: basic tests

- Twofold test   : structure and size
                         : a concentration with a Community
                           dimension

- Concentration   : control = the ability to exercise decisive
                           influence

- Community dimension: three questions

    (i) world-wide turnover

    (ii) Community turnover

    (iii) which Member States

- Prenotification discussions with Merger Task Force

- Mandatory notification within one week of signing or offer/
  announcement

A "concentration"

There are two types of concentration which are covered by the Merger Regulation. These arise where:

(i) a business or businesses (or a person or persons who already control a business)("the acquirer(s)") acquire direct or indirect control of another business (or parts of it) ("the target"); or

(ii) there is a merger of two previously independent businesses.

The question of whether an acquirer will have control of the target requires consideration of all the rights that person will be able to exercise directly or indirectly. This may include voting rights arising from the acquisition of shares and/or contractual rights under a management contract or joint venture.

Control

Does a company (or individual) acquire control of a business or its assets? There are two questions: what rights are acquired, and do they give the acquirer decisive influence over the target?

In order to determine whether a potential acquirer will have control of the target, it is necessary to consider all the rights that person will be able to exercise directly or indirectly (even if there is no intention to exercise such rights to secure control). This may include:

- rights arising from the acquisition of securities (for example, voting rights on shares in the target); or

- contractual rights (for example, under a management contract or joint venture agreement); or

- other rights; or

- a combination of different rights (for example, a minority equity investment together with contractual rights in a shareholders' agreement).

"Control" as used in the Merger Regulation does not mean outright control in the sense of a 51% shareholding in the target. It is defined by reference to the "possibility of exercising decisive influence" on the target.

Decisive influence is not itself defined – it is something less than outright control but something more than mere influence. It is particularly important to consider rights in respect of the "composition, voting or decisions" of the board or committees of the target. Although less common, decisive influence can also arise through the ownership or "the right to use" the assets of the target.

When is decisive influence acquired?

The question of whether the acquirer will have decisive influence depends upon the particular facts of the transaction concerned. In the case of voting rights, much will depend on whether the target is listed or privately held, and the profile of the other shareholdings in the company. Some examples:

- There is unlikely to be any question of decisive influence where the acquirer has a shareholding in the target of less than 15%, providing the acquirer does not have any additional contractual rights and is not "acting in concert" with other shareholders. A shareholding of 19% combined with a permanent seat on the board (this director's prior written approval being required for all significant decisions and his veto extending to shareholder meetings) and the right to appoint the chairman and CEO of the company has been held to constitute control, where the other investors together had only one seat on the board.

- A 25% shareholding in a listed company may or may not confer decisive influence depending on the profile of the other shareholdings in the target.

  - An increase in shareholding from 20.94% to 25.96% gave Company B control where the other shareholdings were widely dispersed. The Commission carried out a projection of attendance at future general shareholders' meetings and concluded that Company B would have a *de facto* majority

  - In another case a 25% shareholder in an unlisted company was held to have decisive influence because of additional contractual rights to appoint two directors whose consent was required for important decisions such as budget, strategic plans and investment. A right of veto on matters of this kind may well confer decisive influence even when the acquirer only has a small shareholding or no shares at all.

- A shareholding of, say, 35% may well give decisive influence over a listed company, but a shareholding of comparable size which could be outvoted by another shareholder with a larger holding may not.

- A shareholding of 50% or more will almost always confer decisive influence.

- In exceptional cases of economic dependence, control on a factual basis may arise without the acquisition of shares, for example where a business is dependent on very important long-term supply agreements or on credits provided by suppliers or customers.

- Receivers, administrators and liquidators may acquire decisive influence when they are appointed, but in some cases the exemptions referred to below will apply.

- A rescue or refinancing may give the lender decisive influence over the borrower where there is debt/equity swap coupled with stringent covenants given by the borrower.

Is joint control acquired by more than one party?

In some situations the rights of several "acquirers" may be aggregated to determine whether they have joint control of the target.

It is therefore possible, for instance, that investors may each acquire only a small percentage of the target's share capital, but that when their rights are aggregated together they are sufficient to give the investors, as a group, joint control over the target.

"Joint control" may also arise in a joint venture situation where neither of the joint venturers individually has outright control of the target, for example, where there is a straight 50:50 split or where the minority shareholder has a right of veto on important decisions. This frequently arises where two companies decide to combine complementary parts of their businesses, or where a group sells a substantial shareholding in one of its subsidiaries.

The Commission has confirmed that the key to determining whether there is joint control is to establish whether the different partners have necessarily to be in agreement on the strategic decisions taken by the joint venture.

- Where A has 60% of capital and appoints four directors and B has 40% of capital and appoints three directors, but all major decisions have to be taken unanimously, A and B have joint control.

The rights of the partners must go beyond those normally conferred on minority shareholders.

- Minority shareholder S did not have joint control with the other parties because S's rights were insufficient; S had no right of veto in matters of business policy, strategy, budgets and corporate planning.

There are complicated (and unsatisfactory) rules to determine whether joint ventures are "concentrative" or "co-operative". In December 1994 the MTF took the opportunity to revise these rules in

Examples of concentration structures

Example A
XCo acquires all the shares of YCo.

XCo————————100%————————>YCo

Example B
A sells 45% of its shares in XYZCo to B.

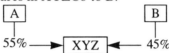

A retains a majority stake in XYZ. B also has decisive influence because the shareholders' agreement provides that both parent companies' consent is required in respect of major decisions regarding the commercial policy and competitive strategy of XYZ. A will appoint 5 members of the board and B will appoint 4. Unanimity will be required in relation to commercial policy, including the annual business plan.

XYZ is jointly controlled by A and B.

Example C
ACo is a subsidiary of the A Group. BCo is a subsidiary of the B Group. A and B decide to concentrate these subsidiaries into ABCo, in which C will be an institutional investor.

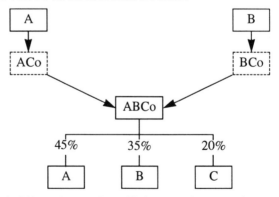

The shareholdings in ABCo will be A 45%, B 35% and C 20%. Each of A, B and C will have a right of veto over the business plan and budget. ABCo is a concentrative joint venture, jointly controlled by A, B and C.

the light of its experience in the first years of the application of the Merger Regulation. Concentrative joint ventures are regulated principally under the Merger Regulation whilst co-operative joint ventures are regulated under Article 85 of the Treaty of Rome.

Does any of the exemptions apply?

Article 3(5) of the Merger Regulation provides an exemption for concentrations arising in three situations.

- Acquisition of securities on a temporary basis
  The first applies where a bank, or other financial institution, acquires securities on a temporary basis with a view to reselling them but various additional criteria have to be satisfied. This exemption might apply, for instance, if an underwriter were left with a significant shareholding after an unsuccessful placing or rights issue. In most cases it would be unwise to rely upon this exemption without discussing the particular case with the Commission.

- Liquidators and administrators
  The second exemption applies where control is acquired by "an office-holder according to the law of a Member State relating to liquidation, winding up, insolvency, cessation of payments, compositions or analogous proceedings". A concentration will not therefore arise when an administrator or liquidator is appointed. There is, however, no exemption, for instance, for a concentration arising when an administrator sells off part of the company's business or for a restructuring/refinancing proposed by an administrator.

- Certain types of investment company
  The third exemption applies to shareholdings acquired by financial holding companies whose investment activities are specifically regulated by an administrative or judicial authority. This exemption is intended to cover particular types of investment company and has been narrowly interpreted.

A Community dimension

The Merger Regulation only catches concentrations which are big enough to have a "Community dimension". To assess this, the following three questions must be answered:

(i) does the combined aggregate world-wide turnover of all the undertakings concerned exceed ECU 5 billion (£3.95 billion approximately)?

(ii) does the aggregate Community-wide turnover of *each* of at least two of the undertakings concerned exceed ECU 250m (£197m approximately)?

(iii)does each of the undertakings concerned achieve more than two thirds of its aggregate Community-wide turnover within one and the same Member State?

The Merger Regulation will only apply if the answer to questions (i) and (ii) is "yes" and the answer to question (iii) is "no".

How to assess turnover

The turnover of the "undertaking concerned" is not the turnover of the individual company but that of the whole parent group. Where an undertaking is acquiring outright just part of another undertaking (say one particular subsidiary of a large group), then the turnover thresholds are applied to the whole of the acquiring group but only to that part of the vendor which is actually being acquired.

Community or Member State turnover refers to the turnover derived from sales to persons in the EU or Member State concerned.

The turnover tests for multiple acquirers

Where there are two or more acquirers who have joint control, each acquirer is treated as being an "undertaking concerned". The Regulation treats such a transaction as being a concentration between the joint controllers themselves as well as between them and the target. The thresholds in questions (i) and (ii) may therefore be exceeded as a result of the group turnover of the joint controllers, even if the target group's turnover is small.

Calculating turnover

Example A

XCo Group merges with YCo Group.
Turnover calculations must be applied to the whole of both groups.

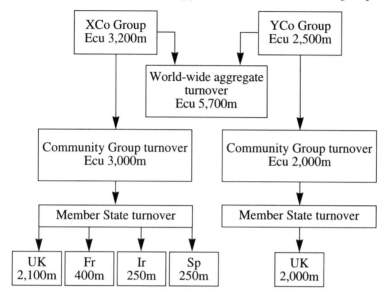

XCo Group and YCo Group each have more than two-thirds of their Community turnover arising from operations in the UK, so the Merger Regulation does *not* apply. The parties should look at the application of the UK Fair Trading Act.

Calculating turnover (*continued*)

Example B

ACo Group acquires the UK and French businesses of BCo Group in order to strengthen its position in those markets. The turnover calculations must be applied to the whole of the ACo Group, but only to the UK and French businesses of BCo Group.

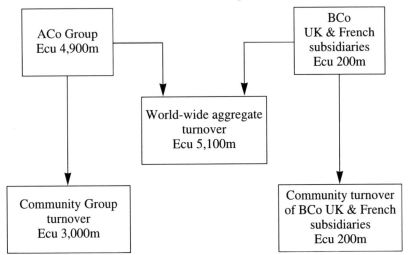

The Community turnover of the target businesses is below the Ecu 250 m threshold. There is no need to answer the third question. The Merger Regulation does *not* apply.

Calculating turnover (*continued*)

Example C

DCo Group (based in the EC) acquires the whole of GCo Inc. (head office in the USA). The turnover calculations must be applied to the whole of both groups.

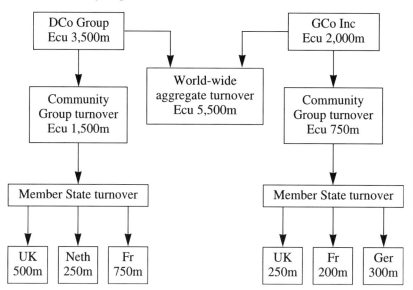

The world-wide and Community aggregate threshold tests are satisfied. Community business of each group is spread across various countries. The transaction has a Community dimension. The Merger Regulation applies.

Calculating turnover (*continued*)

Example D

A Group and B Group merge their subsidiaries ACo and BCo into
ABCo, in which C, an institutional investor, will have a minority
shareholding.

The proposed structure after the merger is:

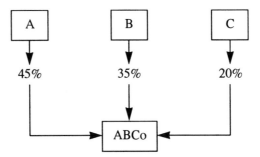

World-wide turnover calculations are applied to aggregate the group
turnover of A, B and the institutional investor C. The total is more
than ECU 5000 m.

Community wide turnover calculations are applied separately to each
of A, B and C. Of these, B and C have Community turnover of more
than Ecu 250 m.

The two-thirds test is applied to each of A, B and C. They do not each
have two-thirds of Community turnover in the same Member State.
The Merger Regulation applies.

Possible lowering of the thresholds

In July 1993, the Commission decided not for the present to seek
lower turnover thresholds. They come up for review again in 1995.

Transactions outside the EU

It is not only companies based in the EU which are subject to the Merger Regulation.

Several transactions involving only US or Japanese companies, as well as many cases involving both EU and third country undertakings, have had to be notified under the Regulation because the groups concerned were sufficiently large world-wide and the companies, or their subsidiaries, had sufficient sales to the EU, to exceed the Community-wide turnover threshold.

Large scale concentrations may be caught not only by the Merger Regulation but also by, for example, the merger controls of the United States. There is an agreement between the EU and the United States designed to promote co-operation between their respective competition/anti-trust authorities. One consequence of this is that when the Merger Task Force (MTF) is investigating a concentration which involves US businesses, it may ask for help from the US authorities. A second point is that if a merger has to be cleared both by the European Commission under the Merger Regulation and by the US Department of Justice under the Hart-Scott-Rodino legislation, the parties and their lawyers will need to liaise to ensure that the necessary notifications are consistent.

Transactions outside the EU

USCo Inc is a conglomerate whose parent company is based in Cincinnati. It has subsidiaries world-wide, although 60% of its business is in the United States.

Japco's head office is in Japan, but it too has subsidiaries world-wide – about 40% of the business is in Japan and the Pacific Rim, another 30% in the United States and the rest in various Scandanavian and other countries.

USCo wants to acquire Japco. Will the EC Merger Regulation apply? Is there a concentration with a Community dimension?

- USCo takes control of Japco – this is a concentration.

- Does the concentration have a Community dimension?

Non EC transactions (*continued*)

The turnover tests are applied to the whole of the USCo group and to the Scandinavian operations of Japco.

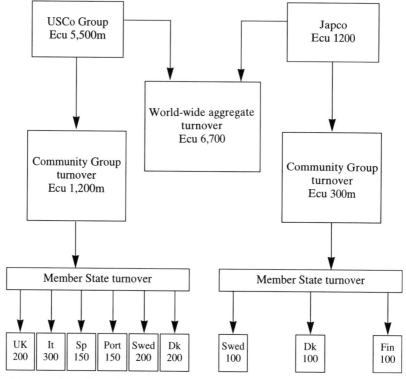

| UK 200 | It 300 | Sp 150 | Port 150 | Swed 200 | Dk 200 | Swed 100 | Dk 100 | Fin 100 |

The combined world-wide turnover is more than Ecu 5,000 m. The aggregate Community-wide turnover of each of USCo Group and of Japco is more than Ecu 250 m.

Each group has Community business spread over several countries; the answer to the two-thirds test is "no".

The EC Merger Regulation applies to the acquisition by a US group of a Japanese group.

Financial institutions

The turnover questions above cannot be applied to banks and other financial institutions. Alternative criteria are used based on the banks' assets and the geographical spread of their lending. World-wide turnover is replaced by one-tenth of total assets. Total Community-wide turnover is replaced by one-tenth of total assets, multiplied by the ratio between loans and advances to credit institutions and customers in transactions with Community residents and the total sum of those loans and advances. The Member State percentage test is determined by taking the ratio of loans and advances to banks and customers in the Member State concerned, as a percentage of loans and advances to EC banks and customers.

The MTF appreciates that these alternative criteria are difficult to apply in practice and may produce unrepresentative snapshots of, for example, the spread of a bank's international business. It is hoped that this policy may be changed. The adoption of a "banking income method", whereby the allocation of "turnover" would be made to those branches and subsidiaries of a bank where the business was carried out, apparently found favour in some quarters, but not with the central banks. Further thought and a long waiting period are therefore now needed before a new way of dealing with financial institutions emerges.

Does the Merger Regulation apply? The basic questions

1. Is there a concentration?

   Is the transaction one where:

   – a business (or businesses or the person(s) who controls it or them) acquires direct or indirect control of another business or part of it; or

   – two businesses are merging?

2. Does a company (or individual) acquire control of a business or its assets?

   Refer to main text for definitions of:

   – direct/indirect control: "the ability to exercise decisive influence";

   – ways in which decisive influence may be obtained: shares, voting rights, contractual rights, combination of elements.

Does the Merger Regulation apply? The basic questions (*continued*)

3. Is joint control acquired by more than one party?

    Is the transaction:

    –   a concentrative joint venture?

    –   the acquisition of control by a group of investors (or a rescue/ refinancing by banks or some similar arrangement) who will pursue a common policy towards the target?

4. Do any of the exemptions apply?

    Refer to main text for situations involving:

    –   temporary acquisition of securities for resale;

    –   liquidation, administration, winding up (but note that the exemption does not apply when, for example, an administrator sells off part of a company's business or when a restructuring is proposed by an administrator).

    –   the activities of certain financial holding companies.

5. Does the concentration have a Community dimension?

    The questions are:

    (i) Is the combined aggregate world-wide turnover of all the undertakings concerned more than Ecu 5,000 m?

    If yes:

    (ii) Is the aggregate Community-wide turnover of each of at least two of the undertakings concerned more than Ecu 250 m?

    If yes:

    (iii) Does each of the undertakings concerned achieve more than two-thirds of its aggregate Community-wide turnover within one and the same Member State?

    The concentration has a Community dimension only if the answers to questions i and ii are "yes" and the answer to question iii is "no".

Does the Merger Regulation apply? The basic questions (*continued*)

6. If the transaction is a concentration and has a Community dimen-
    sion, the Merger Regulation applies. Preparations for discussion
    with the MTF and notification must be started immediately.

7. If the transaction is a concentration without a Community dimen-
    sion, the Merger Regulation does not apply. Checks should be
    made to see what national merger control legislation applies.

The information you gather in response to your lawyer's checklist (see
page 79) should help you to answer these basic questions.

Notification

It is compulsory to notify to the European Commission all concentrations caught by the Merger Regulation. The Commission must clear
transactions before they can be completed. Failure to notify may
affect the validity of the transaction.

Merger Regulation notifications are handled by a special team at
DGIV, the MTF.

Notifications are made on Form CO (reproduced in Annex 8). The
preparation of a Form CO is lengthy and complex. It requires
turnover data on the companies concerned (including where appropriate with reference to the EFTA States), ownership and control,
personal and financial links, information on the product/
geographical markets affected by the merger, general conditions
prevalent in those markets, how the transaction is likely to affect the
interests of intermediate and ultimate consumers and the development of technical progress.

If there are market share implications, it may be necessary to
commission economic analysis from outside experts.

A short form notification is proposed for joint ventures below
certain thresholds and which are not expected to have more than *de
minimis* activities within the EEA. The form of the notification is
anyway in effect "negotiated" with the Commission during meetings
at which drafts are reviewed. It is not advisable to deliver a notification out of the blue, particularly as one often needs to get derogations

from the Commission in respect of some of the requirements in Form
CO. Information provided to the Commission should be verified and
appropriate caveats made in respect of assumptions, beliefs etc.

Preliminary meetings with the Merger Task Force

A meeting with the MTF can normally be arranged at short notice –
often in a matter of days. Unless the transaction is very simple,
however, it is helpful to prepare a briefing memorandum for the
meeting, setting out the structure of the transaction including details
of the key provisions relevant to the questions of "control". In the
case of complex transactions it can take some time to prepare a
briefing memorandum of this kind. After the meeting the MTF will
either issue an informal comfort letter stating that the Regulation
does not apply, or will ask for a full notification on Form CO before
it decides whether the Merger Regulation applies.

Timing

The notification in its final form must be delivered to the Commission
not more than one week after the conclusion of the agreement, or the
announcement of a public bid, or the acquisition of a controlling
interest (whichever occurs first). This one week period starts to run
immediately even if the agreement is conditional upon clearance
under the Merger Regulation. In practice, a short extension of time is
available in some cases.

It is, however, very important that the preparation of the notification is started several weeks before the date for the signing of the
agreement/ announcement of the offer. Even after preliminary meetings with the MTF, the time needed to pull together all the information required by Form CO must not be under-estimated.

After receipt of the notification, the Commission will publish a
notice inviting interested parties to give their views. In a non-
contentious case, clearance will normally be given a month later.

Grounds for objection and the Commission's powers

The intention of the Merger Regulation is to prevent concentrations
which would create or strengthen a dominant position which would

significantly impede competition in the Common Market or a substantial part of it. The Commission is not therefore concerned with wider issues of public interest which could apply under domestic regulations.

A full-scale investigation may be launched by the Commission three to four weeks after notification, if it feels that the concentration may be anti-competitive. A further four month period is then allowed for the investigation to be completed. The transaction will finally be put to the full Commission, which may prohibit it outright, allow it to go ahead but subject to conditions (*e.g.*, divestment of competing interests) or permit it to proceed as planned. To date few transactions have been prohibited outright; the tendency has been for the parties to agree conditions or changes.

Ancillary restrictions

Where a notified transaction includes contractual restrictions on the parties, one has to determine whether they are ancillary to the concentration.

Restrictions which are directly related and necessary to the implementation of a concentration are assessed by the Commission as part and parcel of the merger. They do not require separate consideration under Article 85.

Ancillary restrictions will include non-compete clauses, provided these are limited to what is strictly necessary to achieve the merger in terms of duration, geographical field of application, subject matter and persons subject to them. Licences of industrial and commercial property rights and of know-how, and purchase and supply agreements necessary to maintain continuity of business, are all commonly exempted as part of the merger clearance. The Commission has published a Notice explaining its approach.

If restrictions are not ancillary, then Article 85 and/or the UK Restrictive Trade Practices Act or other domestic legislation in the relevant countries may apply.

Concentrations without a Community dimension

The system provides that all concentrations with a Community dimension (except those covered by the special provisions for referral to Member States and for protection of particular interests) fall within the jurisdiction of the Commission. In principle, concentrations below the Community dimension thresholds are to be controlled by the relevant Member States applying their domestic law. This rule is not infallible.

Referral to Member State authorities

The situation can arise where a Member State believes that a concentration with a Community dimension may have a substantial and harmful effect on competition at national level ("competition would be impeded on a market . . . which presents all the characteristics of a distinct market"), whilst being inoffensive at EU level. In this case the Member State can request that the Commission does take action or refer the merger across to the relevant national authorities so that they can deal with it at the domestic level.

This procedure is rarely used.

Investigation of mergers below the thresholds

At the opposite end of the scale, a Member State can also ask the Commission to investigate a merger which does not have a Community dimension because it is likely to have an adverse effect on competition in a particular country. The idea here is for there to be Commission controls available for mergers in Member States which still do not have effective domestic merger legislation. Most EU countries do now have their own systems so the provision is little used.

The Regulation and domestic legislation

How does the Regulation affect the need for domestic clearance from the authorities of individual Member States, for example from the OFT/DTI under the Fair Trading Act 1973?

Where the Regulation applies, the general principle is that Member States are not allowed to apply their own laws on merger control or competition to the transaction concerned. They can, however, maintain controls on certain other grounds, for example, prudential

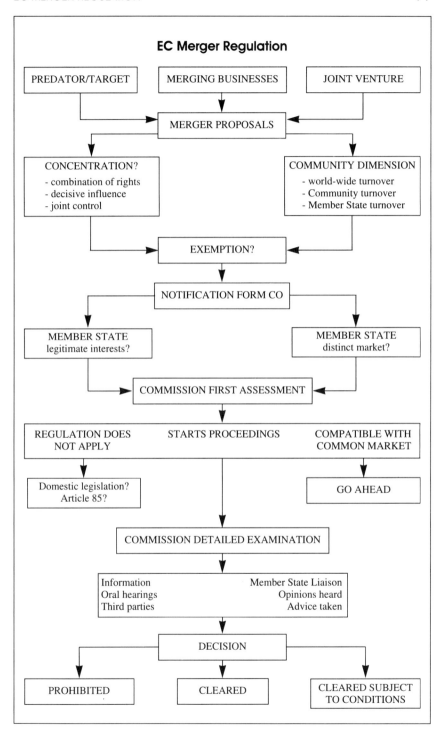

(Bank of England consent under the Banking Act) and plurality of the media (control of newspaper mergers under the Fair Trading Act). Even where there are no specific issues of this kind, it is normally advisable to notify the OFT at least on an informal basis.

Guidance from the Commission

In addition to the Regulations setting out the basis of EC merger control and the notification and timing procedures, the Commission initially issued Notices in the interpretation of concentrative and co-operative joint ventures and on how it deals with restrictions ancillary to concentrations. The Regulations and Notices have been revised to take account of the MTF's experience in its four years of dealing with large-scale transactions, and additional guidelines, for example on the definition of a concentration, are being drafted. The whole revised package was published at the end of December 1994. Its contents are listed in Annex 4.

**Checklist of information required to determine whether
the EC Merger Regulation applies:
What your lawyer will ask you**

1. Give a brief description of the proposed transaction including any transactions which are linked to it.

2. What rights are to be acquired?
    For example: shares and associated voting rights; rights in relation to the appointment/removal of directors of the target; contractual terms which may give the acquirer(s) the ability to restrict/control/veto decisions of the board of the target, its business operations or particular decisions such as those relating to capital expenditure, business plans, sales of assets, borrowings etc.

3. Does the acquirer already have an interest in the target?

4. Describe any other shareholders in the target.

Checklist of information required to determine whether the EC Merger Regulation applies: What your lawyer will ask you (*continued*)

5. Does the transaction involve any form of consortium, syndicate or grouping (including of family members)?

6. What is the world-wide turnover of the acquiring group(s)?

7. What is the world-wide turnover of the target group?

8. What is the Community-wide turnover

   (a) of the acquiring group(s)
   (b) of the target group?

9. Is the Community turnover of the acquiring group (or each acquiring group in the case of joint control) and that of the target group concentrated in one and the same Member State? If so, please give an indication of the percentage involved.

10. What is the proposed timetable for the transaction?

11. What are the main businesses of the acquiring group(s) and the target group and what sort of overlap is there? Are the businesses the same/upstream/downstream of each other/in related areas?

12. Does the transaction involve any party accepting restrictions of any kind (e.g. non compete, use of information, restriction on business activity, exclusivity, supply or purchasing obligations etc)?

CONTENTS OF
CHAPTER 3

*How to Enforce your
EC Rights in Commercial
Disputes: Attack and Defence*

3. HOW TO ENFORCE YOUR EC RIGHTS IN COMMERCIAL DISPUTES: ATTACK AND DEFENCE

Introduction

In earlier chapters this book has outlined how a company must analyse the potential problems in competition terms whenever it is contemplating a new deal or defining a commercial policy or simply on the point of signing a distribution agreement. This chapter looks at what a company should do when it believes it is the victim of an anti-competitive practice or when it is on the receiving end of a complaint. It must be aware of all possible rights of action so that it can decide on the most cost effective way of defending its rights.

Several procedures may be involved because:

- there is a variety of sanctions for breaches of the rules:
  - fines, damages, injunctions, nullity
- there is a variety of authorities which may judge the issues:
  - European Commission, European courts, national authorities, domestic and national courts.

Although this chapter focuses on a company's risks and rights under EC competition rules, one cannot ignore national rules when assessing the risks. National rules must be approached from two angles:

- national rules/EC rules: how do they interrelate?

- rules of different Member States: this is important where a deal or a commercial policy is implemented in more than one Member State.

What are your rights and risks in relation to the competition rules? These must be considered as regards the European Commission and your national court.

The powers of the European Commission

There are three areas which are particularly important:

- powers of investigation;
- powers to terminate infringements; and
- powers to impose fines.

The Commission's powers of investigation

The Commission has wide powers including:

- power to obtain information – such as background information and market data, details of alleged infringements, copies of documents;
- power to make inquiries into sectors of industry – general inquiry into a specific sector (rare in practice); and
- power of investigation – investigations may be carried out by Commission officials either with or without prior notice to the undertakings involved. Dawn raids are not uncommon. Commission officials are entitled to examine the company's books and other business records, to take copies, to ask for oral explanations on the spot, to enter any premises, land or means of transport of undertakings.

The Commission's powers to terminate infringements

The Commission may by decision require an undertaking to terminate infringements.

Fines

The Commission may impose fines where undertakings "intentionally or negligently" infringe Articles 85 or 86.

Fines may range from ECU1,000 to ECU1m, or up to 10% of

turnover of the undertakings concerned in the preceding business year, whichever is greater.

The Commission has some discretion as to whether it will impose a fine and as to the amount of the fine. The general trend is that fines are getting higher.

- In its XXIst Report on Competition Policy, the Commission indicated its intention to make fuller use of the possibility of imposing fines of up to 10% of annual turnover in order to reinforce the deterrent effect of EC penalties.

- Three cases in 1994 illustrate the Commission's strong views. New fines imposed in the steel beams case in February and in the cartonboard case in July totalled more than ECU236m (nearly £190m). Commenting on these decisions, Competition Commissioner van Miert said that the same attitude would be taken towards any other industry where such blatant anti-trust violations were uncovered. A further shock at the end of 1994 was the Commission's imposition of a $200m fine on 42 companies and associations in the cement industry.

- The amount of a fine will be determined by reference to the gravity and duration of the infringement. Factors taken into account include:

  Gravity
  - nature of the infringement – policies which have an adverse effect on cross-border trade (for example, export bans);
  - market share and turnover;
  - effect of infringement;
  - effect on third parties (for example, competitors, consumers);
  - benefits accruing from the infringement.

  Duration
  - the duration of the infringement is reviewed in the light of all other circumstances.

- Mitigation

  If parties promptly terminate a breach of EC rules, remedy a situation or co-operate with the Commission, the fines may be reduced. Evidence of a genuine effort to comply (*e.g.* a compliance programme – see Chapter 8) may also help.

- Limitation of actions
  Five years from the date of the infringement (*e.g.* a refusal to supply) or five years from the date on which the infringement ceased for continuing or repeated infringement (*e.g.* an export ban in a 10-year contract).

- Warning: ignorance of EC rules is not an excuse, especially if the action is a well-known infringement of EC rules.

- Immunity: notification of an agreement to the Commission may provide immunity from fines.

The European Courts in action

Competition cases may reach the Court of First Instance (CFI), for example, if a company challenges the validity of a Commission decision under Article 85. They may also reach the European Court of Justice (ECJ) on appeal from the CFI or by way of a question for a preliminary ruling whereby a national court may seek guidance from the ECJ on the interpretation of Articles 85 or 86.

Remedies available

The first point to remember is that provisions in an agreement which are contrary to Article 85(1) and have not been given an exemption by the Commission are void. So, if a party tried to enforce such a provision through the courts, the defendant could plead Article 85 as a defence on the basis that the provisions were void and unenforceable – sometimes referred to as "nullity".

- Scope of nullity
  The nullity will only cover the provisions of the agreement concerned which are in breach of Article 85(1). It is for the relevant national law to decide on the effect of the nullity on the remaining provisions of the agreement.
  The "doctrine of severance" may spare non-infringing provisions.

In the example, only the minimum resale prices provisions are in breach of Article 85. These are severable from the remaining provisions which will still be enforceable.

RPM not enforceable

- A supplier introduces minimum resale prices in a distribution agreement. The distributor ignores these prices.

- The supplier cannot enforce the resale prices provisions: they are void.

- So there is still an agreement between the supplier and the distributor, but the distributor is free to set his own price.

Other remedies

There is no harmonised system at the EU level. It is for the national system to decide which remedies should be available for a breach of EC competition law. However, the ECJ has held that the remedies cannot be less favourable than those applying in the context of a breach of national competition rules.

The distributor in the above case was happy to get his supplies confirmed and to be able to charge what he wanted. In another situation, a distributor may want an action stopped or to claim damages for the loss he has suffered. What could the court do for him? Damages and/or injunctions may be available.

Damages

In the United Kingdom, although the availability of damages where appropriate is clearly recognised, there are still discussions about the most appropriate cause of action: is breach of Article 85 a breach of statutory duty or an "economic tort"?

The assessment of damages would be based on the principle of *"restitutio in integrum"*. The court will award a sum of money which will put the party who has suffered in the same position as he would have been if he had not sustained the wrong.

Claiming damages

- Supplier A stops supplying certain contract goods to Distributor B because the latter exports them outside his territory.

- This proves to be an illegal export ban.

- Distributor B could claim the profits he has lost because he has not been able to sell the contrast goods which Supplier A refused to supply to him.

Injunctions

Injunctions have been granted, or at least considered, to prevent or to stop a breach of Articles 85 or 86.

In the United Kingdom, the granting of an injunction is an equitable remedy and as such is a matter of discretion for the court. Therefore, the plaintiff must come to court with "clean hands". If he is in any way responsible for the anti-competitive behaviour (for example he is party to an agreement in breach of Article 85), the injunction could be refused.

There must be a "serious question" to be tried or an arguable case. It must be the case that damages would not be an adequate remedy as a substitute for an injunction.

Further, the court looks at the balance of convenience. For instance, the court will assess the degree of disturbance the granting of an interim injunction would cause to the defendant's business, and also the risk of doing an injustice should the injunction be refused. This is a matter of fact in each case.

Finally, it is normal for a court to require cross-undertakings from the plaintiff when granting an injunction.

Injunction granted

The plaintiff had agreements with several public houses for the supply of amusement machines. The new manager of the public houses required them to deal with nominated suppliers of amusement machines. This list did not include the plaintiff.

The High Court granted an injunction to restrain what was considered a breach of Article 85.

Damages were not an adequate remedy since the denial of an injunction would put an end to the plaintiff's business.

Injunction not granted

The Outer House (Scotland) had to consider a motion brought by Company A for interim interdict against two companies from taking any steps towards a proposed merger of those two companies.

Company A claimed that the merger would amount to an abuse of a dominant position (Article 86).

The Court refused to grant the injunction on the balance of convenience so that both Company A's bid and the other company's bid could remain open to the target's shareholders.

(This case was decided before the Merger Regulation came into force in September 1990.)

Choice of forum: Commission or national court

If a company is victim of an anti-competitive practice, which forum does it go to? European Commission or national courts? Does the company have a choice?

In principle, national courts have concurrent jurisdiction with the European Commission to apply Articles 85(1) and (2) and Article 86. However, the trend is towards decentralisation/ subsidiarity.

The Commission is not required to investigate every complaint it receives. In its Notice on co-operation with the national courts, the Commission states that:

"the Commission intends, in implementing its decision-making powers, to concentrate on notifications, complaints and own-initiative proceedings having particular political, economic or legal significance for the Community."

Where these conditions are not met, "the complaints should, as a rule, be handled by national courts or authorities".

The choice between Commission or national court will therefore be subject to these criteria. They will also be important in assessing the risk of a complaint being investigated by the Commission. Some of the questions to be addressed in making a choice are:

(i) What are the company's objectives?

- getting damages for a loss suffered (past behaviour)?

- bringing an end to the infringement (future behaviour)?

- is the infringement from which a company suffers pan-European or limited to one (or two) Member States?

- costs – what can a company afford to spend on its action?

(ii) What is the best forum to achieve these objectives?

The pros and cons of the options are outlined below.

Commission	
Pros	*Cons*
• Cost: making a complaint is relatively inexpensive	• Cannot award damages
• If the complaint is not successful, no liability for costs	• Injunctions take a long time
• Only authority able to grant individual exemption/ negative clearance	• May refuse to take action in smaller cases
• Expertise	
• Better placed for pan-European infringements	

National courts

Pros	Cons
• Damages: more efficient deterrent	• Not always experts *but* co-operation with the Commission
• Injunctions: more quickly	• Need for specialised tribunals – sophisticated economic analysis
	• Cannot grant individual exemption/negative clearance *but* may apply block exemptions
• May review claims under both EC and national competition law	• Cost involved
• Plaintiff in control of litigation (settlement)	

Settlement out of court

The number of actions brought under Articles 85 and 86 is regularly increasing. Distribution agreements seem to be the main source of disputes. Taking the United Kingdom as an example, most of these actions are settled out of court, as indeed are most commercial actions. This may be explained, in particular, by the stringent English rules of evidence. For instance, parties are subject to the discovery requirement whereby they have to disclose to their opponent all documents which are relevant to the action, whether or not they are in their favour. Companies may be reluctant to disclose information relating to their commercial operations and therefore would have a strong impetus to settle. Another element in favour of settlements out of court in the United Kingdom is the rule on costs; in most cases, the losing party will pay at least part of his opponent's costs. There is no clear sign that more actions will reach trial in the near future. In this context, it is for the plaintiff to show a strong case under Articles 85 and 86 in order to obtain as good a settlement as possible.

Some typical scenarios

Company X needs parts made by Company B in order to develop new products and markets.

BCo is the largest supplier of these parts and Company X thinks it is probably dominant, at least in France.

BCo refuses to supply the parts to Company X.

Refusal to deal by a dominant company is a breach of Article 86 – an abuse of its dominant position. What can Company X do?

- Can Company X threaten to complain to the Commission as part of its negotiations with BCo? It will need to consider:

  - whether French law or Article 86 is the relevant law;

  - whether it is seeking damages or an injunction.

- If Company X chooses to complain to the Commission: how does it file a complaint?

  - Company X must have a legitimate interest (significant and direct).

  - No particular form is required, an ordinary letter may be accepted by the Commission.

  - However, the Commission has issued a Form C for the purpose of lodging a complaint.

The complaint would identify in particular:

- the nature of Company X's interest;

- the facts alleged;

- Company X's reasons for alleging that there has been a *prima facie* case of infringement;

- a request for the Commission to act, explaining why this is the case (having sufficient political, economic or legal interest) which the Commission should investigate; and

- possibly a request for interim measures.

- If Company X chooses the national court route: which court would have jurisdiction?

    The rules are in the Brussels Convention. There may be scope for "forum shopping". The general rule is that the court of the defendant's domicile should hear the case. But there are also additional and special rules.

    - A case in tort may be heard where the harmful event occurred.

    - A case in contract may be heard at the place of performance of the obligation in question.

    Company X needs to:

    (i) identify which courts may have jurisdiction;

    (ii) select the most appropriate forum by reference to the courts' respective rules on

    - remedies,

    - costs,

    - evidence/discovery,

    - length of proceedings, etc.

These rules also apply if it is Company X which is in breach of the competition rules.

Although it is having problems breaking into the French market, Company X does have an established distribution network in other EU Member States. This is organised as follows:

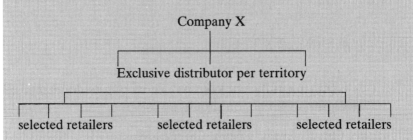

Retailers are admitted to the country networks on the basis of selective criteria – "selective distribution". The rule is that all retailers who fulfil the selection criteria should be allowed to join the network.

Company X instructs its exclusive distributor, whose territory is Italy and Spain, to refuse a particular retailer in Spain access to the selective network. The retailer complains. What happens next?

The Spanish retailer may sue the distributor and possibly Company X in Italy, because the exclusive distributor is domiciled in Italy. Spanish courts could also have jurisdiction because the harm resulting from this refusal is felt in Spain.

Relationships between EC law and national law

In the Spanish situation above, Company X needs to consider both EC law and national competition rules in parallel because some practices may be acceptable under Article 85 but not under national rules.

For example, refusal to supply is prohibited *per se* under French rules even if the undertaking refusing to supply is not in a dominant position. This may only be a problem under EC competition law if the undertaking does hold a dominant position.

There are also differences between the respective national laws to be taken into account. Company X needs to be aware that some practices may be acceptable under the competition rules of Member State A but not under the rules of Member State B.

To encourage sales in the French and English markets, Company X decides to offer free gifts with certain packages of its goods. To what extent is this possible?

Under English law, this is not a problem. Under French law, this may be a problem where, for example, the gift is not negligible or is not of the same nature as the main product supplied under the contract. Thus Company X always needs to make sure it has taken advice on EC law and on the domestic law of the country in which it is operating.

CONTENTS OF CHAPTER 4

*Competition Rules
of the EEA*

4. COMPETITION RULES OF THE EEA

Introduction

What is the EEA?

The European Economic Area came into being on 1 January 1994. As a result, certain of the EFTA countries came to share with the EU the four fundamental freedoms of the single market – freedom of movement of goods, services, persons and capital. At the time of the creation of the EEA, five of the EFTA countries were members: Austria, Sweden, Norway, Iceland and Finland. Three of those countries 12 months later became full members of the EU.

Switzerland voted to remain outside the EEA. The position of Liechtenstein was more complicated. Liechtenstein's close fiscal and other ties with Switzerland had to be revised before the EEA Agreement could apply to it.

At 1 January 1995, therefore, the position is:

European Union	15 Member States Austria, Belgium, Denmark, Finland, France, Germany, Greece, Ireland, Italy, Luxembourg, the Netherlands, Portugal, Spain, Sweden, the United Kingdom.
EFTA	4 countries Norway, Iceland, Liechtenstein, Switzerland

Although Switzerland is in fact a member of EFTA, references to EFTA countries in this book are to those EFTA Members which are in fact also EEA countries.

European Economic Area	15 EU Member States plus Norway, Iceland and Liechtenstein from mid-1995

One of the main objectives of the EEA Agreement is the "setting up of a system ensuring that competition is not distorted". In order to achieve this objective, the EEA Agreement extends the EU competition rules to EFTA countries and sets up a surveillance system. The EEA Agreement introduces a two-pillar system (EU/EEA competition rules; European Commission/EFTA Surveillance Authority) and the "one-stop shop" principle.

The relevance of the EEA competition rules

The EEA was for just one year – 1994 – a large market with a need for a separate competition regime and a real possibility that from time to time it would be EEA rules and EEA authorities which would have to deal with the problems of business. That year has passed, leaving us with a complex regime and several new institutions essentially operating for the benefit of two small countries, Norway and Iceland, with a third to join them in mid-1995.

It is not therefore very likely that business will often need to refer specifically to the EEA competition rules rather than to the EC ones. For those particular instances, however, this chapter outlines the rules, the institutions which apply them, and the complicated system of attribution of cases which straddle EU and EEA countries.

EC or EEA competition rules?

Where only trade between EU Member States is affected, Community competition rules continue to apply. EEA competition rules only apply where there is an effect on trade between one or more Member States of the EU and one or more EFTA States or between EFTA States.

EEA institutions

The Agreement created new institutions whose task is to monitor the implementation and development of the EEA. The EEA institutions concerned with monitoring competition are listed below.

The EFTA Surveillance Authority (ESA)

The ESA has similar powers and functions to those of the European Commission:

- the ESA investigates complaints and breaches of EEA competition rules and may impose sanctions;

- if there is a breach of their EEA duties by the EFTA countries, the ESA can bring an action against an EFTA State before the EFTA Court (see below), in the same way as the European Commission may bring an action against an EU Member State before the European Court of Justice.

Unlike the European Commission, the ESA plays no role in the legislative process. Its headquarters is in Brussels.

The EFTA Court

The seat of the EFTA Court is in Geneva.

The role of the EFTA Court is very similar to that of the European Court of Justice. The EFTA Court has been granted jurisdiction, in particular, in the following areas, which include competition matters:

- infringement proceedings initiated by the ESA against an EFTA State;

- advisory opinions (equivalent to the ECJ's "preliminary rulings") requested by an EFTA National Court on a point of EEA law;

- actions to annul ESA's decisions;

- settlement of disputes between two EFTA countries.

The EEA Joint Committee

The Joint Committee, consisting of representatives of the EU and EFTA countries, takes formal decisions regarding the implementation and operation of the EEA Agreement. It has established a system for passing on of information from the EFTA States to the EFTA Surveillance Authority and the EFTA Standing Committee and for the exchange of information between the ESA and the European Commission.

The EEA competition rules

The competition rules of the Agreement on the EEA (concluded between the Community, the Member States and the EFTA States) are based on the same principles as those contained in the Community competition rules and have the same purpose, that is, to prevent the distortion of competition in the EEA territory by restrictive practices or the abuse of a dominant position. They apply to any enterprise trading directly or indirectly in the EEA territory, wherever established.

Restrictive arrangements

Article 53(1) of the EEA Agreement (which is closely modelled on Article 85(1) of the EC Treaty) prohibits restrictive agreements between undertakings, decisions by associations of undertakings and concerted practices which may affect trade between the Community and one or more EFTA States (or between EFTA States). Article 53(2) declares agreements or decisions containing such restrictions void (although, following the decisions of the European Court of Justice, if restrictive terms of agreements are severable, only those terms are void). A notification procedure for exemption of practices with beneficial effects and which satisfy the conditions of Article 52(3) exists in parallel to that available in the Community under Article 85.

Abuse of dominant position

Article 54 of the EEA Agreement (identical in substance to Article 86 of the EC Treaty) prohibits any abuse by undertaking(s) of a dominant position which may affect trade between the Community and one or more EFTA States, or between EFTA States.

Agreements of minor importance, block exemptions and guidance notices

The regulations for certain types of agreement which may benefit from automatic exemption from Article 85(1) – the block exemptions – have their exact parallel in EEA regulations.

Similarly, the EFTA Surveillance Authority has issued Notices and guidelines modelled on those in use in Member States of the EU. These include notices on agreements of minor importance, the interpretation of various block exemptions (*e.g.*, on exclusive distribution and exclusive purchase), and on the application of the competition rules to co-operation agreements, exclusive dealing contracts with commercial agents and on sub-contracting.

Merger control

Article 57 of the EEA Agreement declares incompatible with the EEA Agreement concentrations which create or strengthen a dominant position as a result of which effective competition would be significantly impeded within the EEA territory or a substantial part of it. This rule applies to concentrations with a Community dimension (as defined by the Merger Regulation discussed above or concentrations with an EFTA dimension (the thresholds relating to the EFTA dimension are identical to those set out in the EC Merger Regulation). Notifications are made on Form CO (issued either by the Commission or by the EFTA authorities) as described above.

The ESA has issued notices in parallel to those of the European Commission on the definition of concentrative and co-operative operations, and on the assessment of restrictions ancillary to concentrations.

State aid

Articles 61 and 62 of the EEA Agreement and various protocols and ESA Decisions have established a system of substantive and procedural rules on the availability of state aid in the EFTA countries. Again, these parallel the EU regime. There are rules on state ownership of enterprises and on aid to public enterprises, on regional aid and on horizontal aid.

European Commission or ESA?

The European Commission and the ESA are together in charge of supervising the application of the EEA competition rules under the dual system mentioned above. The ESA is entrusted with similar powers and functions to those of the European Commission. For example, the ESA can impose fines, and has wide powers of investigation including the right to raid undertakings' premises.

The EEA Agreement lays down complex rules for the attribution of cases between the authorities. The attribution of cases works as follows.

- The European Commission has exclusive competence where:
  - a restrictive agreement affects only trade between European Union Member States; or
  - the dominant position is found to exist within the European Union; or
  - the concentration has a "Community dimension".

- The ESA has exclusive competence where:
  - a restrictive agreement affects only trade between EFTA States; or
  - the dominant position is found to exist within the EFTA territory; or
  - the concentration has an "EFTA dimension" but does not fall within the scope of the EC Merger Regulation.

Mixed cases

What about mixed cases which involve companies in both the EU and EFTA states, or which affect markets in both areas?

Restrictive agreements and abuse of dominant position

Mixed cases are cases where the restrictive agreement affects trade between the EU and one or more EFTA States, or the dominant position exists within both the EFTA States and the European Union. The attribution of cases is fairly complex.

The competence of the Commission and of the EFTA Surveillance Authority to apply the EEA competition rules follows from Article 56 of the EEA Agreement. Notifications and applications relating to restrictive agreements, decisions or concerted practices liable to affect trade between Member States, should be addressed to the Commission, unless their effects on trade between Member States, or on competition within the Community, are not appreciable in the sense of the Commission Notice of 1986 on Agreements of Minor Importance.

All restrictive agreements, decisions or concerted practices affecting trade between one Member State and one or more EFTA States should be notified to the Commission, provided the undertakings concerned achieve more than 67% of their combined EEA-wide turnover within the Community. However, if the effects of such agreements, decisions or concerted practices on trade between Member States or on competition within the Community are not appreciable, the notification should be addressed to the EFTA Surveillance Authority.

All other agreements, decisions and concerted practices falling under Article 53 of the EEA Agreement should be notified to the EFTA Surveillance Authority.

Merger control

Where a concentration has a Community dimension, it will be appraised by the European Commission, including in cases where it also exceeds the turnover thresholds in the EFTA States (in other words, where the concentration has both a Community and an EFTA dimension).

Notifications

The forms which are used in the notification of agreements for exemption under Article 85(3), in making complaints, in notifying mergers and concentrative joint ventures under the Merger Regulation and so forth have been revised, to aid the implementation of the EEA competition rules.

Companies notifying pursuant to the EC and the EEA competition rules use the same types of form. Notifications made on forms issued by the Commission and those issued by the EFTA authorities are equally valid. Applications and notifications made pursuant to the EEA rules may be in one of the official languages of the EFTA States or the working language of the ESA (English) or, in fact, any of the EU official languages. Notes to the various forms explain in brief the purpose of the competition rules and the competence of the European Commission and the ESA to apply the EEA competition rules, as well as the nature and purpose of the forms themselves. Forms are available from the national competition authorities in the EFTA countries.

Co-operation and choice of authorities

The European Commission and the ESA co-operate in order to develop and maintain a uniform surveillance throughout the EEA in the field of competition.

Where a notification or a complaint is addressed to the authority which is not competent under the EEA rules, this authority refers the case without delay to the competent authority.

CONTENTS OF CHAPTER 5

UK Competition Law

5. UK COMPETITION LAW

Introduction

The basis of UK domestic competition law is in:

- Fair Trading Act 1973
- Restrictive Trade Practices Act 1976 and 1977
- Resale Prices Act 1976 and
- Competition Act 1980.

The law is administered by a number of domestic bodies:

- The Department of Trade and Industry (the "DTI")
- Office of Fair Trading (the "OFT")
- Monopolies and Mergers Commission (the "MMC")

There are also various regulatory bodies for particular sectors, each having its particular regulator:

- Director-General of Telecommunications who heads the Office of Telecommunications (OFTEL) under the Telecommunications Act 1984
- Director-General of Gas Supply who heads the Office of Gas Supply (OFGAS) under the Gas Act 1986
- Director-General of Water Services who heads the Office of Water Services (OFWAT) under the Water Act 1989
- Director-General of Electricity Supply who heads the Office of Electricity Regulation (OFFER) under the Electricity Act 1989
- Rail Regulator who heads the Office of Rail Regulator under the Railways Act 1993

- Director-General of the National Lottery who heads the Office of the National Lottery (OFLOT) under the National Lottery Act 1993

- The Civil Aviation Authority under the Airports Act 1986

The Competition and Services (Utilities) Act 1992 may also be relevant.

The OFT, and in particular the Director-General of Fair Trading (the "DGFT"), has been given additional important functions under the Financial Services Act 1986, the Gas Act 1986, the Channel Tunnel Act 1987, the Companies Act 1989, the Electricity Act 1989, the Broadcasting Act 1990, the Courts and Legal Services Act 1990 and the Water Industry Act 1991.

The decisions and reports of the MMC investigations are a reflection of policy from time to time, whilst authorities on legal issues are to be found in the decisions of the Restrictive Practices Court and the judgments of other courts which have reviewed executive decisions in this area.

This book does not deal with the common law which relates primarily to the doctrine of the restraint of trade, and under which the courts will, as a matter of public policy, refuse to enforce a contract which is an unreasonable restraint of trade.

Restrictive Trade Practices Act 1976 and 1977

The Restrictive Trade Practices Act (the "RTPA") establishes a system of registration of restrictive goods and services agreements and information agreements as to goods. It has been supplemented by various statutory amendments.

Many inoffensive agreements have to be registered, whilst some agreements with a real anti-competitive effect can escape registration by careful drafting. The emphasis on form rather than substance is inconsistent with modern competition legislation. Moreover, the blanket exemptions (for instance, for agreements relating to professional services) are no longer considered to be justifiable.

There has been talk for a number of years of repealing the RTPA and adopting legislation more in line with EC law where the effect of the agreement is more important than the form. Despite much criticism from business and the legal profession, and various proposals in Green and White Papers for changes to the UK law on anticompetitive agreements, the RTPA seems to be here to stay. Various amendments are, however, now being brought in as the Deregulation and Contracting Out Act 1994 (the "Deregulation Act") comes bit by bit into effect. They are incorporated into the text below.

Warning

- The Restrictive Trade Practices Act is highly technical and will often apply to agreements which appear to be innocuous and to have little or no effect upon competition. This does not absolve the parties from the obligation to register.

- For various reasons the RTPA is frequently (deliberately or inadvertently) overlooked. Such oversight can have serious consequences for the businesses involved.

- Failure to register a registrable agreement may have unwelcome consequences. All purported restrictions will be void and unenforceable.

- There are various exemptions from the registration requirement, such as the sale and purchase and share subscription agreements exemptions, or the schedule of "excepted agreements". They have, however, been narrowly construed and should not be relied upon without suitable and careful analysis.

Scope of the RTPA

The RTPA deals with arrangements and agreements which restrict trade. It provides a system for such agreements to be registered with the Office of Fair Trading so that they can, if necessary, be referred to the Restrictive Practices Court (the "RP Court") which determines whether or not such agreements are expected to operate against the public interest.

The distinctions under the RTPA as to what does, or does not, constitute an agreement which is subject to registration are not based on an assessment of the agreement's economic effect but rather on its technical form. Hence some agreements which may have a minimal effect on competition may still have to be registered. On the other hand, some agreements which may have a considerable anti-competitive effect may fall outside the ambit of the RTPA. It is therefore important, when negotiating and drafting agreements which may be affected by the RTPA, to determine at an early stage whether it is possible to structure the agreement in such a way that it will not have to be registered. If so, agreements must be carefully drawn. If an agreement is, in fact, to be registered, additional provisions will be required to enable the parties to comply with their obligations under the RTPA.

Why register?

Remember that failure to register a registrable agreement could have unpleasant consequences:

- the agreement is void in respect of all relevant restrictions accepted under it;

- it is unlawful to enforce or purport to enforce any such restrictions;

- third parties adversely affected may sue for damages;

- the Court may make an Order restraining any party from giving effect to or enforcing the restrictions in the agreement;

- the OFT can act on its own initiative to investigate a registrable but unregistered agreement. It can respond to a complaint from a third party which may believe it has been injured by the operation of an unregistered agreement; or

- a subsequent investigation may lead to an order being made restraining a party from failure to register future agreements. Breach of such an order can result in proceedings for contempt of court and fines or possible prison sentences.

Restrictive Trade Practices Act Summary

- Provides for the registration of arrangements where:
  - two or more persons carry on business in UK, and
  - listed restrictions are accepted by at least two parties
- Registration is obligatory or restrictions are void
- The system is technical and treacherous
- "Fail safe" registrations can be helpful
- The RTPA can apply in addition to other controls

Criteria for registration

The main types of agreement covered by the RTPA are those relating to goods, services, information as to goods, and agreements of trade or services supply associations or between members of such associations. The RTPA deals separately with each of these types of agreement.

How does the RTPA work?

The Act applies to agreements between two or more persons carrying on business within the United Kingdom in the production or supply of goods, or in the supply of services, under which two or more parties accept restrictions of a type listed in the Act. You may, however, get the benefit of some exemptions. You need to address the following questions in the order suggested below:

(i) Is there a registrable agreement? You need to check the criteria for registrability set out below.

(ii) Does the agreement contain any restrictions which may be disregarded by virtue of certain exemptions? These restrictions will not be taken into account when counting relevant restrictions.

(iii) Are there any remaining restrictions binding at least two parties? If there are, the next question is:

(iv) Does the agreement fit into one of the exempt categories of agreements?

What constitutes an agreement?

The RTPA applies to all sorts of agreements. The concept of an agreement is very widely construed : it includes any arrangement or understanding, however informal, including oral agreements and agreements which are not legally enforceable. Information agreements as to goods may be registrable; the RTPA does not apply to information agreements relating solely to services.

In order to assess registrability it is necessary to look at all the agreements which may be linked together and which form part of an "overall arrangement". For example, where there is a "main agreement" for subscription of shares which refers to other agreements in a conditions precedent clause (shareholders' agreement, services agreement etc.), then all those agreements are together subject to an RTPA analysis and possible registration.

Who are the persons who are parties to the agreement?

A person means an individual, company or partnership. Connected companies are treated as a single person for the purpose of "counting heads" under the Act. An agreement between a parent company and a subsidiary would not be registrable as there would be only one party to that agreement. Similarly, it is usually (but not always) the case that if restrictions are accepted by two or more subsidiaries of the same group, or by a parent company on behalf of itself and its subsidiaries, then the RTPA regards them as being accepted by only one "party". This is important to the overall analysis.

Are there two or more persons carrying on business within the United Kingdom?

Business is construed widely. The test of where a business is being carried on is a factual one. A company incorporated in the United Kingdom will usually be carrying on business here, regardless of the nationality of its parent. A foreign company may be carrying on business in the United Kingdom even though it does not have a branch here.

Goods agreements, services agreement and mixed agreements

The Act deals separately with goods agreements and with services agreements. To be registrable, an agreement needs to meet either all the requirements relating to "goods agreements" or all the requirements relating to "services agreements".

Goods agreements

Are there two or more persons parties to the agreement carrying on business in the United Kingdom in the production or supply of goods? These need not be the same sort of goods. If so, are restrictions of a type listed below (section 6 RTPA) and specific to goods accepted by two or more parties? If so the Act will apply. If not, the goods provisions of the Act will not apply. You need to check whether the agreement may fall within the Act as an agreement relating to services.

Services agreements

Are there two or more persons parties to the agreement carrying on business in the United Kingdom in the supply of services? These need not be the same sort of services. If so, are restrictions of a type listed below (section 11 RTPA) and specific to services accepted by two or more parties? If so, the Act will apply. If not, the services provisions of the Act will not apply.

This distinction between goods and services agreements means, in theory, that an agreement between just two persons, where one of them produces or supplies only goods, and the other supplies only services, is not registrable.

Are there two or more parties accepting relevant restrictions?

The two or more parties who accept restrictions need not be the same as the two or more persons who are carrying on business in the United Kingdom.

What is a restriction?

Parties accept a restriction when they accept some limitation on the freedom (which they enjoyed prior to the agreement) to make their own decisions in relation to matters to do, for example, with the production or supply of goods or services. Both negative and positive obligations are included.

A party is not generally regarded as accepting a restriction within the meaning of the Act when it accepts a limitation on rights it would not have at all were it not for the agreement (the "open door" principle).

As a result, where a lessee or licensee accepts restrictions on the use of the property which is being leased to him, those restrictions will not normally be relevant to the question of registration. Similar principles apply in relation to the licensing of intellectual property rights.

Restrictions may arise as an express term of the contract or by implication and may be qualified or unqualified. A restriction may also come about not only from a simple negative obligation but also where compliance with conditions confers privileges, benefits or penalties, or additional obligations.

Only restrictions in respect of matters listed in the RTPA are relevant to the question of registrability.

A registrable agreement

- Is there an agreement?

    - written and/or oral: include everything in the "overall arrangement"

- Name the persons who are parties to the agreement

    - connected companies are one person

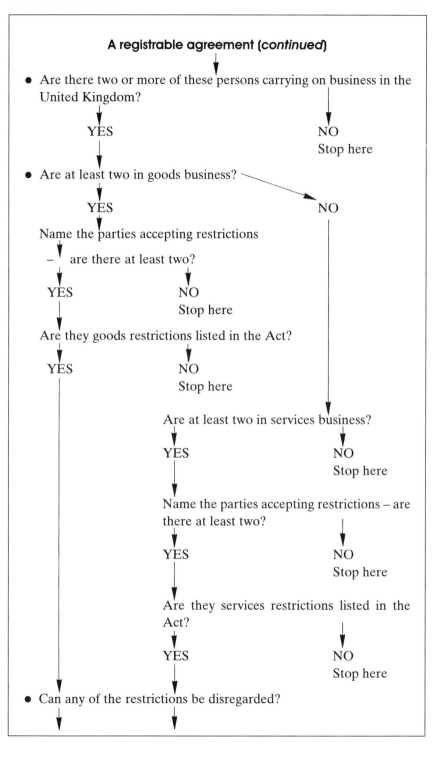

A registrable agreement (*continued*)

• Are there two or more of these persons carrying on business in the United Kingdom?

YES   NO
                                             Stop here

• Are at least two in goods business?

YES   NO

Name the parties accepting restrictions

– are there at least two?

YES   NO
                         Stop here

Are they goods restrictions listed in the Act?

YES   NO
                         Stop here

Are at least two in services business?

YES   NO
                         Stop here

Name the parties accepting restrictions – are there at least two?

YES   NO
                         Stop here

Are they services restrictions listed in the Act?

YES   NO
                         Stop here

• Can any of the restrictions be disregarded?

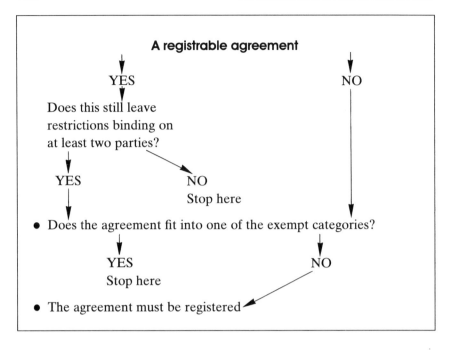

The system in practice: goods agreements

The system may be illustrated by the example of goods agreements. A goods agreement will have to be registered if it is made between two or more persons carrying on business in the United Kingdom, producing or supplying goods or applying a manufacturing process to goods, and two or more parties (who need not be the persons carrying on business in the United Kingdom) accept restrictions as a result of the agreement on any of the following matters:

(i) prices or charges to be made or recommended for the acquisition or supply or resale of goods;

(ii) the terms or conditions on which the goods are to be supplied or acquired or processed;

(iii)the quantities or descriptions of goods to be produced, supplied or acquired;

(iv)the manufacturing process to be used, or the levels or amounts of goods to be processed;

(v) the persons to or from whom, or the areas or places within which, the goods are to be supplied or manufacturing processes applied.

Getting all the documents together

In considering whether an agreement is subject to registration, it is important to consider the whole scope of the arrangements between the parties, and to identify not only provisions expressed as restrictions but also those which may apply by implication or in consequence of a term expressed in the form of a positive obligation. Similarly, one must look at all the documents, memoranda, oral agreements and so forth which together make up the whole arrangement, since it is this which must in the event be copied and described to the OFT.

Restrictions to be disregarded

An agreement which at first sight appears registrable may be saved from registration because certain types of restriction can be disregarded under the RTPA.

Terms relating exclusively to the goods/services

In particular, a term which relates exclusively to the goods or services supplied under a vertical agreement (*e.g.*, between supplier and reseller) can be disregarded.

The phrase "relates exclusively to" is difficult to explain and is not defined in the RTPA.

Examples

- restrictions in various everyday supply contracts concerning the amount of goods to be supplied by A to B at a fixed charge;

- restrictions whereby a dealer agrees to sell goods under a specified trade mark, or to advertise goods as specified by supplier.

Employment

There are also provisions enabling one to disregard certain restrictions relating to employment and workers to be employed.

Example

- supplier requiring dealer to employ staff with specific
qualifications.

Quality standards

Restrictions by which parties agree to comply with BSI standards or
the quality standards of any other statutory body can also be ignored.
As a general rule, no restriction is registrable if it merely seeks to
enforce the provisions of the general law between the parties.

Financing terms

The RTPA 1977 deals with financing terms, *e.g.*, loans, credit facilities or the lease or hire of property. It enables one to disregard
certain restrictions intended:

- to maintain a person's ability to discharge any liability incurred by
him under or in connection with the financing terms;
- to protect a person against the consequences of another person's
default in discharging such a liability.

The "financing terms" exemptions are narrow and will not always
apply. Loan structures can be complex and may involve terms which
bankers may not regard as restrictions but which are technically
caught by the Act.

Special rules for sale and purchase and share subscription agreements

Sale of Shares or Business Agreements and Share Subscription
Agreements may be exempted from registration under the RTPA by
virtue of the Restrictive Trade Practices (Services)(Amendment)
Order 1989 and the Restrictive Trade Practices (Sale and Purchase
and Share Subscription Agreements)(Goods) Order 1989 (the "1989

Orders"), provided all the conditions laid down in the 1989 Orders are met.

When considering whether an agreement may benefit from this exemption all the related agreements which together with the Sale or Share Subscription Agreement form part of the overall arrangement must be considered together. In other words, it is the overall arrangement and not simply the Sale or Subscription Agreement which needs to comply with the 1989 Orders.

The restrictions which can be ignored under the 1989 Orders are limited in terms both of type and categories of person. The net result is that the Orders allow the exemption of only certain straightforward agreements.

Exemption by category

Some specific types of agreement may in certain circumstances be exempted under the RTPA. They include agreements authorised by statute, exclusive dealing agreements, trade mark agreements, patents and registered designs, know-how agreements, copyright agreements and agreements with overseas operations. These are not general exceptions for categories of agreement, but particular exceptions for narrowly defined types of arrangement between two parties only and where the sole restrictions are those specifically listed in the relevant schedule. They must therefore be approached with care.

There is an exemption for agreements of importance to the national economy which have been approved by the Secretary of State. Certain agreements relating to the coal and steel industry, wholesale co-operative societies, agriculture, forestry and fishing and the Stock Exchange may be outside the RTPA. Similarly, there are exemptions for certain categories of agreement relating to international shipping, air transport, road passenger transport, insurance, unit trusts and certain financial matters. Finally, many categories of professional service (including legal, medical and accounting services) are excluded from the Act altogether.

RTPA action plan

- Is the basic test for application satisfied?

    - two persons carrying on business in the United Kingdom, and
      at least two parties accepting relevant restrictions?

    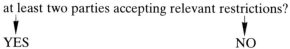

        YES   NO
                                                         Stop here

- Can any restrictions be disregarded?

    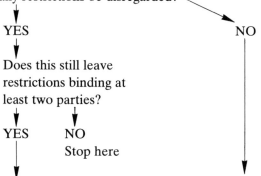

        YES   NO

        Does this still leave
        restrictions binding at
        least two parties?

        YES   NO
                   Stop here

- Does the agreement fit into any of the exempt categories?

    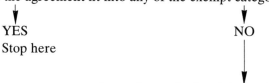

        YES   NO
        Stop here

- The agreement must be registered – furnish particulars to the OFT.

How to register an agreement: "Furnishing particulars"

The process of registering an agreement is known as "furnishing particulars". The parties are required to provide to the OFT:

- two copies of all documents setting out the terms of the agreement; and

- the statutory certificate known as RTP(C).

There is also an Annex to form RTP(C) which the OFT encourages parties to complete. It is in the form of a questionnaire about the purpose of the agreement, the parties and their market shares and the restrictions they have agreed. Use of the Annex is obligatory if "fast track" registration is being sought (see below).

All the documents need to be supplied to the OFT before the restrictions in the agreement come into effect, and in any event within three months of the signing of the agreement.

Furnishing particulars

- Prepare 2 copies of all agreements, memoranda and other documents forming the arrangements

- Complete statutory certificate RTP(C)

- Complete Form RTP(C) Annex questionnaire

- Request section 21(2) waiver

- Consider secret section (confidentiality) application

- Send complete package to OFT within 3 months of signing

- Notify other parties that the restrictions are in force

What if you are not sure

In cases of uncertainty as to whether an agreement is registrable it is advisable to make a "fail-safe furnishing" to the OFT explaining why you doubt that the agreement is registrable. If there is sufficient time, you can discuss the particular case informally with the OFT first.

Suspensory or safety clauses and timing

If an agreement is or may be registrable you should insert a clause to provide that any registrable restrictions it contains do not come into effect until the day after the agreement has been received by the OFT. This is known as a "suspensory" or "safety" clause. It allows you to furnish the agreements to the OFT after signing but within three months. There are proposals to simplify the system so that clauses will be unnecessary, but the three month time-limit will remain.

Failure to provide details within the permitted time period renders the restrictions void and unenforceable. The parties will have to re-execute in order to register (see below).

Termination and variation

There is a duty to notify the OFT of certain subsequent variations to the agreement. Those include variations whereby:

- a further restriction is accepted by one or more of the parties; or
- a restriction ceases to have effect; or
- the scope of an existing restriction is extended or reduced (for example, as regards the areas or persons or goods or services to which it relates); or
- the restrictive terms or conditions on which goods or services are to be supplied or acquired are varied.

The timing for the registration of relevant variations depends on the nature of the variation concerned. However, in order to avoid any difficulty, the RTPA position should be considered in advance of any variation being made and coming into force.

Details of the termination of a registered agreement must also be furnished to the OFT (within three months from the date of termination).

What happens when an agreement is registered?

Registration involves the whole agreement (not just the relevant restrictions) being placed on a register which is open to public inspection on weekdays from 10 am to 4.30 pm at the OFT's London EC4 offices. Once an agreement is registered anyone can inspect its terms and take copies for a small fee.

What about confidentiality?

There are provisions in Section 23(3) of the Act for certain details to be entered on the special section of the register which is not open to public inspection. This is where the particulars furnished to the OFT contain information whose publication would, in the Secretary of State's opinion, substantially damage a company's legitimate business interests.

It is the Secretary of State whom the parties have to convince on this point. The Secretary of State can refuse a request for confidentiality where he believes that it is actually in the public interest for the information to be published, even though the information is substantially damaging to the parties' business interests.

Although the scope of the confidentiality provisions has been broadened (until the coming into force on 3 January 1995 of the relevant section of the Deregulation Act 1994 they were limited primarily to protecting secret processes and the location of mineral deposits), parties still need to establish their claim for protection. The key issue lies in the identification of substantial damage to business interests. It remains to be seen how wide an interpretation the OFT will make of this new section.

Applications for documents to be placed on the special section must be made at the same time as all particulars are furnished for registration. The OFT has said that if agreements are furnished with an indication that the parties might wish at a later date to submit a special section application, the parties will receive a letter from the OFT stating that if the special section application is not made within 14 days, the whole of the agreement will be placed on the public register.

The OFT passes requests for special section treatment to the DTI. Applicants must provide signed explanatory memoranda giving specific reasons why each clause for which special treatment is claimed meets the criteria in section 23(3). Where appropriate, they must also state the precise nature of the damage to business interests which disclosure would cause and why this would be substantial. The DTI will aim to give a decision within six or seven weeks of the OFT's passing on of the application.

The Secretary of State can also direct that information be placed on the secret register where he believes publication on the main register would be contrary to the public interest.

What happens next?

The OFT considers whether the agreement is registrable. If it is, details are entered on the register. Some agreements can benefit from a fast track procedure – see below.

Dealing with the OFT

The DGFT is under a duty to refer registrable agreements to the RP Court but will not do so if he is satisfied that the restrictions are not significant (unlikely to reduce competition so as to harm the public or unlikely to produce discriminatory results).

Almost invariably, parties will apply for an exemption from reference to the RP Court on the grounds that the restrictions in their agreement are not significant in their anti-competitive effect. This is known as making representations under section 21(2) RTPA. In many cases, therefore, agreements will have to be registered because they contain relevant restrictions on the parties, but they will not be referred to the RP Court because they are unlikely to have any significant anti-competitive effect. In certain circumstances, where time permits, it is possible for the parties to consult with the OFT before signing an agreement to discuss the question of whether the OFT is likely to recommend an exemption from reference to the RP Court.

The OFT assesses whether the restrictions are likely to produce discriminatory or unfair results or restrict or reduce competition to a level that would be harmful to the public. For example, price fixing agreements will almost always be thought to contain significant restrictions.

What happens if the agreement does not get section 21(2) clearance?

If the OFT indicates that an agreement is not considered suitable for section 21(2) waiver from reference to the RP Court, it is usually in the parties' interests to negotiate with the OFT a compromise satisfactory to all concerned, rather than to leave it to the RP Court to declare whether the restrictions are contrary to the public interest. If a compromise proves impossible (for example because the parties to the agreement cannot agree to an amendment acceptable to the OFT) then the matter will be referred to the Court.

Where an agreement is registered and referred to the RP Court it will be declared contrary to the public interest unless the parties satisfy the Court that the restrictions meet one or more specific criteria – usually referred to as the "gateways" – which are set out in the RTPA. The parties have to show that the anti-competitive effect of a restriction is balanced by a corresponding benefit in one of these areas. The parties must also establish that any restrictions are reasonable.

Fast track registration

Parties to certain types of agreement can expect a response from the OFT within two months of the date on which they furnish particulars. These are agreements which either

- are *de minimis* because the aggregate turnover of the parties to the agreement in their business activities as a whole is less than £5m *or* the market share of the parties in the goods or services subject of the agreement is less than 5%; or

- have already been granted a specific individual exemption from Article 85 *or* are covered by a block exemption

and

- the agreement contains no price fixing restrictions or information provisions on the prices of goods; and

- no application for the agreement to be placed on the special (secret) section of the register has been made; and

- the parties believe the agreement is registrable (that is, they are not furnishing it on a fail-safe basis); and

- the parties have completed a form RTP(C) Annex and make a declaration that they fulfil all the above criteria

The OFT may take longer than two months if it has to refer back to the parties on any questions of registrability. In its response, the OFT will say whether in its view the agreement is registrable and, if so, whether it will be referred to the RP Court or simply placed on the Register.

Consequences of non-registration

It is not a criminal offence to fail to register an agreement within the time allowed. If registration is not effected, however, the restrictions in the agreement are void and it is unlawful for any of the parties to attempt to enforce them.

An injured third party has a right to sue for damages in respect of any loss suffered from the effects of a registrable but unregistered agreement. The DGFT also has powers which enable him to determine whether there has been a failure to register a registrable agreement, in which case he can refer the matter to the RP Court for an order prohibiting the enforcement of the restrictions.

What about EC competition law?

It is frequently necessary both to submit an agreement for registration under the RTPA and to notify it to the European Commission for negative clearance/exemption/ a comfort letter under Articles 85 and/or 86. Always consider whether Article 85 may apply.

The OFT's targets

The January 1994 code of practice for the operations of the OFT established targets for dealing with particulars furnished under the RTPA. As well as using the fast track procedure for *de minimis* agreements noted above, the OFT will:

- acknowledge agreements furnished for registration within five working days;

- register and assess for significance of restrictions all the agreements over the *de minimis* thresholds within six months (provided all the relevant information was given to the OFT). The initial target is to get 60% of agreements assessed within this timetable.

It is no longer necessary to pass automatically to the OFT details of EC notifications in relation to registrable documents. Conversely, agreements granted an EC clearance or covered by a block exemption may benefit from the fast track procedure.

Deregulation and Contracting Out Act : further proposed changes

Although the Deregulation Act as such is being brought into force step by step in 1995, its effects on the RTPA are not all immediate. This is because in many cases the Act simply grants powers to enable the Secretary of State to do something. He then has to get his Department to produce further secondary legislation in the form of Statutory Instruments before businesses can know exactly what the new law will be, and what advantages and disadvantages it brings them. The Deregulation Act 1994 includes a power to exempt from notification certain categories of restrictive agreements. The UK Government proposes that any agreements which meet the conditions set out in certain EC block exemptions will be non-notifiable under the RTPA. In theory, therefore, if this proposal is adopted a company should only have to check that its agreement would (if it has an effect on trade between Member States) be exempt from Article 85(1) under one of the block exemptions to be sure that it was also exempt from notification under the RTPA. For an explanation of Article 85 and the block exemptions, see Chapter 1.

There would be certain riders to this basic rule and the DGFT would retain power to ask companies for details of non-notifiable agreements if he thought they might be anti-competitive.

This Act also includes powers to introduce *de minimis* thresholds below which agreements will not require RTPA notification. At the time of writing, the DTI's intention is to introduce thresholds to apply where the parties to restrictive agreements have a combined turnover of less than £5–10m or a combined market share of less than 10–10% of the relevant market. So companies with large market share but low turnover would be exempt, as would companies with high turnover but a small share of the market. The turnover threshold would be applied to the combined total UK turnover of all the companies parties to the agreement and of the whole of the groups to which they belong. The market share test would apply to those groups' combined total share of the market for the products covered by the agreement, together with products viewed as substitutable for them, in the whole or any part of the UK.

The third major improvement is that the DTI proposes to simplify the time limits for registration so that agreements would not become void for want of a suspensory clause. Agreements would still have to be furnished within three months of their being made and it would be unlawful for companies to give effect to restrictions until the agreements had been furnished.

Relevant Annexes

- OFT Code of Practice on enforcement at Annex 6.

- Useful addresses and publications at Annexs 6 and 7.

- Copies of registration forms at Annex 8.

**Checklist of information required to determine whether
the RTPA applies:
What your lawyer will ask you**

A. General information

1. Detailed information about all the parties to the agreement: full
    name of each party, its main business, name and business of any
    group to which it belongs, legal status and place of registration.

2. Do two or more parties to the agreement carry on business in the
    UK? If not UK incorporated, do companies show other evidence
    of UK activity?

3. Are two or more of those parties who carry on business in the UK
    in business in goods? In services?

4. What goods or services are the subject of the agreement, *i.e.* what
    is the relevant business?

5. List all the documents, letters (including side and disclosure
    letters), memoranda, oral agreements etc which form part of the
    overall contractual arrangement.

6. The arrangement will then be analysed to assess the nature and
    extent of the restrictions accepted. If these demonstrate that the
    arrangement is caught by the RTPA (there are two or more
    parties accepting relevant restrictions), then your advisers will ask
    for further information.

*B. Information indicating effect of restrictions and required for
OFT questionnaire*

1. What purpose are the restrictions intended to achieve?

2. What are the parties' shares of the market in the relevant business
    in the UK in terms of percentages (for the purposes of calculating
    market shares for each party, include the market shares of any
    group company)?

Checklist of information required to determine whether the RTPA applies:
What your lawyer will ask you (*continued*)

3. What is the turnover of each of the parties in the UK in terms of both the relevant business and their business activities as a whole?

4. Who are the parties' main competitors in the relevant business? What are the market shares of those competitors?

5. Why are the restrictions necessary?

6. What is the geographical extent of the parties' business?

7. Why do the restrictions not have a significant effect upon competition?

C. EC competition law

1. Has a specific exemption from Article 85 been obtained or sought or is the agreement covered by a block exemption?

Resale Prices Act 1976

The Resale Prices Act is concerned with the prohibition of resale price maintenance whether collectively or individually. The principle at stake is that dealers should always be free to decide their own resale prices.

Collective resale price maintenance

Collective resale price maintenance is prohibited under sections 1 and 2. This makes unlawful any agreement or arrangement between suppliers:

(i) to withhold supplies of goods from dealers who resell or have resold goods in breach of any resale price maintenance condition (a dealer boycott);

(ii) to refuse to supply goods to such dealers except on terms and conditions (for example as to credits and discounts) less favourable than those normally applied to similar dealers (dealer discrimination);

(iii) to supply goods only to other persons who agree themselves to boycott or discriminate against dealers as described above.

Trade associations are subject to the Resale Prices Act and their recommendations as to prices may also be registrable under the RTPA. Dealers will be caught by the Act if they agree to withhold orders for goods from suppliers who supply price cutting retailers. It is also unlawful to participate in proceedings to penalise any dealer who so acts.

Individual resale price maintenance

Individual resale price maintenance is dealt with in section 9. This makes void any term or condition in a contract between a supplier and a dealer which purports to establish a minimum price for the resale of goods within the United Kingdom. It is also unlawful to include such a term in a contract or to notify to a dealer a price which is calculated to be understood as a minimum price.

This Act does not prevent a supplier's setting a maximum price and recommending resale prices provided it is clear that dealers do in fact retain the freedom to resell at below the stipulated price.

Enforcement

The Act provides for actions to be taken in court against suppliers who maintain resale prices. It is much more common, however, for disgruntled dealers to complain to the OFT and for the OFT to investigate. Where the OFT finds a complaint to be justified, it will seek undertakings from the supplier as to future compliance with the law. For example, the supplier might be required to circulate to all its dealers a statement telling them that they are free to sell, advertise and display for sale its goods at whatever price they may choose.

Mergers under the Fair Trading Act 1973

The Fair Trading Act (the "FTA") contains the main domestic legislation on the control of mergers involving one or more UK businesses. There are separate provisions dealing with transactions where the parties have connections with newspapers. The newspapers provisions are not covered in this book. Transactions falling within the newspapers provisions may be prohibited unless the Secretary of State has given his consent in advance.

The relationship between the FTA and the EC Merger Regulation is explained on page 77. In the case of large transactions parties may need to explain why their transaction is not caught by the Merger regulation.

Connections with the United Kingdom

The FTA applies to "merger situations" involving two or more enterprises of which at least one is carried on in the United Kingdom or by or under the control of a company incorporated in the United Kingdom. A merger between two UK companies naturally falls within this definition, but so also would the acquisition by a US or Japanese company of a UK business. Less obvious, perhaps, is the fact that the FTA also catches merger situations between two non-UK companies which happen to include the transfer of the activities of a UK subsidiary. So if a French company buys an Italian company and that Italian company has a business in the United Kingdom, then the FTA could apply to that transaction.

What merger situations does the FTA cover?

The FTA then defines a "merger situation qualifying for investigation". A merger which does not so qualify is unaffected by the FTA. Two questions arise:

- what is a "merger situation"?

- where a merger situation exists, what makes it qualify for investigation?

This chapter looks at each of these questions in turn.

Investigation is first by the OFT and then, if necessary, by reference to the MMC. References can be made to the MMC either where a merger is proposed or, subject to certain time limits, after it has taken place.

What is a merger situation?

A merger for these purposes is widely defined as arising when "enterprises cease to be distinct". This happens when enterprises are brought under common ownership or control, or where there are arrangements whereby one or more enterprises ceases to be carried on in order to prevent competition. An "enterprise" means the activities, or part of the activities, of a business. A sale of assets which does not also include the sale of any business activity or contracts or goodwill will therefore not be covered by the FTA.

A merger can therefore arise either where there is a change of control in a company (*e.g.*, upon a sale or issue of shares) or where there is a change of control or ownership of a business.

There are three levels of influence over an enterprise which constitute a change of control:

- the acquisition of the ability to exercise material influence

   A shareholding of 25% enabling the shareholder to block special resolutions will usually amount to material influence even if all the other shares are held by one person. A shareholding of between 15% and 25% may give material influence depending on the size of the other shareholders. A shareholding below 15% (without any additional contractual rights) is unlikely to involve material influence unless the target is a large listed company with no other substantial shareholders.

- the acquisition of the ability to control policy

   This amounts to *de facto* control. It arises when the acquirer has a sufficiently large shareholding and/or other rights in the target to enable it, in practice, to control the policy of the target, even though it has less than 50% of the voting rights.

- the acquisition of a controlling interest

   This is outright or "legal" control, which normally means a shareholding with more than 50% of the voting rights in the target.

The first threshold of material influence is lower than the decisive influence test under the Merger Regulation (see Chapter 2) and can arise on the acquisition of a shareholding as small as 10–15%.

A merger arises either when control, at whatever level, is first acquired by the party concerned, or when someone who already has control (at the material influence or *de facto* control level) acquires a higher level of control.

Common control by associated persons

For the purpose of determining whether enterprises come under common ownership or common control, associated persons and any companies which they or any of them control are treated as one person. Separate holdings by spouses and relatives, by partners, their spouses and relatives, or by two or more persons acting together to secure or exercise control of an enterprise, are therefore aggregated as one holding.

Examples of transactions where individual investors/shareholders may be treated as "associated persons" include:

- joint bids and concert parties;

- a placing to a syndicate of institutional investors;

- a refinancing/restructuring involving a large number of banks swapping debt for equity in the borrower.

The individual investors/lenders may each only take a small shareholding, but when their rights are aggregated together they may confer control with the result that a qualifying merger arises.

Merger situations

- ACo owns 100% of the shares in XYZ. BCo acquires 30% of the shares and the ability to block special resolutions. BCo acquires the ability to exercise material influence over XYZ.

- D Inc, an American company, acquires all the shares of UK-based Masset Ltd from ECo.

- JapCo, whose head office is in Tokyo, acquires the French Groupe Parico. Groupe Parico has a UK subsidiary.

Qualifying criteria

There are two separate criteria, either of which may cause a merger
to qualify for investigation:

- the market share test;
- the size of assets test.

The market share test is satisfied where, as a result of the merger, at
least 25% of all the goods or services in a particular market are
supplied or consumed in the United Kingdom (or a substantial part
of it) by the acquiring and target group. If the merger does not result
in any increase in market share at all, this test is not satisfied. If,
however, one of the parties already has a market share exceeding
25%, any enhancement, no matter how small, will have the result
that the merger qualifies for investigation.

There is also an absolute "size of assets" test. A merger will qualify
under this test, irrespective of market share, where the gross value of
the assets of the target enterprise exceeds £70m (raised from £30
million in February 1994). It is important to note that this text is
applied on a gross rather than a net basis and to assets world-wide.

Does the merger qualify for investigation? The market shares test

UK market share Acquirer AaCo	UK market share Target BeeCo	Qualifies for investigation?
20%	3%	no
20%	5%	yes
25%	5%	yes
30%	5%	yes
30%	0%	no

What should parties to a merger do?

There is no duty to pre-notify a merger. Pre-notification does, however, carry the benefit of legal certainty. Where the merger is thought
by the parties and their advisers to have no possible anti-competitive

effect – for example because the asset value of the target is over £70m but the acquirer and target are in unrelated businesses – then they may decide that no notification is necessary.

If the parties do not pre-notify, however, the purchaser/controller runs various risks arising from the possibility of a reference being made to the MMC after contractual commitments have been made and even after completion of the merger. If there were an adverse report from the MMC, the purchaser might be required to divest itself of all, or part, of the acquired enterprise which may necessitate a "forced sale". The OFT monitors the press, trade journals and industry contacts to identify mergers which have not been notified to it by the parties concerned.

A reference can be made up to six months after the later of:

- the date of completion of the transaction, or

- the earlier of the date on which relevant facts about the merger were made public or the date on which it was notified to the authorities.

This creates a long period of uncertainty for the companies involved and the DTI now proposes to shorten the period to four months.

There are three procedures available to the parties to a prospective merger which qualifies for investigation.

Confidential guidance

The OFT operates a procedure under which the parties can obtain confidential guidance (in fact issued by the Secretary of State) as to whether a proposed merger qualifying for investigation is likely to be referred to the MMC. This is confidential in that the OFT is not concerned to ask the opinion of third parties. The OFT responds to requests for confidential guidance on the basis that the request itself, as well as the terms of the advice given, are kept secret. The procedure is not available if the proposals are already in the public domain.

The OFT aims to advise the Secretary of State on confidential guidance cases within 19 working days.

On the basis of the advice received from the OFT, the Secretary of State will normally be able to confirm that there is little likelihood of a reference being made ("favourable guidance") or the transaction is likely to be referred ("unfavourable guidance"). A third possibility is that the Secretary of State is unable to give any guidance because of the need to consult third parties.

If the transaction proceeds, the parties will have to decide whether to make a formal notification (which the OFT will expect) and fees will be payable at that stage.

Fair Trading Act merger summary

- Provides for notification of
    - a merger situation
    - which qualifies for investigation because
        - it creates or enlarges market share over 25%, or
        - assets acquired over £70m
- Voluntary pre-notification procedure available
- Confidential guidance can be requested from OFT
- Fees are payable
- RTPA may also apply

Fast track notification

Although there is no general duty to pre-notify mergers (other than under the newspapers provisions), the Companies Act 1989 introduced a "fast track" procedure for voluntarily pre-notifying mergers. This procedure is only available where there has been a public announcement and where the merger will not take place until clearance is obtained.

The parties complete a Merger Notice which gives the OFT 20 working days to consider the proposed merger. The consideration period is subject to one single possible extension of 15 working days.

Informal applications

The parties may make an informal application to the OFT in writing with a view to obtaining clearance. In this case the statutory fast track time limits for a decision do not apply, but the OFT's Code of Conduct includes a target of 39 days in which the OFT should make its decision.

Where the DGFT has announced target periods in the Code of Conduct, these are maxima and will run from the day on which the OFT receives sufficient information to enable it to begin its assessment (a "satisfactory submission") until the OFT sends its advice to ministers.

Qualifying mergers: should we notify?

- Assets taken over exceed £70m world-wide, but companies are in substantially different areas of business : no combined market shares above 10% can be identified in any UK business sector. The companies are certain there could be no effect on competition in their respective markets as a result of the acquisition.

  Decision: no pre-notification made.

- Assets to be taken over valued at £42m. Merger plans are still secret and no announcement has been made. The companies are in related business areas, making different ranges of kitchen cabinets, tables and other fittings. They are unsure of the correct definition of the market. If the market is for "kitchen furniture" then it includes many suppliers, from the bespoke handmade to the self-assembly chain store, and the companies' combined market shares are about 5%. On the other hand, a narrowing down of the market to the "upper" or "luxury" end might produce a market share of 30% (Company A's 20% plus Company B's 10%).

  Decision: confidential guidance sought.

- XCo, which has 62% of the market for domestic heating units suitable for use in bathrooms, announces that it intends to acquire a 40% interest in the shares of YCo. The transaction will also give XCo contractual rights which enable it to control YCo's business plan. YCo has 4% of the relevant market; it is the specialist bathroom business unit of WCo, which also makes complete domestic central heating systems. If the deal goes well, XCo will probably acquire the other 60% of YCo next year.

  Decision: confidential guidance not available, so XCo pre-notifies the transaction to the OFT.

Giving information to the OFT: the Merger Notice

The standard Merger Notice reproduced in Annex 8 requires in Part One brief information about the party notifying, the proposal being notified and any steps taken to publicise it. Part Two of the Notice demands responses to a series of questions, some quite complex and not all relevant in every case. The time periods for consideration by the OFT can only start to run when all the relevant information has been provided.

It is an offence punishable by fine of up to £2,000 and/or a maximum prison sentence of two years knowingly or recklessly to supply false or misleading information directly or indirectly to the OFT.

Merger Notices may be withdrawn by written notice to the OFT.

What the OFT wants to know

The OFT finds it helpful if your submission includes:

- a summary of the transaction – parties and type;

- whether there are external timetable constraints (*e.g.* under the Take-over Code);

- a description of the business being acquired;

- a note on the areas of overlap between acquirer and target;

- the reasons for the acquisition; and

- copies of the parties' most recent Annual Report and Accounts.

The OFT will assess the effects, if any, of the merger on competition. The question of what markets are affected is vital. Businesses will put forward their own definitions and reasoning, but in the end it is the OFT's opinion which counts. It is therefore essential to have access to good unbiased information. The OFT considers "demand side substitutability" – whether there are products which customers would happily use as an alternative to your products, for example, if you were to put up your prices. It also looks at "supply side sub-stitutability" – what other companies might be considered to be in the same market as you, even if at the moment they do not supply exactly the same goods/services, for example because they could easily begin to make those products. It is also important to identify the correct geographical market, whether, for example, it is regional, national or European.

Fees

Fees for merger clearance are payable to the OFT on a sliding scale depending on the size of the gross assets of the target.
    The amounts payable are:

- where the assets to be taken over do not exceed £30m but the market share test is satisfied   £5,000

- where the assets to be taken over are between £30m and £100m and if the value is less than £70m the market share test is satisfied   £10,000

- where the assets to be taken over exceed £100m   £15,000

Where a Merger Notice is used, the relevant fees must be paid when the Notice is delivered to the OFT. In other cases, the fees are payable when the Secretary of State announces whether or not a reference is to be made, and are payable even when the parties have not themselves given any notification to the OFT.

OFT investigations

Once the OFT has been informed that a qualifying merger is about to take place, or it learns from its own investigation that such a merger has already taken place, it will conduct an investigation with a view to advising the Secretary of State on whether to make a reference to the

MMC. A large proportion of mergers which qualify on the size of assets tests alone are allowed to proceed without a reference.

Grounds for reference to the MMC

The Government has emphasised that the primary consideration in determining whether or not to make a reference is the likely effect of the merger on competition. Under the FTA, however, the Secretary of State has a wide discretion as to whether to refer a merger. Once a merger is referred the MMC is required to investigate its effect on the public interest. Again, the primary considerations are normally those relating to competition, although the public interest is defined in the FTA in very general terms.

MMC merger views

- Thomson Travel wanted to acquire Horizon Midlands. Both companies were in the air package holiday market. Combined, the two would have 38% of the market; the next largest player would have 14%.

The MMC cleared the acquisition.

- Kingfisher Group, owners of general stores (Woolworth), DIY stores (B&Q) and electrical retailers (Comet) planned to buy the Dixon Group, owners of two other well-known electrical retailers (Dixon and Curry's). The definition of the market was difficult; combined shares would be between 21% and 26%, depending on the definition.

The MMC blocked the deal.

- Why this difference of opinion? The MMC is pro-consumer; it looks at the creation of market power and the possibility of abuse; it considers how easily new competitors could enter the market. In this comparison, the last question was important. The MMC's report stresses that "barriers to entry into tour operating are very low ... the costs of entering the market are low ... accommodation and aircraft seats are generally readily available".

Undertakings as an alternative to a reference

The Secretary of State is, by virtue of the Companies Act 1989, able to accept undertakings from parties to a merger as an alternative to a reference to the MMC. Companies may already offer divestment undertakings as an alternative to a merger reference, that is, they may for example accept that in order to proceed with the proposed acquisition, they must sell off certain of their existing business units, or they must within a certain period sell off certain units of the target company. The Deregulation Act will extend the Secretary of State's power so that he may accept other sorts of undertaking as well, including those about the future behaviour of the companies concerned. This part of the Act was not at the time of writing in force.

The role of the MMC

When a reference is made in respect of a proposed merger, the parties are automatically prohibited from acquiring shares in each other unless a consent from the Secretary of State is applicable. In the case of a completed merger, measures may be taken to restrict the purchaser's involvement in the target's business during the MMC investigation.

If a merger is referred, the MMC compiles an analytical report and concludes whether the merger is likely to have an adverse effect on the public interest. This report is published.

If the MMC concludes that the merger is not expected to have an adverse effect, then the Secretary of State and the OFT have no further powers to intervene. If, on the other hand, the MMC makes an adverse finding, the Secretary of State has wide-ranging powers to intervene, including ordering divestment of part of the merged enterprises' business. He is not, however, obliged to exercise these powers and has on a few isolated occasions effectively refused to accept the MMC's conclusion. Very often the Secretary of State will not need to exercise his formal powers because the parties will themselves offer undertakings or other steps to deal with the adverse effects identified by the MMC.

Checklist of information required to determine whether the merger provisions of the Fair Trading Act 1973 apply: What your lawyer will ask you

1. What sort of a transaction is this and are there any linked transactions?
   - Explain what rights are being acquired – shares, voting rights, contractual rights in relation to business operations and so forth;
   - Who are the other shareholders in the target (if any) and what are their shareholdings?
   - Does the acquirer already have any interest in the target?

2. Is the acquirer "associated" with any other person who has, or will have, an interest in the target (*e.g.* family relations or partners)? Does the transaction involve any form of consortium, syndicate or grouping?

3. What is the book value of the world-wide gross assets of the target group as stated in the most recent Report and Accounts? If the current value is thought to be very different, explain why.

4. Please describe the business of the acquiring and target groups and their market position in the United Kingdom. Are they in the same or similar businesses? What are their market shares and those of their main competitors?

5. Explain the reasons for the acquisition.

6. Does the City Code apply to the transaction and is a whitewash to be applied for?

7. Does the target group have any newspaper interests?

8. What is the proposed timetable for the transaction?

9. Does the transaction involve any party accepting restrictions of any kind (*e.g.* non compete, use of information, restrictions on business activity, exclusivity, supply or purchasing obligations, etc)? If so, please provide details.

Monopolies under the Fair Trading Act 1973

The Fair Trading Act gives the Secretary of State, and in most cases the DGFT, the right to refer "monopoly situations" to the Monopolies and Mergers Commission (the "MMC") for investigation. Monopoly situations can arise in relation to goods, services and exports. There are two types of monopoly under the FTA.

Structural or scale monopoly

The first type of monopoly considered by the Act is sometimes called a structural or scale monopoly, where one company or group of companies has a market share in excess of 25%. The company may supply more than 25% of the goods or services of the relevant market, or may be supplied with 25% of those goods or services. In its definition of a structural monopoly, the FTA is concerned with market shares in relation to the supply of goods and services and not in relation to their production.

Complex or behavioural monopoly

The second type of monopoly is referred to in the FTA as a complex monopoly situation. Economists also call it a behavioural monopoly. More than one company is involved. A complex monopoly arises where any number of different companies, whose combined market shares in the production or supply of certain goods in the United Kingdom is 25% or more, so conduct their respective affairs as to prevent, restrict or distort competition in connection with the production or supply of those goods in the United Kingdom. The same test applies to markets for services. The companies will not necessarily have entered into any particular agreement but their parallel actions will demonstrate an anti-competitive effect.

Monopoly situation in relation to exports

There is a little-used section in the FTA which allows the MMC to investigate export of goods from the United Kingdom, where the

Monopoly situations

Structural	Complex
XCo makes wall lights for domestic use and also imports wall lights from other countries. XCo distributes all these products in the UK. It supplies 45% of all wall lights bought in the UK for domestic use.	
	ACo, BCo and ECo are brewers of beer. Together they supply more than 55% of all bitters and 60% of all lagers sold in the public houses in the UK. They each own many public houses and severely limit the number of "guest beers" such pubs can sell; the publicans in these tied houses have to pay whatever wholesale prices the brewers set.
YCo is a pharmaceutical company. Many of its OTC products are supplied in capsules of which the main ingredient is a particular type of edible gel ("E gel"), which it obtains from a variety of suppliers. YCo buys 29% of the "E gel" on the UK market.	

exporters have a market share of at least 25% in the production of such goods in the United Kingdom. In fact export investigations usually include an examination of the UK market as well.

Investigations and reports

Where the DGFT has reason to believe that a monopoly situation may be being abused he will make informal investigations, which may lead to a reference to the MMC. If a reference is made, the MMC has to determine whether a monopoly situation exists and whether it operates or may be expected to operate against the public interest. Various different types of reference can be made according to whether the MMC is to investigate generally or to investigate specific complaints.

A detailed report of the MMC's findings is published. In the case of an adverse finding, the MMC also publishes its recommendations as to what action should be taken to prevent damage to the public interest. The Secretary of State has wide-ranging powers to enable him to prevent abuses of monopolies following a report by the MMC.

Industry investigations

A monopoly investigation, particularly of a behavioural or complex monopoly, often amounts to an investigation of a whole industry or sector.

The MMC has investigated the market for the supply of beer for retail sale in the United Kingdom. Its report in 1989 led to the publication of two statutory instruments which, *inter alia*, limited the number of tied premises that brewers could own as well as requiring brewers to publish wholesale price lists above which they cannot charge.

In 1994 the MMC investigated the market for private medical services in the United Kingdom and found that the BMA guidelines on private consultant work operated against the public interest. As a result, the guidelines were abandoned. The BMA gave undertakings not to publish similar guidance on the fees to be charged for private medical services.

The Secretary of State can make references to the MMC on general practices operated in a number of different sectors and can also refer restrictive labour practices for investigation.

MMC reports

Pre-recorded music

Five major record companies with a combined market share of over two thirds of the market were provisionally found to:

- adopt similar pricing policies to each other for various formats – CD, cassettes, and vinyl;

- have restrictive licensing practices;

- enter into restrictive recording contracts with artists.

A complex monopoly situation therefore existed.

The MMC also found that:

- there was strong competition both among record companies and among retailers and neither were making excessive profits;

- the companies were not able to exercise market power in a way which enabled them to exploit their monopoly positions.

Conclusions: a complex monopoly situation existed but the companies were not taking any steps to maintain or exploit it. There were no facts which might be expected to operate against the public interest.

Films

In its third investigation into the supply of films, the MMC found:

- distributor/exhibitor alignment in sharing distribution markets;

- distributors refusing to supply, requiring minimum exhibition periods, imposing exclusivity and restrictions on screen use and having influence over admission prices.

A complex monopoly system therefore existed. A structural or scale monopoly was also found to exist in favour of one particular cinema group.

MMC reports (*continued*)

The MMC found that these practices:

- reduced competition for screens amongst aligned distributors;
- reduced the pressure on the big cinema chain exhibitors to ensure that their cinemas could compete for prints of first released films on merit;
- reduced consumers' choice of cinema in which to see a given film.

Conclusions: a complex monopoly operated against the public interest. The MMC recommended that the practice of alignment be prohibited, and that minimum exhibition periods must be limited to a maximum of two weeks on first release and one week subsequently.

Compliance costs

As part of reforms to its practice announced at the end of January 1994, the OFT is to consider ways in which the compliance costs on companies subject to undertakings can be reduced (time limits, consideration of representations to lift undertakings, automatic five-year review).

Register of undertakings

In April 1994, a Register of Undertakings and Orders under the Competition Act 1980 and the monopoly provisions of the Fair Trading Act 1973 was established. It includes a list of existing undertakings where the DGFT has responsibility for keeping those under review. The first issue of the Register was up to date to 31 March 1994 to be followed by a revised version to 31 December 1994. Thereafter the Register should be updated annually incorporating any amendments; the update will also include the removal of entries where the company concerned has been released from its undertakings by the Secretary of State.

The Register is open to the public, free of charge, and copies can be obtained from the OFT.

Competition Act 1980

The Competition Act (the "CA") is concerned with "anti-competitive practices". There is no absolute prohibition of such practices under the CA (in contrast to EC competition law in relation to the abuse of dominant positions). Instead there is a procedure, similar to that under the FTA for monopolies, for alleged anti-competitive practices to be investigated and ultimately for a determination as to whether they are expected to operate against the public interest.

There has been a surprisingly small number of CA investigations since the introduction of this Act in 1980. Many of these have involved relatively minor sectors of industry.

Anti-competitive practices

Courses of conduct likely to come under CA scrutiny:

- price discrimination
- predatory pricing
- tie-in sales/full-line forcing
- refusal to supply
- resale price maintenance

What is an anti-competitive practice?

An anti-competitive practice is defined in the CA as a course of conduct pursued by a person in the course of business which "of itself or when taken together with a course of conduct pursued by persons associated with him, has or is intended or is likely to have the effect of restricting, distorting or preventing competition in connection with the production, supply or acquisition of goods in the United Kingdom or any part of it or the supply or securing of services in the United Kingdom or any part of it".

The CA does not proscribe particular practices, but instead the definition is directed at the effect of the particular practice in its particular circumstances.

The concept of a "practice" is a wide one. The procedures of the firm under investigation are considered both *per se* and in the light of the market position of its competitors. The effect of the practice has to be considered in the context of the relevant market (see below) and it may have an effect at several different levels of distribution. The intention of the firm under investigation is also relevant, because the CA specifically refers to a practice which "has or is intended to have" an anti-competitive effect. It is not necessary to establish "market dominance" in the terms of Article 86, but some market power is necessary if a firm's practices are to have an anti-competitive effect.

Possible anti-competitive practices include those relating to price discrimination, predatory pricing, vertical price squeezing, tie-in sales, full-line forcing, rental-only contracts, exclusive supply, exclusive purchase and selective distribution. These often involve a refusal to deal which is intended to have an anti-competitive effect.

Predatory pricing

It is often difficult in practice to draw a distinction between what is predatory behaviour (what the OFT calls "predation") and what is rigorous (but not anti-competitive) competition.

The OFT has through its practice over a period of years and in compiling Competition Act reports defined a three-part approach to identifying "predation". It looks in particular at:

- the structure of the market and the characteristics of the alleged predator, to see whether predation really is a feasible strategy for him;

- the effects of the alleged action on the profitability of the alleged predator;

- whether the alleged predator intends to eliminate a specific competitor from the market.

Excluded sectors

Under the CA and related regulations a number of areas are excluded from investigation:

(i) Agreements which are subject to registration under the Restrictive Trade Practices Act are not also subject to the CA. This reflects the policy under the monopoly provisions of the Fair Trading Act, that restrictive trade practices agreements should be considered solely under the RTPA and not under the other domestic competition legislation.

(ii) Firms whose groups have an annual turnover of less than £10m *or* who have less than 25% of a relevant market are exempted from investigation. These criteria were introduced by the Anti-Competitive Practices (Exclusions)(Amendment) Order 1994. The threshold was previously that turnover should be less than £5m *and* that the business should have less than 25% of a relevant market.

(iii)There are further exemptions in relation to certain sectors, such as international shipping and international civil aviation.

Investigations by the OFT

The responsibility for the initial investigation of alleged anti-competitive practices rests with the OFT, which normally reacts to complaints from trade competitors. If it believes that a complaint may be justified, the OFT will undertake an initial informal investigation of the practice concerned. This provides an opportunity for the company under investigation to change its practices so as to avoid any formal investigation.

If a formal investigation procedure is begun, the first stage is an investigation by the OFT itself solely into the question of whether a firm under investigation is conducting an anti-competitive practice. The OFT's report is published. If the OFT concludes that an anti-competitive practice is being carried on, it provides an opportunity for the firm under investigation to offer undertakings to the satisfaction of the OFT. If undertakings of this sort are not forthcoming, the matter will be referred to the MMC for a full investigation into the practice itself and into the effect on the public interest.

Formal powers to prevent the practice only arise once the MMC has reported and concluded that the practice was both anti-competitive and likely to have an adverse effect on the public interest. The firm under investigation will then have a final opportunity to offer satisfactory undertakings, failing which the Secretary of State can proceed to make the appropriate order.

Competition Act reports

- A manufacturer of bicycles operated a selective distribution policy in which it supplied specialist cycle shops but refused to sell to certain multiple retailers. It was found to be the market leader.

  Decision: the practice was anti-competitive.

- A new free-sheet newspaper was launched in the South of Scotland. The main newspaper publisher in the region retaliated by itself launching a free-sheet in which, for an initial period, it provided free advertising space on condition that the advertisers did not use any other free-sheet in the region. After the introductory period, advertising space was offered at rates below cost.

  Decision: the practice was anti-competitive.

- The operators of a bus station on the Isle of Wight refused competitors access to the station. These other bus companies were thus unable to tell potential passengers at the station about their services.

  Decision: the practice significantly restricted competition.

- A bus company in West Yorkshire was accused of predatory pricing on routes where it faced competition, and may not have been making enough to cover its overheads on some parts of the service.

  Decision: no evidence that the bus company's actions did in fact restrict or prevent competition or that it wanted to do so.

The Register

Undertakings given as a result of Competition Act investigations are now listed in the Register of Undertakings and Orders under the Competition Act 1980 and the monopoly provisions of the Fair Trading Act 1973, established by the OFT in April 1994. See page 154 for more details.

CONTENTS OF
CHAPTER 6

French Competition Law

6. FRENCH COMPETITION LAW

Introduction: the law and the administration

The main statutes

French competition law is chiefly regulated by the ordinance of 1 December 1986 on freedom of prices and competition ("l'Ordonnance du 1er décembre 1986 relative à la liberté des prix et de la concurrence", the "1986 Ord") completed by a Decree of 29 December 1986 (the "1986 Decree"). The 1986 Ord applies to all types of undertakings involved in goods or services-related activities. The 1986 Ord includes three main sets of competition rules:

- those which prohibit anti-competitive behaviour (such as cartels, abuse of dominant position and abuse of economic dependence). Some of these provisions are similar to the corresponding provisions in Articles 85 and 86 of the Treaty of Rome;

- those which prohibit specific restrictive trade practices (such as refusal to supply, resale at a loss);

- those which govern merger control.

Rules governing tortious liability and, in particular, Article 1382 of the French Civil Code, may be relied upon to sanction anti-competitive behaviour such as "concurrence déloyale" (or disloyal competition).

Anti-trust authorities

Competition law in France is enforced by both administrative and judicial authorities.

Administrative authorities

The Competition Council (Conseil de la concurrence) is the main competition authority. Its members are judges, representatives of the main economic sectors and other competent persons. The Competition Council has both an enforcement and a consultative role. It may be approached by a wide range of persons (including, in particular, the Minister of Economy, victims of anti-competitive practices, professional organisations and consumer associations) in relation to anti-competitive practices falling within the ambit of the 1986 Ord. The Council can also act at its own discretion.

Every procedure before the Competition Council begins with an enquiry. The Council's agents may enter business premises and request communication of documents. The Competition Council is empowered:

- to order undertakings concerned to stop their anti-competitive practices;

- to grant injunctions;

- to impose administrative fines of up to 5% of the undertakings' annual turnover;

- to refer any fraudulent practices to the public prosecution office.

The Competition Council may be consulted by the Minister of Economy in relation to merger control, or by the Government or the Parliament on all issues relating to competition. It may also be consulted by a court whenever a competition issue arises.

The Competition Council has no jurisdiction to deal with certain restrictive trade practices such as disloyal competition or refusal to sell.

The Minister of Economy

The Minister of Economy has the ultimate power to clear or veto mergers. It may also exercise its authority whenever an undertaking abuses its dominant position or a situation of economic dependence.

The DGCCRF

The DGCCRF is the abbreviation of the Direction Générale de la Concurrence, de la Consommation et de la Répression des Fraudes.

This office, which is part of the Minister of Economy, has a wide-ranging role. It is empowered to monitor the markets in order to detect any anti-competitive practices and to collect evidence of such practices.

Judicial authorities

The Competition Council has no power to award damages or to pronounce the nullity of an anti-competitive practice. The victim of such a practice will have to seek these remedies from the courts, which are likely to be commercial tribunals. There may therefore be two parallel procedures: one before the Competition Council and one before a court. The courts have exclusive jurisdiction to deal with cases of "disloyal competition" and other specific restrictive trade practices such as refusal to supply.

French competition law terminology		
French	*Abbreviation*	*English*
Conseil de la Concurrence		Competition Council
Ministre de l'Economie		Minister of the Economy
Direction Générale de la Concurrence, de la Consommation et de la Répression des Fraudes	DGCCRF	Office of Competition, Consumer Affairs and Fraud
Ordonnance du 1er décembre 1986 relative à la liberté des prix et de la concurrence	1986 Ord	Ordinance of 1 December 1986 on freedom of prices and competition

---

French competition law terminology (*continued*)

Décret du 29 décembre 1986 fixant les conditions d'application de l'ordonnance du 1er décembre 1986	1986 Decree	Decree of 29 December implementing the 1986 Ord
Concurrence déloyale		Unfair or disloyal competition
Refus de vente		Refusal to supply
Vente à perte		Sale at a loss
Vente avec prime		Sale with a free gift
Ventes liées		Tie-in/tied sales

Rules governing anti-competitive behaviour

Agreements between undertakings and concerted practices

The 1986 Ord prohibits any agreements or concerted practices which have as their object or effect the prevention, restriction or distortion of competition, in particular where they aim to:

- limit access to the market or free competition. For example, loyalty rebates may hinder access to the market as customers will have no incentive to deal with other suppliers;

- hinder free fixation of prices (as a result, prices are kept artificially low or high);

- limit or control production, markets, investments or technical development. Cartels of this sort are punished severely by the competition authorities;

- share markets or sources of supply.

The scope of the 1986 Ord is particularly wide, as it applies to all types of cartels (vertical or horizontal) whatever their forms. Oral and written agreements, express or tacit arrangements may all be caught.

Abuse of a dominant position

The 1986 Ord prohibits the abuse of a dominant position held by a single undertaking or group of undertakings in the French market or a substantial part thereof. The concept of dominant position is not expressly defined in the 1986 Ord. It is assessed by reference, in particular, to market share, financial strength, the ability to act independently from competitors and barriers to entry in the relevant market.

Examples of abuses listed in the 1986 Ord include refusal to supply, tie-in and discriminatory conditions of sale. These provisions and the way they have been interpreted are very similar to Article 86 of the Treaty of Rome (see Chapter 1 on EC competition law).

Economic dependence

The 1986 Ord prohibits the abuse of a state of economic dependence. This exists where a customer or a supplier does not have any alternative source of supply at equivalent conditions. The narrow scope of the concept of economic dependence explains why only a small number of cases have been referred to the Competition Council on that ground.

This prohibition applies only to relationships between business undertakings. It does not affect relationships between undertakings and their consumers (that is, persons acting outside their trade or profession). The concept of economic dependence requires more than a mere inequality between the parties.

The ongoing contractual relationships must be vital to one of the parties and essential to its commercial survival. There will be abuse of such economic dependence where the strong party imposes conditions on the dependent party which the latter would not have accepted had it been economically independent.

The concept of economic dependence is one peculiar to French competition law and has no equivalent under EC law.

Exemptions

Agreements, as well as abuses of dominant positions or abuses of economic dependence, may be exempted under Article 10 of the 1986 Ord from the prohibitions mentioned above provided:

- they result from the application of a statute. This is a very strict condition: the anti-competitive practice must be the direct and inevitable result of a statute and not only allowed by that statute; or

- they may guarantee economic progress; consumers must obtain a fair share of the resulting benefits and the undertakings involved must not have the ability to eliminate competition in respect of a substantial part of the relevant products. Finally, the restrictions must be indispensable to meet the objective of economic progress.

These conditions are very similar to those enshrined in Article 85(3) of the Treaty of Rome. There are, however, two major differences. First, the exemption applies to abuses of dominant position (or economic dependence), whereas such abuses cannot be exempted under Article 86 of the Treaty of Rome. Second, the exemption is not subject to prior notification of the practice concerned to the competition authorities. It will be for the Competition Council or the courts to undertake an overall assessment of the anti-competitive practices to determine whether they qualify for exemption under Article 10.

Specific restrictive trade practices

The rules governing specific restrictive trade practices aim to guarantee the transparency of the market. These practices may be either civil or criminal offences. Here are a few examples.

Refusal to sell

Refusal to sell is prohibited *per se* even if it is not committed by a dominant undertaking or as the result of a cartel. This is another instance where French competition law is very different from EC or other national anti-trust laws.

It is prohibited to refuse to sell to a consumer (that is, a person acting outside his trade or profession) unless there is a legitimate reason. A legitimate reason may be that the products requested are not available in stock. Refusal to sell to a consumer is a criminal offence and may be punished by fines or a prison sentence.

Although refusal to sell occurring between businesses is no longer a criminal offence, it is prohibited where:

- the customer's orders are not "abnormal". The normality of the orders is assessed by reference to the usual commercial practices in the relevant market. For example, the quantities ordered may be considered unusually too high or too low. The customer may not be qualified to sell the products concerned (for example his staff does not have the proper training). This is particularly relevant in the context of selective distribution;

- the customer is acting in good faith. The customer may not be acting in good faith where, for example, he places a second order before paying the first invoice. A distributor selling the products at a discount or cheaper than other resellers would not be regarded as acting in bad faith. It may prove very difficult for the supplier to establish his customer's bad faith.

Resale price maintenance

The 1986 Ord prohibits any person from imposing, either directly or indirectly, minimum resale prices or minimum margins. Resale price maintenance is punished by a fine from FF5,000 to FF100,000.

Recommended prices are allowed provided they are not, in practice, compulsory. Maximum prices may be imposed provided they do not result in the reseller selling at a loss.

Resale at a loss

The resale of a product at a price inferior to the purchase price is forbidden. It is a criminal offence punishable by a fine (from FF5,000 to FF100,000).

Discriminatory prices between businesses

Discrimination between businesses regarding prices, terms of payment and conditions of sale is prohibited where it is based on no actual consideration and it results in an advantage or disadvantage in terms of competition.

Discrimination between customers may be justified where, for example, the quantities ordered are different, the customer deals with the packaging or transportation of the goods or where a distributor offers after-sales service.

Tie-in

Tie-in with a consumer (acting outside his trade or profession) is a criminal offence whereas it is only a civil offence when dealing with a professional. It is subject to the same sanctions as refusal to sell.

Free gift

It is forbidden to offer a free gift to consumers unless the free product (or service) is identical to the products (or services) supplied, is a sample or is of small value.

Other requirements aimed at transparency

Any producer, wholesaler or importer must communicate to any reseller who so requires his price list and conditions of sale including terms of payment and any discounts. Failure to comply with this requirement is a criminal offence.

Invoices must be issued in relation to any supply of goods or services. Invoices must include in particular the names of the parties, their address, the date of the sale, quantities supplied, price without VAT and any discount.

Disloyal or unfair competition

An undertaking is guilty of unfair or "disloyal" competition ("concurrence déloyale") when it is using disloyal practices to solicit customers away from a competitor. The victim of such practices may claim damages under the general rules on tortious liability or seek an injunction to stop the practice.

Unfair competition would include, for example, smear campaigns over a competitor's products, introducing confusion as to the companies' products or commercial names (because of their similarities) or soliciting away a competitor's employees.

Merger control

Merger control is a relatively recent development in French competition law. It was first introduced in 1977 and is now governed by the 1986 Ord. It covers "concentrations".

There is "concentration" whenever one or more undertakings acquire the ability to exercise decisive influence over one or more other undertakings.

This wide concept is therefore very similar to the EC Merger Regulation definition of a concentration. The manner in which decisive influence is acquired is irrelevant.

The relevant thresholds

A merger or concentration may qualify for investigation by the Minister of Economy when the following conditions are met:

- the merger will create or strengthen a dominant position as a result of which competition will be impeded; and
- the undertakings which are parties to the merger or which are the subject thereof or which are economically linked to such undertakings have either:
  - (i) a combined market share of 25% on the French market or a substantial part thereof; or
  - (ii) an aggregate turnover on the French market of more than FF7 billion, provided that at least two undertakings have a turnover of at least FF2 billion.

Notification

The parties to a concentration which falls within the ambit of the 1986 Ord have three options:

(i) they may pre-notify the proposed merger to the Minister of Economy; or

(ii) they may notify the merger within three months of completion.

Notification of a merger is not compulsory. When a merger is notified, the Minister of Economy has two months to reach a decision (or six months if he refers the merger to the Competition Council). If the Minister of Economy takes no action within the relevant time period, the merger is deemed to have been cleared.

The Competition Council will assess the overall impact of the concentration on competition and determine to what extent the merger's contribution to economic progress compensates for any restrictions on competition.

(iii) the third option open to the parties is not to notify. This may be a risky decision as the Minister of Economy has no time limit to investigate a concentration falling within the scope of the 1986 Ord.

Following the review of a merger, the Minister of Economy also has three options:

(i) he may authorise the merger unconditionally;

(ii) he may veto the merger. If the merger has already been completed, the buyer may have to divest itself of the target;

(iii) he may authorise the merger subject to conditions. For example, the Minister of Economy may order the parties to take any measure necessary to contribute to social and economic progress so as to compensate for the restrictions on competition resulting from the concentration. The parties are obliged to comply with those conditions if they want to go ahead with the merger. Failure to comply is punishable by a fine of up to 5% of the turnover.

In case of an abuse of dominant position (or of economic dependence) the Competition Council may require the Minister of Economy to order the parties to review or terminate the concentration, even if the latter was subject to the control (and clearance) of the Minister of Economy under the 1986 Ord procedure.

CONTENTS OF CHAPTER 7

German Competition Law

7. GERMAN COMPETITION LAW

Introduction: the main statutes

German competition law is mainly regulated by the Act Against Restraints of Competition (GWB, Gesetz gegen Wettbewerbsbeschränkungen; the "Anti-trust Act") and the Act Against Unfair Competition (UWG, Gesetz gegen den unlauteren Wettbewerb). Whereas the basic aim of the Anti-trust Act is the preservation and protection of the freedom of competition by maintaining competitive market structures, the Act Against Unfair Competition is designed to prevent unethical business practices and to provide a certain standard of fair play. Certain types of behaviour such as boycotts or abuses of dominant positions may violate both acts.

Unfair competition law is also regulated in several laws dealing with specific competitive practices such as the Act Concerning Price Discounts (Rabattgesetz), the Regulation on Complementary Extras (Zugabeverordnung) and the Regulation Concerning the Quotation of Prices (Preisangabenverordnung). However, there are strong political leanings towards the abolition of the Act Concerning Price Discounts. Further special regulations for the pharmaceutical and drug business exist in the Drug Advertising Act (HWG, Heilmittelwerbegesetz), and labelling requirements under the Food Law (LMBG, Lebensmittel- und Bedarfsgegenständegesetz). Finally, the Wine Law (Weingesetz), the Regulation on Cosmetics (Kosmetikverordnung) and the Act Concerning the Closing Time of Stores (Ladenschlußgesetz) contain further unfair competition rules.

Some of the legal areas are developing rapidly in the light of the process of harmonisation with EC Law. There are also vehement political controversies about liberalising or even abolishing in part or in whole the legislation on the closing time of stores, on price discounts and on "complementary extras".

German competition law terminology

German	Abbreviation	English
Gesetz gegen Wett-bewerbsbeschrä-kungen	GWB	Act Against Restraints of Competition
Gesetz gegen den unlauteren Wettbe-werb	UWG	Act Against Unfair Competition
Rabattgesetz	RabattG	Act Concerning Price Discounts
Zugabeverordnung	ZugabeV	Regulation on Complementary Extras
Preisangabenverord-nung	Preisanga-benV	Regulation Concerning the Quotation of Prices
Heilmittelwerbege-setz	HWG	Drug Advertising Act
Lebensmittel– und Bedarfsgegenstände-gesetz	LMBG	Food law
Weingesetz	WeinG	Wine law
Kosmetikverordnung	KosmetikV	Regulation on Cosmetics
Ladenschlußgesetz	LandenschlG	Act Concerning the Closing Time of Stores
Bundeskartellamt	FCO	Federal Cartel Office
Bundesministerium für Wirtschaft		Federal Ministry of Economic Affairs
Landeskartellbe-hörden		State Cartel Offices
Monopolkommission		Monopoly Commission
Zusammenschluß		Merger
Anzeige		Post merger filing

Anti-trust law

Anti-trust authorities

There is no authority in Germany comparable to the OFT in Britain. However, there are a number of different anti-trust authorities with different competences such as:

Bundeskartellamt

The Federal Cartel Office in Berlin (Bundeskartellamt, the "FCO"), is the most important anti-trust authority. Although the FCO is a federal authority which is attached to the Federal Ministry of Economic Affairs, it enjoys a fair degree of independence from the Government. The FCO is competent for all cartel matters which have effect in more than one German State (Land). As such it has almost exclusive domain over the implementation of German anti-trust law and is only supplemented by the local cartel authorities of the German States.

Bundesministerium für Wirtschaft

The Federal Ministry of Economic Affairs (Bundesministerium für Wirtschaft) is competent to authorise certain cartel agreements and mergers which have been prohibited by the FCO. In some cases, the Ministry has indeed overridden negative decisions of the FCO and has allowed a merger based on special public interest to take place.

Landeskartellbehörden

The State Cartel Offices of the individual German States (Landeskartellbehörden).

Monopolkommission

The Monopoly Commission (Monopolkommission) in Cologne consists of a number of experts dealing with mergers and important anti-trust law problems. The commission issues reports and recommendations on merger control and plays an important role in the development and interpretation of anti-trust law.

Procedure

Proceedings before the anti-trust authorities can be initiated *ex officio* at the reasonable discretion of the cartel authorities or upon the filing of an application by undertakings or individuals. Although there is no formal complaint procedure available to third parties, they can invoke the Anti-trust Act in civil law proceedings against the infringing party and obtain injunctions and damages.

The anti-trust authorities may impose administrative fines for major infringements of the Anti-trust Act; these may be up to DM 1 million or three times the proceeds resulting from such infringements (whichever is the higher). Fines will be imposed on the undertaking but also on each person who participated in an infringement such as the sole proprietor or the managing director.

Restraints of competition in horizontal agreements: cartels

Section 1 of the Anti-trust Act contains a general clause which declares all cartel agreements null and void. Cartel agreements are defined as "all agreements between enterprises entered into for a common purpose ... insofar as they are apt to influence production or market conditions ... by restraining competition".

This general prohibition in section 1 of the Anti-trust Act catches not only agreements that fix prices or that co-ordinate production or marketing strategies between competitors, but also agreements which restrict competition in an indirect manner, such as agreements between competitors for the exchange of certain sensitive information.

The cartel prohibition only applies to agreements that are entered into "for a common purpose". This expression is meant to distinguish horizontal cartel agreements from so-called vertical agreements. Such vertical agreements (*e.g.* distribution or licensing agreements) are covered by other provisions of the Anti-trust Act.

Furthermore, the prohibition only applies to cartel agreements which are "able to influence market conditions". This has been interpreted by the Federal Court of Justice as "being noticeable". Agreements which do not significantly affect competitors, suppliers or customers, or where there exists a sufficient number of participants on the market or where the parties have only a relatively small market share will often not be "noticeable". Therefore, the actual influence on market conditions has to be proven by facts.

The Anti-trust Act contains a list of statutory cartel exemptions. Whereas certain types of cartels are generally exempted from the prohibition when notified to the anti-trust authorities, others can be exempted by the anti-trust authorities on an individual basis. The following cartels are specifically listed and dealt with in the Anti-trust Act:

> Condition cartels, discount cartels, cartels to overcome structural crisis, rationalisation cartels, specialisation cartels, cartels of small and medium-sized companies, purchase cartels, import and export cartels.

Agreements which fall within the general cartel prohibition are unenforceable. The practice of such an agreement is subject to administrative fines. Also prohibited are concerted actions with the same effect. Third parties which suffer damage from a violation of the cartel prohibition may obtain an injunction and claim damages in civil proceedings. Since the scope of the general cartel prohibition in the Anti-trust Act is wider in certain areas than the EC competition rules, exemptions granted under EC law may have a limiting effect. Therefore, the anti-trust authorities will not pursue an agreement which has been exempted under Article 85(3) of the Treaty of Rome or if the European Commission has granted a comfort letter for a specific agreement.

Restraints of competition in vertical agreements

Sections 15 to 21 of the Anti-trust Act deal with restraints of competition in vertical agreements. Vertical agreements are those between seller and buyer, manufacturer and distributor, lessor and lessee, licensor and licensee, etc. The Anti-trust Act does not prohibit such vertical restrictions in general because they do not have the same impact on market conditions as cartels and are not as dangerous for competition.

Section 15 of the Act deals with retail restrictions such as resale price maintenance, most favourable prices and non-compete clauses.

According to section 15 agreements between undertakings concerning goods or services are prohibited in so far as they restrict a party in its freedom to determine prices or terms in contracts for such goods or services with third parties. Such agreements are considered null and void. According to precedents of the Federal Court of Justice, this does not only apply to direct restrictions on terms and prices, but also to indirect or economic restrictions. Regarding this, the Federal Court has held most favourable prices or treatment clauses to be invalid.

The price recommendations are, in general, permitted only for branded products which are in price competition with similar goods of other manufacturers.

Unlike EC law, non-compete clauses or exclusive dealing agreements or other similar clauses are valid but may be prohibited by the anti-trust authorities if they have a certain negative impact on competition.

Distribution agreements may create problems if they contain provisions which restrict one party in the freedom to use, to purchase or to supply others with goods or services, or if they restrict a party in the sale of the supplied goods to third parties, or if they oblige a party to take unrelated goods or services in connection with the purchase. In this area, the EC block exemptions for exclusive distribution and exclusive purchase agreements play an important role.

Licence agreements are invalid only to the extent that they contain restraints which go beyond the scope of the protected right. However, the law expressly states that " ... restrictions pertaining to the type, extent, quantity, territory or period of the exercise of such right shall not be deemed to go beyond its scope". Further, the law contains a list of restrictions, obligation and prohibitions in licence agreements which are expressly permitted.

Concerted practices and unilateral conduct

Concerted practices are prohibited in the same way as anti-competitive horizontal or vertical agreements. In addition, undertakings are also prohibited from unilaterally inducing third parties to engage in conduct that would be prohibited if it were the subject matter of an agreement.

Abuse of market dominance or market strength

The Anti-trust Act is not a tool to prohibit the monopolisation of markets or to dissolve a monopoly position, but offers strong means to prohibit and avoid abuses of such a dominance. This means that under German law it is not possible to restore competitive structures by dissolving dominant market positions, but the cartel authorities may prohibit abusive practices of companies having market dominance or of enterprises of qualified market strength and declare such agreements to be of no effect.

There exist many different forms of abusive practices which the cartel authorities may prohibit. Pursuant to section 22, paragraph 4 of the Anti-trust Act, the law considers as abusive any behaviour of market dominant companies which:

- impairs, without justification and in a way affecting competition in the market, the opportunities of other enterprises to compete;

- demands prices or business terms which are different from those which would be agreed upon if effective competition existed; in this connection, particular regard must be given to the conduct of other enterprises which are active on comparable markets on which effective competition does exist;

- demands less favourable prices or other business terms compared to those which it demands from similar buyers on comparable markets, unless there is a justifiable cause for the difference made.

The definitions of "relevant market", "market dominance" and "market strength" are very important. Besides the definitions and presumptions provided by the law, the decisions of the Federal Court of Justice are the main source for the interpretation of these terms.

A dominant enterprise

An enterprise is deemed to dominate the market if (section 22, paragraph 1):

- it is without competitors or is subject to no substantial competition; or

- it has a superior market position in relation to its competitors; in this connection, special regard shall be given to its financial strength, its access to the supply and sales markets, and its relationships with other enterprises as well as to legal or factual barriers to the entry of other enterprises into the market.

Two or more enterprises shall be deemed to have market dominance in so far as substantial competition does not exist between them for a specific kind of goods or commercial services, either generally or in specific markets, and in so far as they fulfill the conditions of paragraph 1 in their entirety (section 22, paragraph 2).

It is presumed that:

- an enterprise is dominant in its market if it has a market share of at least one third for a specific kind of goods or commercial services; this presumption shall not apply if the turnover the last fiscal year was less than DM 250m;
- the conditions in section 22, paragraph 2 are fulfilled if, with respect to a specific kind of goods or commercial services,
  - (i) three or fewer enterprises together have a market share of 50% or more; or
  - (ii) five or fewer enterprises together have a market share of two thirds or more.

The most important forms of abuse are monopolistic conduct, predatory pricing aimed at the elimination of competitors, the charging of excessive prices, discriminatory pricing, the grant of certain fidelity rebates or bonuses, discriminatory application of other business conditions, refusals to deal or to supply, and tying-in.

Boycotts and discrimination

The Anti-trust Act prohibits enterprises requesting other enterprises to refuse to deal with third parties. Such a boycott always involves three participants (section 26, paragraph 1).

If one enterprise refuses directly to supply or to deal with another enterprise, this would be considered as abusive use of a dominant position or of market strength or as a discriminatory measure. This provision prohibits dominant enterprises, associations of certain enterprises and enterprises which set resale prices, hindering other enterprises in business activities which are generally accessible to them or to treat them differently from other enterprises of the same kind without justification. Also, dominant enterprises may not exploit their market position by demanding preferential conditions on business transactions.

A violation of these prohibitions (section 26) may give rise to administrative fines. The enterprise against which the boycott or discriminatory measure is directed may also file an injunction or claim damages in the context of civil proceedings.

Exempted sectors

There is a number of economic sectors to which the Anti-trust Act is not or is only partly applicable. These include the air, sea and land transport sectors, agriculture, credit and insurance institutions, as well as coal, steel, electricity, gas, and water industries. However, these exemptions are currently the subject of considerable political debate.

In the meantime, however, the FCO has resorted to EC law (which applies to most exempted sectors) in order to establish competitive conditions in the exempted sectors as well. The FCO, for example, has recently challenged, under Article 85 of the Treaty of Rome, certain exclusivity provisions in a supply agreement between a large German electricity supplier and a German municipality, in an effort to start breaking up the existing transmission and supply monopolies enjoyed by German utility providers.

Merger control

All mergers which have an appreciable effect on the German market are subject to merger control regardless of whether domestic or foreign enterprises are involved.

The definition of the term "merger" (Zusammenschluß) for the purposes of German merger control is substantially broader than the definition of the term "concentration" in the EC Merger Regulation. Therefore, German merger control rules may apply to transactions which meet the EC Merger Regulation turnover thresholds, but which are not caught by the EC Merger Regulation's narrower definition of a "concentration". The following transactions are deemed to be a merger:

- the acquisition of the assets of another enterprise in whole or in substantial part by amalgamation, consolidation, or by other means;
- the acquisition of shares in another enterprise, if such shares, alone or together with other shares already owned by the acquiring enterprise,

  (i) equal or exceed 25% of the voting capital of the acquired enterprise; or

  (ii) equal or exceed 50% of the voting capital of the acquired enterprise; or

  (iii) give the acquiring enterprise a majority participation within the meaning of section 16, paragraph 1 of the Stock Corporation Act.

The definition also includes agreements between companies such as profit and loss transfer and similar arrangements and the acquisition of shares by agreement, articles of association or resolutions, if the buyer is granted the position of a shareholder in a stock corporation with more than 25% of the voting rights (blocking minority) and every other combination of enterprises which result in a similar dominating influence. Further, a "catch-all" clause includes all combinations which enable enterprises or associations of enterprises to exercise a significant competitive influence on another enterprise without reaching the above-mentioned percentages or dominating influence. This catch-all clause certainly goes beyond the scope of the EC Merger Regulation. However, all mergers which are caught by this clause are expressly excluded from the mandatory pre-merger requirement of section 24a of the Anti-trust Act.

Pre-notification

A merger must be pre-notified to the FCO for advance clearance if during the last fiscal year:

(i) one of the enterprises participating in the merger had world-wide turnover of at least DM 2 billion or more; or

(ii) at least two of the enterprises participating in the merger each had world-wide turnover of at least DM 1 billion or more.

Within one month after complete pre-merger filing, the FCO must at least advise the participating enterprises that more time is needed for an investigation. In such a case, the FCO has to complete its investigation within four months. In about 90% of the cases, however, the one month deadline is met.

Post-merger filing

A post-merger filing (Anzeige) of any merger or acquisition of enterprises is required if the participating enterprises had collectively at any time during the last fiscal year turnover of at least DM 500m or more. Participants are usually the acquirer and the target, but the seller also needs to be taken into account when calculating the turnover of DM 500m, except where 25% or more of the shares of the sold or merged enterprise stay with the seller.

Prohibition of mergers

Pursuant to section 24, paragraph 1, the FCO must prohibit a merger or acquisition:

> if it is anticipated that a merger will result in or strengthen a position of market dominance ... unless the participating enterprises demonstrate that the merger will also result in improvement to the competitive situation and that these improvements will outweigh the disadvantages of the market dominance.

The FCO cannot prohibit mergers or acquisitions in certain *de minimis* cases if:

(i) the participating enterprises together had turnover of less than DM 500 million; or

(ii) an enterprise which is not a dependent enterprise and which had during the last fiscal year turnover of not more than DM 50m joins another enterprise, unless the enterprise had turnover of at least DM 4m and the other enterprise had turnover of at least DM 1 billion or more; or (iii)the market concerned has existed for five years or more and is one in which turnover of less than DM 10m was achieved during the last calendar year.

Much stricter rules apply to the press market in order to achieve a diversity of newspapers and periodicals.

Pursuant to section 24, paragraph 3, the Federal Minister of Economic Affairs may grant permission for a merger which has been prohibited by the FCO if the merger's adverse effects are compensated by overall economic advantages or if it is justified by overriding public interest.

Filings and fees

All filings of mergers and acquisitions must be correct and complete. A notice is published in the Federal Gazette: failure to report or incorrect reporting is subject to fines. A merger prohibited by the FCO and not permitted by the Federal Minister of Economic Affairs will be dissolved. The decisions of the Federal Cartel Office and the Federal Minister of Economic Affairs are subject to review by the courts.

The FCO charges fees for both pre-merger and post-merger notifications. However, there is no second fee for a post-merger filing which succeeds a pre-merger notification. The fees may amount up to DM 100,000 and depend on the economic significance of the merger. Average cases should not go beyond a fee of DM 50,000.

Unfair competition law

In addition to the anti-trust law outlined before, unfair competition law provides a second method of protection of free competition by demanding from all participants in trade or business transactions to comply with the rules of fair play. This principle is mainly set out in the Act Against Unfair Competition (Gesetz gegen den unlauteren Wettbewerb: UWG). The following paragraphs briefly outline the main issues.

Applicability and system

German unfair competition law is applicable to all competitive acts occurring on the German market, regardless of whether they are committed by a German or a foreign businessman or enterprise.

Section 1 of the UWG contains a broad statutory general clause followed by a variety of individual competition rules. The combination of this vague general clause and highly specified rules make it difficult for foreign businessmen and enterprises to find out which business methods are possible and accepted and which are prohibited on the German market.

Unfair acts and practices

The general clause in section 1 of the UWG has the following wording:

> Any person who, in the course of its business and for purposes of competition, commits acts contrary to good morals, may be required to cease such acts and held liable to pay damages.

This general clause has been criticised for its broad wording and the generality of its reference to "good morals" as a legal ground for an action to cease or desist or for damages.

However, there has developed a systematic case law approach which divides the acts of unfair competition into five major groups:

(i) fishing for customers

(ii) impeding free competition

(iii)exploitation

(iv)violation of statutory or contractual obligations

(v) disturbance of the market.

Fishing for customers

"Fishing for customers" refers to all attempts to attract customers or suppliers in a way which restrict the customers' or suppliers' freedom of decision. The main categories for such behaviour are: deceptive practices, nuisance or molestation, duress, exploitation of gambling instincts, exploitation of emotions, exploitation of inexperience, advertising to children and enticement.

Impeding free competition

"Impeding free competition" includes all methods and each practice which tends to prevent competitors from showing or promoting their goods or services. The main examples are:

- the expanding of marketing efforts by, for example, concentrating promotional activities in front of a competitor's business establishment in order to lure away customers or to prevent customers from entering the establishment;
- the impeding of a competitor's business by, for example, instigating the competitor's employees to disclose internal know-how or to "go slow";
- cut-throat competition by predatory pricing, boycotts and discrimination ;
- defamation by spreading untrue factual allegations or remarks regarding a competitor;
- critical comparative advertising and product tests.

Exploitation

This category includes methods of imitation, assimilation, labour piracy and customer raiding.

- If a product is not protected by copyright or industrial property rights, the imitation of products can be caught by section 1 of the UWG, if the imitation leads to an unnecessary confusion as to the source of the imitated product. Therefore, the imitated product must have characteristics which enable the customer to distinguish this product from similar products of another source. Also, the systematic imitation of a competitor's promotional campaigns or advertising or of his products will be regarded as unfair competition. Fashion products which are not protected by registered designs or under the copyright statute can be protected against imitations, if their style has been used for the first time during the season for which the product was put on the market. This gives the designer or manufacturer the chance to recover the costs of the creation of the fashion product.

- "Assimilation" is another method of exploiting the efforts and achievements of a competitor which violates section 1 of the UWG. This includes attempts to use a competitor's good image or the good image of his products to work for the promotion of one's own products. This can be done openly or indirectly by using the well-known characteristics of the competitor's products for one's own. The reason behind this is that the good image of a product, an enterprise or a person may be degraded by such exploitation.

- Labour piracy occurs in particular circumstances which go beyond ordinary efforts to attract a competitor's employees. If the competitor's employees are not only induced to give notice of termination but also to violate existing contracts, or if the inducement to terminate the employment has as its sole aim damage to the competitor by exploiting his business secrets, these acts will be considered a violation of section 1 of the UWG.

- Customer raiding follows the same principles and is only prohibited if systematic raiding of customers is undertaken with the help of former employees of the competitor, who have been systematically poached in order to take over know-how, business connections and customer knowledge. In addition, it is regarded as unfair, if the customers of a competitor are systematically induced to break a validly existing contractual obligation in order to switch to, and purchase from, the competitors.

Violations of statutory or contractual obligations

"Violations of statutory or contractual obligations" are not considered as unfair competition *per se*. Such violations, however, may be regarded as unfair, if the behaviour aims to exploit the competitor's correct behaviour. The violation of contractual obligations will be regarded as an act of unfair competition if it tends to destroy the manufacturer's distribution system. Violations of contractual obligations are of particular relevance in the case of contractual price maintenance and selective distribution systems, provided they are permitted by law.

The violation of statutory obligations will only be regarded as an act of unfair competition if such a violation is likely to influence the competitive situation and if the statute violated incorporates moral and legal values of high importance to the public. A violation of other statutes with competitive relevance will only be considered as an act of unfair competition if the purpose of such violation is to provide to the violator an unfair edge on his competitors.

Misleading statements

Section 3 of the UWG contains another general clause prohibiting misleading statements on business matters, provided they are made in the course of business and for the purpose of competition. The question is not whether the statement made is true or untrue, but whether it is apt to mislead a relevant part of the public addressed. In consequence, even a true statement may be misleading and an untrue statement might not be misleading. Whether a statement is misleading depends only on whether a relevant section of the public addressed gains a perspective of the statement made which is different from reality. Therefore, the misleading character of the statement can only be defined after the understanding of the respective statement by the section of the public to which it was addressed has been determined.

Section 3 of the UWG also contains a variety of categories. The most important are misleading statements concerning products (product condition, geographic source of products, composition, health and nature related claim or quantity), misleading statements concerning prices (price calculation, price reductions, price comparisons, price declarations), and misleading statements concerning offers (standing, importance, size, age, business source or business type).

Special rules

Besides the two general clauses noted above, the UWG contains a variety of special rules dealing with special and extraordinary sales, end of season sales, anniversary sales, clearance sales, bankruptcy, kick-backs, spying-out and betrayal of trade secrets, defamation and calumny, and other issues.

Procedure

Pursuant to section 24 of the UWG, the forum for unfair competition proceedings lies (i) at the defendant's place of business, if any, (ii) at the defendant's domicile, if any, and (iii) at the defendant's place of residence. Also, proceedings may be initiated at the place where the unfair act has been committed, if a competitor was directly attacked or if the defendant has no place of business or domicile in Germany. This means that a foreign defendant can become subject to the jurisdiction of German courts in unfair competition matters even if he has no domicile, residence, place of business or property in Germany, as long as the unfair act complained about affects the competitive situation on the German market.

Claims to cease and desist from unfair acts are usually initiated by a warning letter which describes the unfair act complained about, and announces legal proceedings if a letter of submission is not received within a certain deadline. The letter of submission is usually pre-formulated and contains a contractual penalty if a violation of the same kind occurs again. The reason for such a request is the general assumption that the unfair behaviour will be repeated if the obligation to cease and desist is not secured by such a contractual penalty.

If the addressee of a warning letter does not reply within the deadline set, or does not reply in a satisfactory manner or does not offer a contractual penalty, or if the plaintiff considers a warning letter as inappropriate because of reckless and persistent violations, or if the violator repeats his violation despite his promise to cease and desist, the plaintiff may either file an action or apply for a temporary injunction in summary proceedings. In most cases, the application for a temporary injunction is used to enforce unfair competition claims. The applicant for a temporary injunction must show that the order sought is urgent for the avoidance of considerable risks to the enforceability of his rights. However, section 25 of the UWG contains a rebuttable presumption that any application for a temporary injunction is urgent if it is directed against a violation of the Act Against Unfair Competition.

The enforcement of temporary injunctions in unfair competition matters may be sanctioned with up to six months imprisonment or with a fine of up to DM 500,000 or, if such fine cannot be collected from the violator, by up to six weeks imprisonment.

Several provisions of the Act Against Unfair Competition provide for damages claims which can be brought by competitors of the violator. Nevertheless, these claims for damages are of minor importance in most cases since the proof of a certain damage and of its causation by the alleged violation is very difficult in practice.

CONTENTS OF CHAPTER 8

Competition Audits and Compliance Programmes

8. COMPETITION AUDITS AND COMPLIANCE PROGRAMMES

Introduction

The preceding chapters have outlined the variety of competition law issues which can arise in the course of normal business transactions. Some of them are unexpected; some carry heavy penalties for non-compliance. One way to see how far your own business is or might be entangled in the competition rules is to carry out a competition policy audit – a sort of health check.

This chapter looks at how XCo set about its health check and compliance programme. This is one company's approach: it shows various ideas and options which may be more or less relevant or successful depending on your own business circumstances.

XCo's story

XCo is a successful UK company which has been pursuing a fairly rapid programme of acquisition and expansion. One of its major competitors has recently been investigated by the European Commission. The Chairman is worried by this and asks at the following Board meeting whether there are any problems in XCo's subsidiaries of which he ought to be aware. The information is patchy.

The Board decides on a competition law audit. The Company Secretary is given this job. He cannot do it all on his own – the group now has 15,000 employees in six EU Member States.

The Company Secretary decides to organise a two-part programme:

- an audit of existing arrangements;
- a compliance programme for the future.

He identifies key personnel to have responsibility in each subsidiary and sets up reporting lines so that the whole picture can be accumulated in due course. He makes sure that a summary will appear on his desk.

XCo is aware that the audit and compliance programme cannot

ensure 100% technical compliance, but takes practical comfort from the knowledge that:

- the issues will have been addressed;
- everyone in the organisation will be alerted to competition issues and to management's attitude to them;
- any existing major problems will have been identified and sorted out;
- a support structure will be established so that compliance can be monitored;
- there will be procedures in place to deal with complaints should they arise.

Stage 1: the audit

The aim of the competition health check is to isolate any existing problems. To do this XCo needs to examine its arrangements for distribution and licensing, with commercial agents and in relation to pricing policies and its competitors. Corrective action may be needed in some areas. Some examples which arose for XCo were:

Problem	Action	Result
The Belgian subsidiary sets minimum resale prices and refuses to supply dealers who sell below these levels.	Belgian subsidiary told to continue to supply whatever the actual resale price.	Potential actions by disgruntled resellers averted.
A proposed R&D project is not getting off the ground because the other party wants XCo to agree that it will not carry out its own research in other fields.	Assess whether Article 85 applies; use R&D block exemption to settle terms of project and for drafting.	XCo can do its R&D in unrelated fields.

The initial audit must check domestic controls as well as EC ones. These will differ from one country to another, so domestic advice will be needed in each case.

Stage 2: the compliance programme

There are two main stages in setting up a useful compliance programme:

- what does XCo expect the programme to achieve?
- how should the programme be organised?

XCo needs to establish for itself and its employees the main goals of the programme. It is important not to be over ambitious. The programme may cover some or all of the following items, depending on the particular business requirements.

What does a compliance programme do?

- Commitment and responsibility
- Information
- Crime prevention
- Audit existing arrangements
- Aid planning strategy
- Minimise exposure
- Understand what competitors are doing.

- Commitment and responsibility

    The first point is to demonstrate XCo's commitment to a high level of compliance throughout the group and the management's vow to uphold the values set out. XCo might draw up a checklist of target values and line management contact points. A mission statement, encapsulating XCo's commitment, may be circulated; it would need to be supported by the Board and senior management.

- Information

  Employees must be given clear information about competition law, presented in a practical and accessible way. Presentations and manuals are useful.

- Crime prevention

  XCo wants to ensure that, so far as possible, the group does not commit any serious breaches of competition law.

- Audit existing arrangements

  The health check was examined in Stage 1 above.

- Aid planning strategy

  If XCo is confident that its employees understand the basic rules of competition law, then it can use that strength in planning. For example, a new distribution network may confidently be set up according to exclusive block exemption standards or using acceptable selective criteria. XCo will know when and to whom notifications should be made.

- Minimise exposure

  Adherence to the competition rules should minimise opportunities for complaint, for European Commission or national authority investigations, and for domestic court actions.

- Understand what competitors are doing

  If XCo knows the rules it can more easily spot attempts by competitors to bend them. XCo will also know how to respond to business opportunities with minimal competition exposure.

There is evidence that the European Commission and national authorities take a genuine compliance programme into account as a mitigating factor in cases of contravention.

In XCo's situation, setting up a compliance programme may be the only way in which the Company Secretary – the individual given the unenviable responsibility of 'ensuring group compliance with competition law' – can demonstrate that he has done what was required of him.

Organising a compliance programme

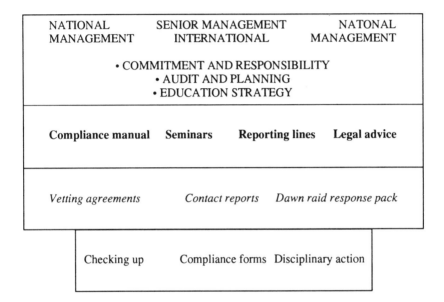

Organising a compliance programme

Again, two main points need to be considered – the role of management, and the strategy for educating personnel through presentations, discussions and the preparation and circulation of compliance handbooks:

- The role of management

  Management at all levels must be aware of the programme and committed to it.

  At international top level, the main board will be responsible for a mission statement, for authorising and giving appropriate funding and technical resources to the programme, and for the general strategy.

National management will have additional responsibilities *vis à vis* domestic law.

- Compliance manuals

A brief and concise manual will be helpful and may be presented to the relevant employees at seminars or discussion groups. Clarity and the giving of practical examples will be more useful than an overcomplicated approach. The manual should state what behaviour is absolutely prohibited and give examples of how to recognise and avoid this.

Employees should be given information on where to find any company guidelines and who is designated to give advice.

The manual may include forms for contact meetings and self-assessment (see below).

Compliance manuals

- Statement of XCo company policy

- Clear, precise and practical

- Prohibited behaviours *e.g.*
  - unauthorised discussions with competitors
  - price agreements
  - market sharing
  - bid rigging
  - fixing resale prices

- Lists XCo standard agreements and guidelines and where to find them

- When and where to go for advice, *e.g.*
  - non-standard distribution, agency, licensing agreements
  - manager? in-house legal?

- Include forms for
  - contact reports of competitor/supplier/distributor meetings
  - annual acknowledgement of copy of manual/attendance at seminars/compliance with company rules and procedures

---

- Presentations

    Presentations should reinforce the practical points. The law and its consequences need to be outlined but detailed technicalities should be avoided. Illustrations are very effective. For example, the story of the cartonboard cartel, heavily fined in July 1994, contains many relevant pointers.

Illustrating the problems

The cartonboard story

The European Commission heard that meetings of an ostensibly legitimate trade association were in fact hiding a clandestine cartel to fix prices and regulate the market in cartonboard. An elaborate institutionalised price-fixing and market-sharing cartel was thought to be operating through a series of committees and conferences whose meetings were usually held in luxury hotels in Zurich. A Swiss fiduciary company provided the secretariat for these meetings and conducted the information exchange system by which the operation of the cartel was monitored and policed.

In April 1991, Commission officials descended simultaneously in dawn raids on 16 locations in the EC. They apparently found private notes (contrary to an understanding that all incriminating evidence was in fact to be destroyed), false minutes of the meetings and a whole network of deception designed to ensure that the cartel was never discovered. What the companies found to their cost, was that the "Swiss hotel hideaway technique" does not work.

After it had become known that a complaint had been made, at least one of the companies engaged lawyers to carry out a "dummy run" or mock Commission investigation.

This story illustrates clearly that:

- it is illegal for competitors to fix prices and regulate their market;

- the investigating officials will strip away measures of concealment;

The cartonboard story (*continued*)

- the Commission, alerted by its own monitoring or by disgruntled competitors or upset clients, will look at what is actually going on in the market and draw their own conclusions about possible causes – investigating officials will then dig around for the evidence;

- carrying on your illegal activities in secret locations outside the EC will not save you;

- the effect on the businesses concerned is unpleasant – quite apart from the large fines, they have to contend with Commission officials with the power to enter every office and open every filing cabinet, taking up many hours of senior management time and disrupting normal business.

The effect on XCo of a breach of competition law could be spelled out by reference to the cartonboard story.

A further use of presentations is, of course, to reinforce the company's commitment and support to a compliance programme.

Compliance presentations

- Emphasise practicalities

- Outline law and consequences (but don't be boring)

- Give effective illustrations *e.g.*

  - information exchange   price coordination   complaint and investigation

  - The "Swiss hotel hideaway technique" won't work

  - What it's like to have DG IV unannounced at the door at dawn

  - The effect on XCo's business: fines
                                                      reputation

  - The effect on the employee's career

- Reinforce company commitment and support

Reporting lines

It is important that everyone involved in competition compliance not only knows the rules but knows to whom he or she goes if a potential problem is spotted, or if there is some uncertainty about taking a particular course of action.

Legal advice

For day-to-day advice on compliance, somebody in each in-house legal team will have responsibility for responding to queries. The legal team will then recognise whether a problem can in fact be handled in-house or whether a situation has arisen where outside counsel may be required.

Vetting agreements

Many companies find it useful, especially if an audit has revealed some discrepancies in the level of competition compliance in its documentation, to include in the compliance system guidelines on who has responsibility to sign off on various types of agreement. Standard contracts or heads of terms settled by the legal team can be useful. Often these will include alternatives or variants suitable for particular situations. They should also carry a warning that when new or unusual variants are being negotiated, somebody in the legal team should be contacted to check whether the variant envisaged will also be in compliance with competition law. It is important to remember that not everything concluded in negotiations or happening in practice is actually recorded on paper. So the job of the legal advisers would also be to make sure that the field negotiators have told them everything that is going on and not simply passed over a piece of paper.

Contact reports

Some companies in sensitive sectors institute contact reports which personnel are required to fill in every time they have a meeting with a competitor or a major supplier or purchaser. These can note any "uncomfortable experiences". They can also be used to demonstrate the innocence of the meetings, should this ever be required.

Dawn raid response pack

When the heavies from DG IV knock on the company's door at six in the morning, it is unlikely to be the managing director who opens it. A compliance programme can thus usefully include a small file to be kept at the reception desk, and therefore available to the receptionist or security people, and which contains simple instructions on what sort of identification they can ask of the unwelcome visitors, which telephone calls to make immediately to company personnel and advisors, and what they can and cannot keep back from the Commission officials pending the arrival of someone in a more senior position.

This will be supplemented by a more complete checklist for the managers who then take charge.

Checking up and compliance forms

A compliance programme will not be of much continuing use unless there is a monitoring procedure. One useful tool is to require the relevant personnel each year to sign a form declaring that they have in the course of the previous 12 months not to their knowledge been involved in any activities nor signed any agreements where competition problems might have arisen, without due reference to the legal department or other designated officer. Where any appraisal system or annual interview or job/salary review is part of the company's general policy, then such forms can form part of those discussions. They can easily be included in the compliance manual.

Disciplinary action

All relevant personnel must be made well aware of the consequences of disregarding the competition rules, not only to the reputation and profits of the company, but also to their own reputation, income and job prospects.

A description of the effect on the career of the employee who gets the company into trouble can also be a very effective warning mechanism. The cartonboard case was large-scale and high-profile and the protagonists included top management. This is not always the case. A surprising number of groups do not know what fixes their subsidiaries may be getting them in to, nor is the board always up to speed on the golf course discussions of the marketing team. All relevant personnel need to be made aware of the company's policy that any practice which involves the company in such costly and uncomfortable experiences must face disciplinary action.

CONTENTS OF ANNEXES

ANNEX 1. THE EUROPEAN UNION, ITS INSTITUTIONS AND TYPES OF LEGISLATION

The European Union

In 1957, six European countries (France, Germany, Italy, Belgium, Luxembourg and the Netherlands) signed the Treaty of Rome which brought the European Economic Community into being on 1 January 1958. In 1973, these countries were joined by the United Kingdom, Ireland and Denmark, in 1981 by Greece, and in 1986 by Spain and Portugal. With reunification in October 1990, the former East Germany was also absorbed into the Community.

The scope of the Treaty of Rome was extended in 1986 by the Single European Act. Then, in November 1993, the Treaty on European Union (the "Maastricht Treaty") came into force.

The Maastricht Treaty has brought further substantial amendments to the European Community (EC). It increased the powers of the European Parliament and introduced various important common policies, including a common foreign and security policy, a common policy on judicial affairs, and the concept of Union citizenship. It was following Maastricht that the then 12 countries became Member States of the European Union (EU).

The Union grew again on 1 January 1995 with the accession of Austria, Finland and Sweden. There are therefore now 15 Member States of the EU:

Austria, Belgium, Denmark, Finland, France, Germany, Greece, Ireland, Italy, Luxembourg, the Netherlands, Portugal, Spain, Sweden, the United Kingdom.

Although as a general rule we now refer to the European Union, the competition rules derive from the original Treaty of Rome and are the competition law of the European Community. This book, therefore, refers to EU Member States, but to EC competition law.

European Economic Area

The European Economic Area (EEA) came into being on 1 January 1994. As a result, certain of the European Free Trade Association (EFTA) countries came to share with the EC the four fundamental freedoms of the Single Market – freedom of movement of goods, services, persons and capital. At the time of the creation of the EEA, five of the EFTA countries were members: Austria, Sweden, Norway, Iceland and Finland. Three of those countries became full members of the EU 12 months later.

Switzerland voted to remain outside the EEA. The position of Leichtenstein was more complicated; its close fiscal and other ties with Switzerland had to be revised before it could join the EEA.

The Member States of the European Economic Area are, therefore, the 15 EU Member States plus Norway and Iceland and, from mid-1995, Leichtenstein.

The EEA was for just one year – 1994 – a large market with a need for a separate competition regime and a real possibility that from time to time it would be EEA rules and EEA authorities which would have to deal with the problems of business. That year has passed, leaving us with a complex regime and several new institutions essentially operating for the benefit of two, shortly to be three, small countries.

Community institutions

The Treaty of Rome and subsequent legislation have established four major Community Institutions: Council, Commission, Parliament and Court. Each has its own highly developed internal structure and each has a part to play in the legislative and administrative processes of the EC.

The Council

It is the function of the Council as the legislative body of the Community both to represent the interests of the Community as a whole and to act as a forum for discussion of national interests. Member States take turns to provide the Council Presidency, which is held for six months according to a strict rotation. Representatives at Council meetings are generally Ministers of the 15 Member State governments. Under Article 145 the Council must ensure co-ordination of the general economic policies of the Member States; it has power to take decisions and to delegate to the Commission matters relating to the implementation of legislation.

The European Parliament

The European Parliament's role in the legislative procedure has been enhanced in recent years. MEPs (Members of the European Parliament) are elected every five years by universal suffrage. They organise themselves into multi-national groupings. The Parliament currently has 20 specialist committees, including working parties on economic and monetary affairs and industrial policy, external economic relations and legal affairs.

The European Commission

The European Commission has been described as the "motive power behind Community policy".

The Commission in Brussels consists of 20 members, including its President. There is at least one but no more than two Commissioners from each Member State, elected in each case for a renewable term of five years. The Commission is an independent body (acting by majority) responsible only to the Parliament. It submits proposals for legislation and ensures that the provisions of the Treaty and other legislation are applied.

In addition to the Secretariat General, the Legal Service and the Spokesman's Service, the Commission is organised into Directorates-General, each responsible for a particular area of interest. Directorate-General IV covers competition issues; it has a special Merger Task Force to deal with transactions caught by the Merger Regulation.

The European Court of Justice

The European Court of Justice (ECJ) in Luxembourg presently consists of 15 Judges (who may sit in plenary session or in chambers) and nine Advocates-General. Its jurisdiction includes individuals, the institutions of the Community and Member States.

There are three main stages to cases before the ECJ: the written stage, the preparatory enquiry stage, and the oral hearings. Before the judges deliver their verdict, they will have considered a full legal and factual analysis prepared by the Advocate-General in the case.

Competition cases are likely to reach the ECJ on appeal from the Court of First Instance or by way of a question for preliminary ruling. The latter are made by national courts under Article 177 of the Treaty, primarily concerning the interpretation of Community law and the validity and interpretation of acts of the EC institutions.

Where a reference is made for the interpretation of a point of Community law, the ruling by the Court is binding on the national court which made the reference and on any other court which hears the case in question. The ruling will also form the basis for the application of that law in subsequent cases, although it will always be open to national courts to apply to the Court for a new interpretation.

The Court of First Instance

The establishment of a Court of First Instance in the autumn of 1989 was intended to speed up the system by relieving the burden on the European Court of Justice. This is the court to which competition cases go. It also hears cases on, in particular, state subsidies, steel cases and all direct actions brought by natural or legal persons, and deals with staff cases.

The judgments of the EC Courts play a major part in the development of Community law.

Community law

Sources of Community law

The first source of the European Economic Community law – its primary legislation – is the Treaty of Rome as amended, in particular, by the Single European Act and the Maastricht Treaty.

Secondary legislation includes law made by the EC institutions. It is fairly complex. Each type of legislation has different characteristics and legal effects. The main sources of secondary legislation are Regulations and Directives.

The ECJ has consistently upheld the principle of the supremacy of Community law. National courts are bound to give precedence to Community law and are under a duty to interpret their national law in the light of the objectives laid down by EC Directives.

Provisions of the Treaty and directly applicable measures of the institutions render automatically inapplicable any conflicting provision of current national law and preclude the adoption of new national law which would be incompatible with Community provisions.

Regulations

Regulations are binding in their entirety and directly applicable in all Member States. They do not have to be transformed into domestic law. So the competition block exemptions, for example, are simply law in all the EU countries, without the need for any domestic law specifically to say so. This means that legislation in the form of Regulations is uniform throughout the EU. Member States, their governing institutions and national courts are directly bound by Regulations.

Directives

Directives are binding "as to the result to be achieved, upon each Member State to which they are addressed but shall leave to the national authorities the choice of form and methods".

Member States must implement Directives through national law. Normally, therefore, there will be domestic law – in the United Kingdom Acts of Parliament or Statutory Instruments ("regulations") – to bring a Directive into force. They are mainly used to achieve "harmonisation" of national laws. The ECJ has rendered several judgments which recognised that Directives may, in certain circumstances, have direct effect.

Decisions

The Council and the Commission can both render Decisions. In competition cases these are usually Decisions addressed to companies telling them whether an agreement is or is not caught by Articles 85(1) or Article 86, and the consequences of that finding, such as the requirement to amend an agreement or pay a fine.

ANNEX 2.   ARTICLES 85 AND 86

The competition rules in the Treaty of Rome

Article 85

1. The following shall be prohibited as incompatible with the common market: all agreements between undertakings, decisions by associations of undertakings and concerted practices which may affect trade between Member States and which have as their object or effect the prevention, restriction or distortion of competition within the common market, and in particular those which:

    (a) directly or indirectly fix purchase or selling prices or any other trading conditions;

    (b) limit or control production, markets, technical development, or investment;

    (c) share markets or sources of supply;

    (d) apply dissimilar conditions to equivalent transactions with other trading parties, thereby placing them at a competitive disadvantage;

    (e) make the conclusion of contracts subject to acceptance by the other parties of supplementary obligations which, by their nature or according to commercial usage, have no connection with the subject of such contracts.

2. Any agreements or decisions prohibited pursuant to this Article shall be automatically void.

3. The provisions of paragraph 1 may, however, be declared inapplicable in the case of:

    –   any agreement or category of agreements between undertakings;

    –   any decision or category of decisions by associations of undertakings;

    –   any concerted practice or category of concerted practices;

which contributes to improving the production or distribution of goods or to promoting technical or economic progress, while allowing consumers a fair share of the resulting benefit, and which does not:

(a) impose on the undertakings concerned restrictions which are not indispensable to the attainment of these objectives;

(b) afford such undertakings the possibility of eliminating competition in respect of a substantial part of the products in question.

Article 86

Any abuse by one or more undertakings of a dominant position within the common market or in a substantial part of it shall be prohibited as incompatible with the common market in so far as it may affect trade between Member States.

Such abuse may, in particular, consist in:

(a) directly or indirectly imposing unfair purchase or selling prices or other unfair trading conditions;

(b) limiting production, markets or technical development to the prejudice of consumers;

(c) applying dissimilar conditions to equivalent transactions with other trading parties, thereby placing them at a competitive disadvantage;

(d) making the conclusion of contracts subject to acceptance by the other parties of supplementary obligations which, by their nature or according to commercial usage, have no connection with the subject of such contract.

ANNEX 3.   PROCEDURAL LAW AND BLOCK EXEMPTIONS

Procedural law and the block exemptions

Procedure

There are various basic Regulations which set out how in practice the Commission and the Member States can apply the broad principles of Articles 85 and 86.

Regulation 17/62, for example, establishes certain supervisory and administrative roles and procedures. It sets out the procedure for notification for individual exemption under Article 85(3) and for negative clearance under Articles 85(1) and 86, for investigations by Member State authorities and by the Commission, for fines and for review by the European Court of Justice. This picture is completed by Regulation 3385/94 (replacing Regulation 27/62) which included the Form A/B used for Article 85/86 notifications. This Regulation also includes a complementary note explaining how the procedure works and how to approach filling in Form A/B.

Regulation 17 provides that, before the Commission takes a decision (for example to impose a fine for breach of the rules), it shall give the companies concerned the opportunity of being heard on the matters to which it has objected. Regulation 99/63 sets out the applicable rules.

All these Regulations should, however, be viewed in the light of further developments – Regulations, Commission Decisions and Notices and case law. For example, there have been several revisions to Form A/B and developments on the role of the Hearing Officer, rights of defence, the right to see the Commission's file and so forth.

The Commission's Notice of 23 December 1992 on the application of Articles 85 and 86 by national courts is one noticeable development, which will over time mean that more cases on the EC competition rules should be brought before local domestic courts.

Enabling regulations

The Council has to give the Commission specific powers to make regulations on competition matters. The legislation that does this is often called an "enabling regulation". The following give the Commission particular powers to apply Article 85(3) to certain categories of agreement.

Regulation 19/65: to make regulations on exclusive supply and exclusive purchase agreements and on the agreements for the use of intellectual property rights.

Regulation 2821/71: to make regulations on Research and Development (R&D) and specialisation agreements.

Regulation 1534/91: to make regulations on certain types of insurance agreement.

Block exemptions

A block exemption is a Regulation which sets out certain terms which can and cannot be included in particular types of agreement in order that such an agreement should benefit from an automatic exemption from Article 85(1). Typically, a block exemption sets out a "white list" of terms which can be included and a "black list" of terms which should on no account be used in the agreement. In addition, there are usually some "grey areas". Where parties can bring their agreements exactly within the terms of the relevant block exemption Regulation, the Commission considers that the agreement is acceptable and does not need to be individually notified. We list below the current block exemptions.

Exclusive distribution and purchasing agreements

Regulation 1983/83: sets the criteria for exclusive distribution agreements.

Regulation 1984/83: sets the criteria for exclusive purchasing agreements.

Commission Notice on Regulations 1983/83 and 1984/83: explains some aspects of the Commission's interpretation of these block exemptions.

Intellectual property agreements

Regulation 2349/84: sets the criteria for patent licence agreements including provisions for exploitation; will expire in July 1995.
Regulation 556/89: sets the criteria for know-how licence agreements.
A new *Regulation on technology transfer agreements* was planned to come into force on 1 January 1995 but is now expected to be available from 1 July 1995. It will replace the patent and know-how block exemptions and cover a wider spectrum of combined patent and know-how agreements. There are transitional arrangements for the use of the existing block exemptions for agreements made before July 1995.

Motor vehicle distribution

Regulation 123/85: sets criteria particular to the distribution of motor vehicles – a sort of mixture of exclusive and selective distribution – and will be substantially revised in 1995. There is an explanatory Notice.

Specialisation and research and development agreements

Regulation 417/85: sets the criteria for certain types of specialisation agreement.
Regulation 418/85: sets the criteria for certain types of research and development agreement.

Franchising

Regulation 4087/88: sets the criteria for standard franchising agreements.

Insurance

Regulation 3932/92: exempts co-operation agreements on:

(a) the establishment of common risk-premium tariffs based on collectively ascertained statistics or on the number of claims;

(b) the establishment of standard policy conditions;

(c) the common coverage of certain types of risks; and

(d) the establishment of common rules on the testing and acceptance of security devices.

ANNEX 4. MERGER CONTROL

The EC Merger Regulation

Regulation 4064/89: on the control of concentrations between undertakings, the "EC Merger Regulation" controls large-scale mergers which have a major effect on EC markets.

Regulation 2367/90: on the notifications, time-limits and hearings provided for in Regulation 4064/89. As well as setting out details of who submits notifications and how the time-limits for the various sections of the procedure are calculated, this Regulation includes the Form CO which has to be used to notify concentrations under the Merger Regulation. Regulation 2367/90 and Form CO have been revised in the light of practical experience.

There are several interpretative notices. In December 1994 some were reformulated and others newly adopted as follows:

- on the notion of undertakings concerned,
- on the notion of a concentration,
- on the calculation of turnover, and
- on the distinction between concentrative and co-operative joint ventures.

There is also a Commission Notice regarding restrictions ancillary to concentrations.

Member State legislation is necessary to complement on various aspects of the operation of the Merger Regulation. For example, in the United Kingdom there are:

- *The EEC Merger Control (Consequential Provisions) Regulations* (SI 1990/1563)
- *The EEC Merger Control (Distinct Market Investigations) Regulations* (SI 1990/1715)

Merger control in the United Kingdom

The *Fair Trading Act 1973* is the main UK law on mergers involving one or more UK businesses. It provides for voluntary pre-notification of mergers where either market share or acquired asset value thresholds are exceeded.

There are additional regulations to complete the picture:

- *Merger (Pre-notification) Regulations 1990* (SI 1990/501) – deal with procedural aspects of giving a Merger Notice.

- *Merger (Fees) Regulations 1990* (SI 1990/1660) – set levels of fees payable and time for payment.

French merger control legislation

Ordonnance du 1er décembre 1986 relative à la liberté des prix et de la concurrence: controls "concentrations" on the French market and provides for notifications and review by the Ministère de l'Economie.

German merger legislation

Gesetz gegen Wettbewerbsbeschränkungen: provides for pre- and post-notification of mergers (very widely defined) depending on the turnover of the participating companies.

Merger control – an outline of notification requirements

Country	Nature	Thresholds	Time Limit	Clearance	Failure to notify	Note
EC	Mandatory pre-notification	The combined consolidated world-wide turnover of all parties concerned exceeds ECU 5 billion; *and* the consolidated Community-wide turnover of each of at least two parties involved exceeds ECU 250m; *and* each party does not achieve more than two-thirds of its Community-wide turnover within one and the same Member State.	Within 1 week of conclusion of the agreement, the bid announcement or the acquisition of a controlling interest.	Within 3–4 weeks unless Commission starts a full investigation (further 4 months) Parties cannot proceed until approved.	Fines from ECU 1,000 to ECU 50,000. Validity of transaction at risk.	Commission may order an appropriate action to restore competition.
United Kingdom	Voluntary, pre-notification	The post-merger UK market share is enhanced to exceed 25% or an existing 25+% share is increased; *or* the gross value of the target's world-wide assets exceeds £70m	Before completion of the deal.	From 20 to 35 days.	Legal uncertainty – risk of a reference to the MMC at any time after merger.	Clearance fee (£5,000 to £15,000) payable.
Germany	Mandatory pre-notification	One party has an annual turnover of at least DM2 billion; *or* two or more parties each have a turnover of at least DM1 billion.	Before completion of the deal.	Within 4 months. Parties cannot proceed until approved.	Fines. The merger may be declared invalid.	A pre-notified merger also requires post notification
	Mandatory post-merger notification	The combined turnover of the parties exceeds DM500m	Without undue delay after completion.	Up to 1 year.		Fees payable.
France	Voluntary post-merger notification	The parties involved have a market share of at least 25%; *or* the parties have a combined turnover of FF7 billion and at least two companies each have a turnover of FF 2 billion.	Within 3 months of completion.	Within 2 months. If no reply, the deal is deemed to be approved	Legal uncertainty – risk of reference to the Competition Council at any time after merger.	Prior submission of the prospective merger possible.

ANNEX 5. MAIN UK LEGISLATION ON RESTRICTIVE PRACTICES AND MONOPOLIES

Restrictive agreements

Restrictive Trade Practices Act 1976: establishes a system of registration of restrictive goods and services agreements where there are at least two parties to the agreement carrying on business in the United Kingdom and at least two parties (not necessarily those in UK business) accepting listed restrictions as a result of the agreement.

Restrictive Trade Practices Act 1977: added to the RTPA system the limited possibility of disregarding certain "financing terms" in analysing agreements for registration purposes.

Restrictive Trade Practices (Information Agreements) Order 1969 (SI 1969/1842): brought information agreements as to goods within the ambit of the RTPA system.

Restrictive Trade Practices (Services) Order 1976 (SI 1976/98): confirmed that all services with the exception of those specifically listed in the relevant RTPA schedule (mainly professional services such as those of lawyers, architects, medical services) are within the RTPA system.

Restrictive Trade Practices (Sale and Purchase and Share Subscription Agreements) (Goods) Order 1989 (SI 1989/1081): exempts such agreements from RTPA registration provided certain strict conditions are met.

Restrictive Trade Practices (Services Amendment) Order 1989 (SI 1989/1082): amends the Restrictive Trade Practices (Services) Order 1976 so that it covers sale and purchase and share subscription agreements as to services business, in parallel with SI 1989/1081.

Restrictive Practices Court Act 1976: establishes the RP Court and procedure for hearings in certain competition matters, including under the RTPA and the Resale Prices Act. It is completed by the *Restrictive Practices Court Rules 1976* (SI 1976/1897)

Resale prices

Resale Prices Act 1976: prohibits individual and collective resale price maintenance.

Anti-competitive practices

Competition Act 1980: sets up a system whereby alleged "anti-competitive practices" can be investigated by the OFT, and, if necessary, by the MMC.

Anti-competitive Practices (Exclusions) (Amendment) Order 1994: provides that firms whose group turnover is less than £10m or which have less than 25% of a relevant market are exempted from investigation under the Competition Act.

Monopolies

Fair Trading Act 1973: provides for the reference to the MMC of abusive monopoly situations.

ANNEX 6. OFT PUBLICATIONS AND CODE OF PRACTICE ON ENFORCEMENT

OFT publications

Information for businesses

The OFT publishes a series of brochures outlining its practice in RTPA and merger/monopoly matters. These can be obtained direct from the OFT at Field House, Bream's Buildings London EC4A 1PR. The following may be of interest:

Restrictive practices

Restrictive agreements (OFT 0037)
A simple guide to the law on restrictive trading agreements.

Restrictive trade practices (OFT 0038)
A detailed guide for the business community and their professional advisers.

Mergers

Mergers (OFT 0036)
A guide to the procedures under the Fair Trading Act 1973.

Monopolies and anti-competitive practices

An outline of United Kingdom competition policy (OFT 0032)
A brief guide to competition policy and its administrative and legislative framework.

Anti-competitive practices (OFT 0033)
A guide to the provisions of the Competition Act 1980.

Cartels: detection and remedies – a guide for purchasers (OFT 0035)

A general guide to help purchasers identify and combat secret cartels.

Annual Reports by the Director General of Fair Trading

The OFT code of practice on enforcement

In January 1994 the Director-General of Fair Trading published a code of practice for the operations of the OFT. In it he established certain time-limits for dealing with notifications, queries and complaints for the business community and set out the OFT's general duties under the code and its particular obligations as regards the Restrictive Trade Practices Act and the Fair Trading Act.

The code includes references to:

- information and openness;
- consultation;
- courtesy and helpfulness;
- complaints.

   "Anyone with a concern or complaint about our procedures or the handling of a case should write to the Director-General, who will ensure that any complaint is fully and properly considered.

   We shall aim to give a response to any such complaint within 30 working days."

- Value for money
- Standards

The code sets standards for OFT enforcement activities for which there are no statutory timetables.

Restrictive trading agreements

"To acknowledge agreements furnished for registration within five working days.

To register an agreement subject to published *de minimis* criteria, and advise on the significance of the restrictions, within two months of receipt.

To register other agreements and, provided all necessary information has been submitted, to assess the significance of the restrictions, within six months of receipt in 60% of cases."

Mergers

"To advise the Secretary of State in confidential guidance cases within 19 working days of receipt of satisfactory information from the parties in 90% of cases.

To advise the Secretary of State in the case of mergers not pre-notified under statutory provisions within 39 working days of receipt of satisfactory information from the parties in 90% of cases."

Monopolies and anti-competitive practices

"To ensure that all parties to an enquiry are kept informed of progress and the issues of concern, and to give a substantive response to complaints and other correspondence within 30 working days in 90% of cases.

To complete an enquiry, by deciding the matter requires no further action, calls for assurances or undertakings or merits reference to the Monopolies and Mergers Commission, within six months in 75% of cases."

Responses to enquiries

"Whenever we receive an enquiry from business about the law, its interpretation, or our own procedures, in any of these areas, we shall aim to reply within 10 working days. If the enquiry is too complex or difficult for us to give a full response within that time, we shall acknowledge it and say how long a full reply is likely to take."

ANNEX 7. USEFUL ADDRESSES

Brussels

Commission of the European Union
200 rue de la Loi
1049 Brussels
Competition Directorate and Merger Task Force are in DG IV

Telephone: +32 2 295 1111 or 299 1111
Fax: +32 2 236 1149

DG IV"Cellule Information"
150 avenue de Cortenberg
1040 Brussels

Telephone: +32 2 295 0094
Fax: +32 2 295 5437

Council
170 rue de la Loi
1048 Brussels

Telephone: +32 2 234 6111
Fax: +32 2 234 8026

European Parliament
97–113 rue Belliard
1040 Brussels

Telephone: +32 2 284 2111
Fax: +32 2 230 7555

European Economic Area

EFTA Secretariat
74 rue de Trèves
1040 Brussels

Telephone: +32 2 286 1711
Fax: +32 2 286 1750

EFTA Surveillance Authority
1–3 rue Marie-Thérèse
1040 Brussels

Telephone: +32 2 226 6811
Fax: +32 2 226 6868

EFTA Court
4 avenue des Morgines
1213 Petit Lancy (Geneva)
Switzerland

Telephone: +41 22 709 0911
Fax: +41 22 709 0998

Luxembourg

European Court of Justice
Plateau de Kirchberg
L 2925 Luxembourg

Telephone: +352 43 031
Fax: +352 43 37 66

Court of First Instance
rue du Fort Niedergrunewald
2925 Luxembourg

Telephone: +352 43 031
Fax: +352 43 03 26 00

United Kingdom

Office of Fair Trading
Field House
Bream's Buildings
London EC4A 1PR

Telephone: 0171 269 8917
Fax: 0171 269 8800

Monopolies & Mergers Commission
New Court
48 Carey Street
London WC2A 2HT

Telephone: 0171 324 1467 or 324 1407
Fax: 0171 324 1400

Department of Trade and Industry
1–19 Victoria Street
London SW1 0NN

Telephone: 0171 215 5000
Fax: 0171 222 4382

DTI European Information Centre

Telephone: 0753 577 877
Fax: 0753 524 644

European Parliament
UK Information Office
2 Queen Anne's Gate
London SW1H 9AA

Telephone: 0171 222 0411
Fax: 0171 222 2713

European Commission
London representative office
8 Storey's Gate
London SW1P 3AT

Telephone: 0171 973 1992

Germany

Federal Ministry of Economic Affairs
Bundesministerium für Wirtschaft
Vielemomblerstraße 76
53123 Bremen

Telephone: +49 228 6152
Fax: +49 228 615 4436

State Cartel Offices
Bundeskartellamt
Meringdham 129
10965 Berlin

Telephone: +49 30 69 011
Fax: +49 30 69 01 400

Monopoly Commission
Monopolkommission
Barbarastraße 1
Cologne

Telephone: +49 221 77 80 11 48/49
Fax: +49 221 77 80 12 81

France

Competition Office
Direction Générale de la Concurrence, de la Consommation et de la
Répression des Fraudes "DGCCRF"
59 boulevard Vincent Auriol
75013 Paris

Telephone: +33 1 44 87 17 17
Fax: +33 1 44 97 30 37

Conseil de la Concurrence
11 rue de l'Echelle
75001 Paris

Telephone: +33 1 42 60 31 61
Fax: +33 1 42 60 60 99

Ministry of Economy
Ministère de l'Economie
Direction de la Concurrence
139 rue de Bercy
75012 Paris

Telephone: +33 1 40 04 04 04
Fax: +33 1 44 97 30 30

ANNEX 8. FORMS

EC law

UK law

RTPA registration

Form A/B*

Introduction

FORM A/B, as its Annex, is an integral part of the Commission Regulation (EC) No 3385/94 of 21 December 1994 on the form, content and other details of applications and notifications provided for in Council Regulation No 17 (hereinafter referred to as "the Regulation"). It allows undertakings and associations of undertakings to apply to the Commission for negative clearance agreements or practices which may fall within the prohibitions of Article 85(1) and Article 86 of the EC Treaty, or within Articles 53(1) and 54 of the EEA Agreement or to notify such agreement and apply to have it exempted from the prohibition set out in Article 85(1) by virtue of the provisions of Article 85(3) of the EC Treaty or from the prohibition of Article 53(1) by virtue of the provisions of Article 53(3) of the EEA Agreement.

To facilitate the use of the form A/B the following pages set out:

- in which situations it is necessary to make an application or a notification (Point A),

- to which authority (the Commission or the EFTA Surveillance Authority) the application or notification should be made (Point B),

- for which purposes the application or notification can be used (Point C),

- what information must be given in the application or notification (Points D, E and F),

- who can make an application or notification (Point G),

- how to make an application or notification (Point H),

- how the business secrets of the undertakings can be protected (Point I),

- how certain technical terms used in the operational part of Form A/B should be interpreted (Point J), and

---

*OJ 1994 L377/31.

– the subsequent procedure after the application or notification
has been made (Point K).

A   In which situation is it necessary to make an application or notification?

I   Purpose of the competition rules of the EC Treaty and the EEA Agreement

1   Purpose of the EC competition rules

The purpose of the competition rules is to prevent the distortion of
competition in the common market by restrictive practices or the
abuse of dominant positions. They apply to any enterprise trading
directly or indirectly in the common market, wherever established.

Article 85(1) of the EC Treaty (the text of Articles 85 and 86 is
reproduced in Annex I to this form) prohibits restrictive agreements,
decisions or concerted practices (arrangements) which may affect
trade between Member States, and Article 85(2) declares agreements and decisions containing such restrictions void (although the
Court of Justice has held that if restrictive terms of agreements are
severable, only those terms are void); Article 85(3), however, provides for exemption of arrangements with beneficial effects, if its
conditions are met. Article 86 prohibits the abuse of a dominant
position which may affect trade between Member States. The original procedures for implementing these Articles, which provide for
"negative clearance" and exemption pursuant to Article 85(3), were
laid down in Regulation No 17.

2   Purpose of the EEA competition rules

The competition rules of the Agreement on the European Economic
Area (concluded between the Community, the Member States and
the EFTA States[1] are based on the same principles as those contained in the Community competition rules and have the same
purpose, *i.e.* to prevent the distortion of competition in the EEA
territory by cartels or abuse of the dominant position. They apply to
any enterprise trading directly or indirectly in the EEA territory,
wherever established.

---

[1] See list of Member States and EFTA States in Annex III.

Article 53(1) of the EEA Agreement (the text of Articles 53, 54 and 56 of the EEA Agreement is reproduced in Annex I) prohibits restrictive agreements, decisions or concerted practices (arrangements) which may affect trade between the Community and one or more EFTA States (or between EFTA States), and Article 53(2) declares agreements or decisions containing such restrictions void; Article 53(3), however, provides for exemption of arrangements with beneficial effects, if its conditions are met. Article 54 prohibits the abuse of a dominant position which may affect trade between the Community and one or more EFTA States (or between EFTA States). The procedures for implementing these Articles, which provide for "negative clearance" and exemption pursuant to Article 53(3), are laid down in Regulation No 17, supplemented for EEA purposes, by Protocols 21, 22 and 23 to the EEA Agreement.[2]

II The scope of the competition rules of the EC Treaty and the EEA Agreement

The applicability of Articles 85 and 86 of the EC Treaty and Articles 53 and 54 of the EEA Agreement depends on the circumstances of each individual case. It presupposes that the arrangement or behaviour satisfies all the conditions set out in the relevant provisions. This question must consequently be examined before any application for negative clearance or any notification is made.

1 Negative clearance

The negative clearance procedure allows undertakings to ascertain whether the Commission considers that their arrangement or their behaviour is or is not prohibited by Article 85(1), or Article 86 of the EC Treaty or by Article 53(1) or Article 54 of the EEA Agreement. This procedure is governed by Article 2 of Regulation No 17. The negative clearance takes the form of a decision by which the Commission certifies that, on the basis of the facts in its possession, there are no grounds pursuant to Article 85(1) or Article 86 of the EC Treaty or under Article 53(1) or Article 54 of the EEA Agreement for action on its part in respect of the arrangement or behaviour.

---

[2] Reproduced in Annex I.

There is, however, no point in making an application when the arrangements or the behaviour are manifestly not prohibited by the abovementioned provisions. Nor is the Commission obliged to give negative clearance. Article 2 of Regulation No 17 states that " ... the Commission may certify ... ". The Commission issues negative clearance decisions only where an important problem of interpretation has to be solved. In other cases it reacts to the application by sending a comfort letter.

The Commission has published several notices relating to the interpretation of Article 85(1) of the EC Treaty. They define certain categories of agreements which, by their nature or because of their minor importance, are not caught by the prohibition.[3]

2   Exemption

The procedure for exemption pursuant to Article 85(3) of the EC Treaty and Article 53(3) of the EEA Agreement allows companies to enter into arrangements which, in fact, offer economic advantages but which, without exemption, would be prohibited by Article 85(1) of the EC Treaty or by Article 53(1) of the EEA Agreement. This procedure is governed by Articles 4,6 and 8 and, for the new Member States, also by Articles 5, 7 and 25 of Regulation No 17. The exemption takes the form of a decision by the Commission declaring Article 85(1) of the EC Treaty or Article 53(1) of the EEA Agreement to be inapplicable to the arrangements described in this decision. Article 8 requires the Commission to specify the period of validity of any such decision, allows the Commission to attach conditions and obligations and provides for decisions to be amended or revoked or specified acts by the parties to be prohibited in certain circumstances, notably if the decisions were based on incorrect information or if there is any material change in the facts.

The Commission has adopted a number of regulations granting exemptions to categories of agreements.[4] Some of these regulations provide that some agreements may benefit from exemption only if they are notified to the Commission pursuant to Article 4 or 5 of Regulation No 17 with a view to obtaining exemption, and the benefit of the opposition procedure is claimed in the notification.

---

[3] See Annex II.
[4] See Annex II.

A decision granting exemption may have retroactive effect, but, with certain exceptions, cannot be made effective earlier than the date of notification (Article 6 of Regulation No 17). Should the Commission find that notified arrangements are indeed prohibited and cannot be exempted and, therefore, take a decision condemning them, the participants are nevertheless protected, between the date of the notification and the date of the decision, against fines for any infringement described in the notification (Article 3 and Article 15(5) and (6) of Regulation No 17).

Normally the Commission issues exemption decisions only in cases of particular legal, economic or political importance. In the other cases it terminates the procedure by sending a comfort letter.

B   To which authority should application or notification be made?

The applications and notifications must be made to the authority which has a competence for the matter. The Commission is responsible for the application of the competition rules of the EC Treaty. However there is a shared competence in relation to the application of the competition rules of the EEA Agreement.

The competence of the Commission and of the EFTA Surveillance Authority to apply the EEA competition rules follows from Article 56 of the EEA Agreement. Applications and notifications relating to agreements, decisions or concerted practices liable to affect trade between Member States should be addressed to the Commission unless their effect on trade between Member States or on competition within the Community are not appreciable within the meaning of the Commission notice of 1986 on agreements of minor importance.[5] Furthermore, all restrictive agreements, decisions or concerted practices affecting trade between one Member State and one or more EFTA States fall within the competence of the Commission, provided that the undertakings concerned achieve more than 67% of their combined EEA-wide turnover within the Community.[6] However, if the effects of such agreements, decisions or concerted practices on trade between Member States or on competition within the

---

[5] OJ No C 231, 12.9.1986, p. 2.
[6] For a definition of "turnover" in this context, see Articles 2, 3 and 4 of Protocol 22 to the EEA Agreement reproduced in Annex I.

Community are not appreciable, the notification should, where necessary, be addressed to the EFTA Surveillance Authority. All other agreements, decisions and concerted practices falling under Article 53 of the EEA Agreement should be notified to the EFTA Surveillance Authority (the address of which is given in Annex III).

Applications for negative clearance regarding Article 54 of the EEA Agreement should be lodged with the Commission if the Dominant position exists only in the Community, or with the EFTA Surveillance Authority, if the dominant position exists only in the whole of the territory of the EFTA States, or a substantial part of it. Only where the dominant position exists within both territories should the rules outlined above with respect to Article 53 be applied.

The Commission will apply, as a basis for appraisal, the competition rules of the EC Treaty. Where the case falls under the EEA Agreement and is attributed to the Commission pursuant to Article 56 of that Agreement, it will simultaneously apply the EEA rules.

C The purpose of this form

Form A/B lists the questions that must be answered and the information and documents that must be provided when applying for the following:

– a negative clearance with regard to Article 85(1) of the EC Treaty and/or Article 53(1) of the EEA Agreement, pursuant to Article 2 of Regulation No 17, with respect to agreements between undertakings, decisions by associations of undertakings and concerted practices,

– an exemption pursuant to Article 85(3) of the EC Treaty and/or Article 53(3) of the EEA Agreement with respect to agreements between undertakings, decisions by associations of undertakings and concerted practices,

– the benefit of the opposition procedure contained in certain Commission regulations granting exemption by category.

This form allows undertakings applying for negative clearance to notify, at the same time, in order to obtain an exemption in the event that the Commission reaches the conclusion that no negative clearance can be granted.

Applications for negative clearance and notifications relating to Article 85 of the EC Treaty shall be submitted in the manner prescribed by form A/B (see Article 2(1), first sentence of the Regulation).

This form can also be used by undertakings that wish to apply for a negative clearance from Article 86 of the EC Treaty or Article 53 of the EEA Agreement, pursuant to Article 2 of Regulation No 17. Applicants requesting negative clearance from Article 86 are not required to use form A/B. They are nonetheless strongly recommended to give all the information requested below to ensure that their application gives a full statement of the facts (see Article 2(1), second sentence of the Regulation).

The applications or notifications made on the form A/B issued by the EFTA side are equally valid. However, if the agreements, decisions or practices concerned fall solely within Articles 85 or 86 of the EC Treaty, *i.e.* have no EEA relevance whatsoever, it is advisable to use the present form established by the Commission.

D   Which chapters of the form should be completed?

The operational part of this form is sub-divided into four chapters. Undertakings wishing to make an application for a negative clearance or a notification must complete Chapters I, II and IV. An exception to this rule is provided for in the case where the application or notification concerns an agreement concerning the creation of a cooperative joint venture of a structural character if the parties wish to benefit from an accelerated procedure. In this situation Chapters I, III and IV should be completed.

In 1992, the Commission announced that it had adopted new internal administrative rules that provided that certain applications and notifications – those of cooperative joint ventures which are structural in nature – would be dealt with within fixed deadlines. In such cases the services of the Commission will, within two months of receipt of the complete notification of the agreement, inform the parties in writing of the results of the initial analysis of the case and, as appropriate, the nature and probable length of the administrative procedure they intend to engage.

The contents of this letter may vary according to the characteristics of the case under investigation:

- in cases not posing any problems, the Commission will send a comfort letter confirming the compatibility of the agreement with Article 85(1) or (3),

- if a comfort letter cannot be sent because of the need to settle the case by formal decision, the Commission will inform the undertakings concerned of its intention to adopt a decision either granting or rejecting exemption,

- if the Commission has serious doubts as to the compatibility of the agreement with the competition rules, it will send a letter to the parties giving notice of an in-depth examination which may, depending on the case, result in a decision either prohibiting, exempting subject to conditions and obligations, or simply exempting the agreement in question.

This new accelerated procedure, applicable since 1 January 1993, is based entirely on the principle of self-discipline. The deadline of two months from the complete notification – intended for the initial examination of the case – does not constitute a statutory term and is therefore in no way legally binding. However, the Commission will do its best to abide by it. The Commission reserves the right, moreover, to extend this accelerated procedure to other forms of cooperation between undertakings.

A cooperative joint venture of a structural nature is one that involves an important change in the structure and organization of the business assets of the parties to the agreement. This may occur because the joint venture takes over or extends existing activities of the parent companies or because it undertakes new activities on their behalf. Such operations are characterised by the commitment of significant financial material and/or non-tangible assets such as intellectual property rights and know-how. Structural joint ventures are therefore normally intended to operate on a medium- or long-term basis.

This concept includes certain "partial function" joint ventures which take over one or several specific functions within the parents' business activity without access to the market, in particular research and development and/or production. It also covers those "full function" joint ventures which give rise to coordination of the competitive behaviour of independent undertakings, in particular between the parties to the joint venture or between them and the joint venture.

In order to respect the internal deadline, it is important that the Commission has available on notification all the relevant information reasonably available to the notifying parties that is necessary for it to assess the impact of the operation in question on competition. Form A/B therefore contains a special section (Chapter III) that must be completed only by persons notifying cooperative joint ventures of a structural character that wish to benefit from the accelerated procedure.

Persons notifying joint ventures of a structural character that wish to claim the benefit of the aforementioned accelerated procedure should therefore complete Chapters I, III and IV of this form. Chapter III contains a series of detailed questions necessary for the Commission to assess the relevant market(s) and the position of the parties to the joint venture on that (those) market(s).

Where the parties do not wish to claim the benefit of an accelerated procedure for their joint ventures of a structural character they should complete Chapters I, II and IV of this form. Chapter II contains a far more limited range of questions on the relevant market(s) and the position of the parties to the operation in question on that (those) market(s), but sufficient to enable the Commission to commence its examination and investigation.

E   The need for complete information

The receipt of a valid notification has two main consequences. First, it affords immunity from fines from the date that the valid notification is received by the Commission with respect to applications made in order to obtain exemption (see Article 15(5) of Regulation No 17). Second, until a valid notification is received the Commission cannot grant an exemption pursuant to Article 85(3) of the EC Treaty and/ or Article 53(3) of the EEA Agreement, and any exemption that is granted can be effective only from the date of receipt of a valid notification.[7] Thus, whilst there is no legal obligation to notify as such, unless and until an arrangement that falls within the scope of Article 85(1) and/or Article 53(1) has not been notified and is, therefore, not

---

[7] Subject to the qualification provided for in Article 4(2) of Regulation No 17.

capable of being exempted, it may be declared void by a national court pursuant to Article 85(2) and/or Article 53(2).[8]

Where an undertaking is claiming the benefit of a group exemption by recourse to an opposition procedure, the period within which the Commission must oppose the exemption by category only applies from the date that a valid notification is received. This is also true of the two months' period imposed on the Commission services for an initial analysis of applications for negative clearance and notifications relating to cooperative joint ventures of a structural character which benefit from the accelerated procedure.

A valid application or notification for this purpose means one that is not incomplete (see Article 3(1) of the Regulation). This is subject to two qualifications. First, if the information or documents required by this form are not reasonably available to you in part or in whole, the Commission will accept that a notification is complete and thus valid notwithstanding the failure to provide such information, providing that you give reasons for the unavailability of the information, and provide your best estimates for missing data together with the sources for the estimates. Indications as to where any of the requested information or documents that are unavailable to you could be obtained by the Commission must also be provided. Second, the Commission only requires the submission of information relevant and necessary to its inquiry into the notified operation. In come cases not all the information required by this form will be necessary for this purpose. The Commission may therefore dispense with the obligation to provide certain information required by this form (see Article 3 (3) of the Regulation). This provision enables, where appropriate, each application or notification to be tailored to each case so that only the information strictly necessary for the Commission's examination is provided. This avoids unnecessary administrative burdens being imposed on undertakings, in particular on small and medium-sized ones. Where the information or documents required by this form are not provided for this reason, the application or notification should indicate the reasons why the information is considered to be unnecessary to the Commission's investigation.

Where the Commission finds that the information contained in the application or notification is incomplete in a material respect, it will, within one month from receipt, inform the applicant or the notifying

---

[8] For further details of the consequences of non-notification see the Commission notice on cooperation betwen national Courts and the Commission (OJ No C 39, 13.2.1993, p 6).

party in writing of this fact and the nature of the missing information. In such cases, the application or notification shall become effective on the date on which the complete information is received by the Commission. If the Commission has not informed the applicant or the notifying party within the one month period that the application or notification is incomplete in a material respect, the application or notification will be deemed to be complete and valid (see Article 4 of the Regulation).

It is also important that the undertakings inform the Commission of important changes in the factual situation including those of which they become aware after the application or notification has been submitted. The Commission must, therefore, be informed immediately of any changes to an agreement, decision or practice which is the subject of an application or notification (see Article 4(3) of the Regulation). Failure to inform the Commission of such relevant changes could result in any negative clearance decision being without effect or in the withdrawal of any exemption decision[9] adopted by the Commission on the basis of the notification.

F   The need for accurate information.

In addition to the requirement that the application or notification be complete, it is important that you ensure that the information provided is accurate (see Article 3(1) of the Regulation). Article 15(1)(a) of Regulation No 17 states that the Commission may, by decision, impose on undertakings or associations of undertakings fines of up to ECU 5,000 where, intentionally or negligently, they supply incorrect or misleading information in an application for negative clearance or notification. Such information is, moreover, considered to be incomplete (see Article 4(4) of the Regulation), so that the parties cannot benefit from the advantages of the opposition procedure or accelerated procedure (see above, point E).

G   Who can lodge an application or a notification?

Any of the undertakings party to an agreement, decision, or practice of the kind described in Articles 85 or 86 of the EC Treaty and

---

[9] See point (a) of Article 8(3) of Regulation No 17.

Articles 53 or 54 of the EEA Agreement may submit an application for negative clearance, in relation to Article 85 and Article 53, or a notification requesting an exemption. An association of undertakings may submit an application or a notification in relation to decisions taken or practices pursued in the operation of the association.

In relation to agreements and concerted practices between undertakings it is common practice for all the parties involved to submit a joint application or notification. Although the Commission strongly recommends this approach, because it is helpful to have the views of all the parties directly concerned at the same time, it is not obligatory. Any of the parties to an agreement may submit an application or notification in their individual capacities, but in such circumstances the notifying party should inform all the other parties to the agreement, decision or practice of that fact (see Article 1(3) of the Regulation). They may also provide them with a copy of the completed form, where relevant once confidential information and business secrets have been deleted (see below, operational part, question 1.2).

Where a joint application or notification is submitted, it has also become common practice to appoint a joint representative on behalf of all the undertakings involved, both in making the application or notification, and in dealing with any subsequent contacts with the Commission (see Article 1(4) of the Regulation). Again, whilst this is helpful, it is not obligatory, and all the undertakings jointly submitting an application or a notification may sign it in their individual capacities.

H   How to submit an application or notification

Applications and notifications may be submitted in any of the official languages of the European Community or of an EFTA State (see Article 2(4) and (5) of the Regulation). In order to ensure rapid proceedings, it is, however, recommended to use, in case of an application or notification to the EFTA Surveillance Authority one of the official languages of an EFTA State or the working language of the EFTA Surveillance Authority, which is English, or, in case of an application or notification to the Commission, one of the official languages of the Community or the working language of the EFTA Surveillance Authority. This language will thereafter be the language of the proceeding for the applicant or notifying party.

Form A/B is not a form to be filled in. Undertakings should simply provide the information requested by this form, using its sections and paragraph numbers, signing a declaration as stated in Section 19 below, and annexing the required supporting documentation.

Supporting documents shall be submitted in their original language; where this is not an official language of the Community they must be translated into the language of the proceeding. The supporting documents may be originals or copies of the originals (see Article 2(4) of the Regulation).

All information requested in this form shall, unless otherwise stated, relate to the calendar year preceding that of the application or notification. Where information is not reasonably available on this basis (for example if accounting periods are used that are not based on the calendar year, or the previous year's figures are not yet available) the most recently available information should be provided and reasons given why figures on the basis of the calendar year preceding that of the application or notification cannot be provided.

Financial data may be provided in the currency in which the official audited accounts of the undertakings(s) concerned are prepared or in Ecus. In the latter case the exchange rate used for the conversion must be stated.

Seventeen copies of each application or notification, but only three copies of all supporting documents must be provided (see Article 2 (2) of the Regulation).

The application or notification is to be sent to:

Commission of the European Communities
Directorate-General for Competition (DG IV)
The Registrar
200, rue de la Loi
B-1049 Brussels

or be delivered by hand during Commission working days and official working hours at the following address:

Commission of the European Communities,
Directorate-General for Competition (DG IV)
The Registrar
158, avenue de Cortenberg
B-1040 Brussels.

I Confidentiality

Article 214 of the EC Treaty, Article 20 of Regulation No 17, Article 9 of Protocol 23 to the EEA Agreement, Article 122 of the EEA Agreement and Articles 20 and 21 of Chapter II of Protocol 4 to the Agreement between the EFTA States on the establishment of a Surveillance Authority and of a Court of Justice require the Commission, the Member States, the EEA Surveillance Authority and EFTA States not to disclose information of the kind covered by the obligation of professional secrecy. On the other hand, Regulation No 17 requires the Commission to publish a summary of the application or notification, should it intend to take a favourable decision. In this publication, the Commission " ... shall have regard to the legitimate interest of undertakings in the protection of their business secrets" (Article 19(3) of Regulation No 17; see also Article 21(2) in relation to the publication of decisions). In this connection, if an undertaking believes that its interests would be harmed if any of the information it is asked to supply were to be published or otherwise divulged to other undertakings, it should put all such information in a separate annex with each page clearly marked "Business Secrets". It should also give reasons why any information identified as confidential or secret should not be divulged or published. (See below, Section 5 of the operational part that requests a non-confidential summary of the notification.)

J Subsequent procedure

The application or notification is registered in the Registry of the Directorate-General for Competition (DG IV). The date of receipt by the Commission (or the date of posting if sent by registered post) is the effective date of the submission (see Article 4(1) of the Regulation). However, special rules apply to incomplete applications and notifications (see above under Point E).

The Commission will acknowledge receipt of all applications and notifications in writing, indicating the case number attributed to the file. This number must be used in all future correspondence regarding the notification. The receipt of acknowledgement does not prejudge the question whether the application or notification is valid.

Further information may be sought from the parties or from third parties (Articles 11 to 14 of Regulation No 17) and suggestions might be made as to amendments to the arrangements that might make them acceptable. Equally, a short preliminary notice may be published in the C series of the *Official Journal of the European Communities*, stating the names of the interested undertakings, the groups to which they belong, the economic sectors involved and the nature of the arrangements, and inviting third party comments (see below, operational part, Section 5).

Where a notification is made together for the purpose of the application of the opposition procedure, the Commission may oppose the grant of the benefit of the group exemption with respect to the notified agreement. If the Commission opposes the claim, and unless it subsequently withdraws its opposition, that notification will then be treated as an application for an individual exemption.

If, after examination, the Commission intends to grant the application for negative clearance or exemption, it is obliged (by Article 19(3) of Regulation No 17) to publish a summary and invite comments from third parties. Subsequently, a preliminary draft decision has to be submitted to and discussed with the Advisory Committee on Restrictive Practices and Dominant Positions composed of officials of the competent authorities of the Member States in the matter of restrictive practices and monopolies (Article 10 of Regulation No 17) and attended, where the case falls within the EEA Agreement, by representatives of the EFTA Surveillance Authority and the EFTA States which will already have received a copy of the application or notification. Only then, and providing nothing has happened to change the Commission's intention, can it adopt the envisaged decision.

Files are often closed without any formal decision being taken, for example, because it is found that the arrangements are already covered by a block exemption, or because they do not call for any action by the Commission, at least in circumstances at that time. In such cases comfort letters are sent. Although not a Commission decision, a comfort letter indicates how the Commission's departments view the case on the facts currently in their possession which means that the Commission could where necessary – for example, if it were to be asserted that a contract was void under Article 85(2) of the EC Treaty and/or Article 53(2) of the EEA Agreement – take an appropriate decision to clarify the legal situation.

K   Definitions used in the operational part of this form

Agreement: The word "agreement" is used to refer to all categories of arrangements, *i.e.* agreements between undertakings, decisions by associations of undertakings and concerted practices.

Year: All references to the word "year" in this form shall be read as meaning calendar year, unless otherwise stated.

Group: A group relationship exists for the purpose of this form where one undertaking:

– owns more than half the capital or business assets of another undertaking, or

– has the power to exercise more than half the voting rights in another undertaking, or

– has the power to appoint more than half the members of the supervisory board, board of directors or bodies legally representing the undertaking, or

– has the right to manage the affairs of another undertaking.

An undertaking which is jointly controlled by several other undertakings (joint venture) forms part of the group of each of these undertakings.

Relevant product market: questions 6.1 and 11.1 of this form require the undertaking – or individual submitting the notification to define the relevant product and/or service market(s) that are likely to be affected by the agreement in question. That definition(s) is then used as the basis for a number of other questions contained in this form. The definition(s) thus submitted by the notifying parties are referred to in this form as the relevant product market(s). These words can refer to a market made up either of products or of services.

Relevant geographic market: questions 6.2 and 11.2 of this form require the undertaking or individual submitting the notification to define the relevant geographic market(s) that are likely to be affected by the agreement in question. That definition(s) is then used as the basis for a number of other questions contained in this form. The definition(s) thus submitted by the notifying parties are referred to in this form as the relevant geographic market(s).

Relevant product and geographic market: by virtue of the combination of their replies to questions 6 and 11 the parties provide their definition of the relevant market(s) affected by the notified agreement(s). That (those) definition(s) is (are) then used as the basis for a number of other questions contained in this form. The definition(s) thus submitted by the notifying parties is referred to in this form as the relevant geographic and product market(s).

Notification: this form can be used to make an application for negative clearance and/or a notification requesting an exemption. The word "notification" is used to refer to either an application or a notification.

Parties and notifying party: the word "party" is used to refer to all the undertakings which are party to the agreement being notified. As a notification may be submitted by only one of the undertakings which are party to an agreement, "notifying party" is used to refer only to the undertaking or undertakings actually submitting the notification.

OPERATIONAL PART

PLEASE MAKE SURE THAT THE FIRST PAGE OF YOUR APPLICATION OR NOTIFICATION CONTAINS THE WORDS "APPLICATION FOR NEGATIVE CLEARANCE/ NOTIFICATION IN ACCORDANCE WITH FORM A/B"

CHAPTER I

Sections concerning the parties, their groups and the agreement (to be completed for all notifications)

Section 1

Identity of the undertakings or persons submitting the notification

1.1 Please list the undertakings on behalf of which the notification is being submitted and indicate their legal denomination or commercial name, shortened or commonly used as appropriate (if it differs from the legal denomination).

1.2 If the notification is being submitted on behalf of only one or some of the undertakings party to the agreement being notified, please confirm that the remaining undertakings have been informed of that fact and indicate whether they have received a copy of the notification, with relevant confidential information and business secrets deleted.[1] (In such circumstances a copy of the edited copy of the notification which has been provided to such other undertakings should be annexed to this notification.)

1.3 If a joint notification is being submitted, has a joint representative[2] been appointed?[3]

If yes, please give the details requested in 1.3.1 to 1.3.3 below. If no, please give details of any representatives who have been authorized to act for each or either of the parties to the agreement indicating who they represent.

1.3.1 Name of representative.

1.3.2 Address of representative.

1.3.3 Telephone and fax number of representative.

1.4 In cases where one or more representatives have been appointed, an authority to act on behalf of the undertaking(s) submitting the notification must accompany the notification.

Section 2

Information on the parties to the agreement and the groups to which they belong

2.1 State the name and address of the parties to the agreement being notified, and the country of their incorporation.

---

[1] The Commission is aware that in exceptional cases it may not be practicable to inform non-notifying parties to the notified agreement of that fact that it has been notified, or to provide them a copy of the notification. This may be the case, for example, where a standard agreement is being notified that is concluded with a large number of undertakings. Where this is the case you should state the reasons why it has not been practicable to follow the standard procedure set out in this question.

[2] *Note:* For the purposes of this question a representative means an individual or undertaking formally appointed to make the notification or application on behalf of the party or parties submitting the notification. This should be distinguished from the situation where the notification is signed by an officer of the company or companies in question. In the latter situation no representative is appointed.

[3] *Note:* It is not mandatory to appoint representatives for the purpose of completing and/or submitting this notification. This question only requires the identification of representatives where the notifying parties have chosen to appoint them.

2.2 State the nature of the business of each of the parties to the agreement being notified.

2.3 For each of the parties to the agreement, give the name of a person that can be contacted, together with his or her name, address, telephone number, fax number and position held in the undertaking.

2.4 Identify the corporate groups to which the parties to the agreement being notified belong. State the sectors in which these groups are active, and the world-wide turnover of each group.[4]

Section 3

Procedural matters

3.1 Please state whether you have made any formal submission to any other competition authorities in relation to the agreement in question. If yes, state which authorities, the individual or department in question, and the nature of the contact. In addition to this, mention any earlier proceedings or informal contacts, of which you are aware, with the Commission and/or the EFTA Surveillance Authority and any earlier proceedings with any national authorities or courts in the Community or in EFTA concerning these or any related agreements.

3.2 Please summarize any reasons for any claim that the case involves an issue of exceptional urgency.

3.3 The Commission has stated that where notifications do not have particular political, economic or legal significance for the Community they will normally be dealt with by means of comfort letter.[5] Would you be satisfied with a comfort letter? If you consider that it would be inappropriate to deal with the notified agreement in this manner, please explain the reasons for this view.

---

[4] For the calculation of turnover in the banking and insurance sectors see Article 3 of Protocol 22 to the EEA Agreement.
[5] See paragraph 14 of the notice on cooperation between national courts and the Commission in applying Articles 85 and 86 of the EC Treaty (OJ No C 39, 13. 2. 1993, p 6).

3.4 State whether you intend to produce further supporting facts or arguments not yet available and, if so, on which points.[6]

Section 4

Full details of the arrangements

4.1 Please summarize the nature, content and objectives pursued by the agreement being notified.

4.2 Detail any provisions contained in the agreements which may restrict the parties in their freedom to take independent commercial decisions, for example regarding:

   – buying or selling prices, discounts or other trading conditions,

   – the quantities of goods to be manufactured or distributed or services to be offered,

   – technical development or investment,

   – the choice of markets or sources of supply,

   – purchases from or sales to third parties,

   – whether to apply similar terms for the supply of equivalent goods or services,

   – whether to offer different services separately or together.

If you are claiming the benefit of the opposition procedure, identify in this list the restrictions that exceed those automatically exempted by the relevant regulation.

4.3 State between which Member States of the Community and/or EFTA States[7] trade may be affected by the arrangements. Please give reasons for your reply to this question, giving data on trade flows where relevant. Furthermore, please state whether trade between the Community or the EEA territory and any third countries is affected, again giving reasons for your reply.

---

[6] *Note:* In so far as the notifying parties provide the information required by this form that was reasonably available to them at the time of notification, the fact that the parties intend to provide further supporting facts or documentation in due course does not prevent the notification being valid at the time of notification and, in the case of structural joint ventures where the accelerated procedure is being claimed, the two month deadline commencing.

[7] See list in Annex II.

Section 5

Non-confidential summary

Shortly following receipt of a notification, the Commission may publish a short notice inviting third party comments on the agreement in question.[8] As the objective pursued by the Commission in publishing an informal preliminary notice is to receive third party comments as soon as possible after the notification has been received, such a notice is usually published without first providing it to the notifying parties for their comments. This section requests the information to be used in an informal preliminary notice in the event that the Commission decides to issue one. It is important, therefore, that your replies to these questions do not contain any business secrets or other confidential information.

1. State the names of the parties to the agreement notified and the groups of undertakings to which they belong.

2. Give a short summary of the nature and objectives of the agreement. As a guideline this summary should not exceed 100 words.

3. Identify the product sectors affected by the agreement in question.

CHAPTER II

Section concerning the relevant market

(to be completed for all notifications except those relating to structural joint ventures for which accelerated treatment is claimed)

Section 6

The relevant market

---

[8] An example of such a notice figures in annex 1 to this Form. Such a notice should be distinguished from a formal notice published pursuant to Article 19(3) of Regulation No 17. An Article 19(3) notice is relatively detailed, and gives an indication of the Commission's current approach in the case in question. Section 5 only seeks information that will be used in a short preliminary notice, and not a notice published pursuant to Article 19(3).

A relevant product market comprises all those products and/or services which are regarded as interchangeable or substitutable by the consumer, by reason of the products' characteristics, their prices and their intended use.

The following factors are normally considered to be relevant to the determination of the relevant product market and should be taken into account in this analysis:[1]

–   the degree of physical similarity between the products/services in question;

–   any differences in the end use to which the goods are put;

–   differences in price between two products;

–   the cost of switching between two potentially competing products;

–   established or entrenched consumer preferences for one type or category of product over another;

–   industry-wide product classifications (*e.g.* classifications maintained by trade associations).

The relevant geographic market comprises the area in which the undertakings concerned are involved in the supply of products or services, in which the conditions of competition are sufficiently homogeneous and which can be distinguished from neighbouring areas because, in particular, conditions of competition are appreciably different in those areas.

Factors relevant to the assessment of the relevant geographic market include[2] the nature and characteristics of the products or services concerned, the existence of entry barriers or consumer preferences, appreciable differences of the undertakings' market share or substantial price differences between neighbouring areas, and transport costs.

6.1 In the light of the above please explain the definition of the relevant product market or markets that in your opinion should form the basis of the Commission's analysis of the notification.

In your answer, please give reasons for assumptions or findings, and explain how the factors outlined above have been taken into

---

[1] This list is not, however, exhaustive, and notifying parties may refer to other factors.
[2] This list is not, however, exhaustive, and notifying parties may refer to other factors.

account. In particular, please state the specific products or services directly or indirectly affected by the agreement being notified and identify the categories of goods viewed as substitutable in your market definition.

In the questions figuring below, this (or these) definition(s) will be referred to as "the relevant product market(s)".

6.2 Please explain the definition of the relevant geographic market or markets that in your opinion should form the basis of the Commission's analysis of the notification. In your answer, please give reasons for assumptions or findings, and explain how the factors outlined above have been taken into account. In particular, please identify the countries in which the parties are active in the relevant product market(s), and in the event that you consider the relevant geographic market to be wider than the individual Member States of the Community or EFTA on which the parties to the agreements are active, give the reasons for this.

In the questions below, this (or these) definition(s) will be referred to as "the relevant geographic market(s)".

Section 7

Group members operating on the same markets as the parties

7.1 For each of the parties to the agreement being notified, provide a list of all undertakings belonging to the same group which are:

   7.1.1 active in the relevant product market(s);
   7.1.2 active in markets neighbouring the relevant product market(s) (*i.e.* active in products and/or services that represent imperfect and partial substitutes for those included in your definition of the relevant product market(s)).

Such undertakings must be identified even if they sell the product or service in question in other geographic areas than those in which the parties to the notified agreement operate. Please list the name, place of incorporation, exact product manufactured and the geographic scope of operation of each group member.

Section 8

The position of the parties on the affected relevant product markets

Information requested in this section must be provided for the groups of the parties as a whole. It is not sufficient to provide such information only in relation to the individual undertakings directly concerned by the agreement.

8.1 In relation to each relevant product market(s) identified in your reply to question 6.1 please provide the following information:

  8.1.1 the market shares of the parties on the relevant geographic market during the previous three years;

  8.1.2 where different, the market shares of the parties in (a) the EEA territory as a whole, (b) the Community, (c) the territory of the EFTA States and (d) each EC Member State and EFTA State during the previous three years.[3] For this section, where market shares are less than 20%, please state simply which of the following bands are relevant: 0 to 5%, 5 to 10%, 10 to 15%, 15 to 20%.

For the purpose of answering these questions, the market share may be calculated either on the basis of value or volume. Justification for the figures provided must be given. Thus, for each answer, total market value/volume must be stated, together with the sales/ turnover of each of the parties in question. The source or sources of the information should also be given (*e.g.* official statistics, estimates, etc), and where possible, copies should be provided of documents from which information has been taken.

Section 9

The position of competitors and customers on the relevant product market(s)

------

[3] i.e. Where the relevant geographic market has been defined as world wide, these figures must be given regarding the EEA, the Community, the territory of the EFTA States, and each EC Member State. Where the relevant geographic market has been defined as the Community, these figures must be given for the EEA, the territory of the EFTA States, and each EC Member State. Where the market has been defined as national, these figures must be given for the EEA, the Community and the territory of the EFTA States.

Information requested in this section must be provided for the group of the parties as a whole and not in relation to the individual companies directly concerned by the agreement notified.

For the (all) relevant product and geographic market(s) in which the parties have a combined market share exceeding 15%, the following questions must be answered:

9.1 Please identify the five main competitors of the parties. Please identify the company and give your best estimate as to their market share in the relevant geographic market(s). Please also provide address, telephone and fax number, and, where possible, the name of a contact person at each company identified.

9.2 Please identify the five main customers of each of the parties. State company name, address, telephone and fax numbers, together with the name of a contact person.

Section 10

Market entry and potential competition in product and geographic terms

For the (all) relevant product and geographic market(s) in which the parties have a combined market share exceeding 15%, the following questions must be answered:

10.1 Describe the various factors influencing entry in product terms into the relevant product market(s) that exist in the present case (*i.e.* what barriers exist to prevent undertakings that do not presently manufacture goods within the relevant product market(s) entering this market(s)). In so doing take account of the following where appropriate:

– to what extent is entry to the markets influenced by the requirement of government authorization or standard setting in any form? Are there any legal or regulatory controls on entry to these markets?

– to what extent is entry to the markets influenced by the availability of raw materials?

– to what extent is entry to the markets influenced by the length of contracts between an undertaking and its suppliers and/or customers?

– describe the importance of research and development and in
particular the importance of licensing patents, know-how and
other rights in these markets.

10.2 Describe the various factors influencing entry in geographic
terms into the relevant geographic market(s) that exist in the
present case (*i.e.* what barriers exist to prevent undertakings
already producing and/or marketing products within the relevant product market(s) but in areas outside the relevant geographic market(s) extending the scope of their sales into the
relevant geographic market(s)?). Please give reasons for your
answer, explaining, where relevant, the importance of the following factors:

– trade barriers imposed by law, such as tariffs, quotas, etc.;

– local specification or technical requirements;

– procurement policies;

– the existence of adequate and available local distribution and
retailing facilities;

– transport costs;

– entrenched consumer preferences for local brands or
products;

– language.

10.3 Have any ncw undertakings entered the relevant product mar-
ket(s) in geographic areas where the parties sell during the last
three years? Please provide this information with respect to both
new entrants in product terms and new entrants in geographic
terms. If such entry has occurred, please identify the under-
taking(s) concerned (name, address, telephone and fax numbers, and, where possible, contact person), and provide your
best estimate of their market share in the relevant product and
geographic market(s).

CHAPTER III

Section concerning the relevant market only for structural joint ventures for which accelerated treatment is claimed

Section 11

The relevant market

A relevant product market comprises all those products and/or services which are regarded as interchangeable or substitutable by the consumer, by reason of the products' characteristics, their prices and their intended use.

The following factors are normally considered to be relevant[1] to the determination of the relevant product market and should be taken into account in this analysis:

–   the degree of physical similarity between the products/services in question;

–   any differences in the end use to which the goods are put;

–   differences in price between two products;

–   the cost of switching between two potentially competing products;

–   established or entrenched consumer preferences for one type or category of product over another;

–   different or similar industry-wide product classifications (*e.g.* classifications maintained by trade associations).

The relevant geographic market comprises the area in which the undertakings concerned are involved in the supply of products or services, in which the conditions of competition are sufficiently homogeneous and which can be distinguished from neighbouring areas because, in particular, conditions of competition are appreciably different in those areas.

Factors relevant to the assessment of the relevant geographic market include[2] the nature and characteristics of the products or

---

[1] This list is not, however, exhaustive, and notifying parties may refer to other factors.
[2] This list is not, however, exhaustive, and notifying parties may refer to other factors.

services concerned, the existence of entry barriers or consumer preferences, appreciable differences of the undertakings' market share or substantial price differences between neighbouring areas, and transport costs.

Part 11.1

The notifying parties' analysis of the relevant market

11.1.1 In the light of the above, please explain the definition of the relevant market or markets that in the opinion of the parties should form the basis of the Commission's analysis of the notification.

In your answer, please give reasons for assumptions or findings, and explain how the factors outlined above have been taken into account.

In the questions figuring below, this (or these) definitions(s) will be referred to as "the relevant product market(s)".

11.1.2 Please explain the definition of the relevant geographic market or markets that in the opinion of the parties should form the basis of the Commission's analysis of the notification.

In your answer, please give reasons for assumptions or findings, and explain how the factors outlined above have been taken into account.

Part 11.2

Questions on the relevant product and geographic market(s)

Answers to the following questions will enable the Commission to verify whether the product and geographic market definitions put forward by you in Section 11.1 are compatible with definitions figuring above.

Product market definition

11.2.1 List the specific products or services directly or indirectly affected by the agreement being notified.

11.2.2 List the categories of products and/or services that are, in the opinion of the notifying parties, close economic substitutes for those identified in the reply to question 11.2.1. Where more than one product or service has been identified in the reply to question 11.2.1., a list for each product must be provided for this question.

The products identified in this list should be ordered in their degree of substitutability, first listing the most perfect substitute for the products of the parties, finishing with the least perfect substitute.[3]

Please explain how the factors relevant to the definition of the relevant product market have been taken into

---

[3] Close economic substitute; most perfect substitute; least perfect substitute. These definitions are only relevant to those filling out Chapter III of the form, *i.e.* (those notifying structural joint ventures requesting the accelerated procedure).

For any given product (for the purposes of this definition "product" is used to refer to products or services) a chain of substitutes exists. This chain is made up of all conceivable substitutes for the product in question, *i.e.* all those products that will, to a greater or lesser extent, fulfil the needs of the consumer in question. The substitutes will range from very close (or perfect) ones (products to which consumers would turn immediately in the event of, for example, even a very small price increase for the product in question) to very distant (or imperfect) subsites (products to which customers would only turn to in the event of a very large price rise for the product in question). When defining the relevant market, and calculating market shares, the Commission only takes into account close economic substitutes of the products in question. Close economic substitutes are ones to which customers would turn to in response to a small but significant price increase for the product in question (say 5%). This enables the Commission to assess the market power of the notifying companies in the context of a relevant market made up of all those products that consumers of the products in question could readily and easily turn to.

However, this does not mean that the Commission fails to take into account the constraints on the competitive behaviour of the parties in question resulting from the existence of imperfect substitutes (those to which a consumer could not turn to in response to a small but significant price increase (say 5%) for the products in question). These effects are taken into account once the market has been defined, and the market shares determined.

It is therefore important for the Commission to have information regarding both close economic substitutes for the products in question, as well as less perfect substitutes.

For example, assume two companies active in the luxury watch sector conclude a research and development agreement. They both manufacture watches costing ECU 1,800 to 2,000. Close economic substitutes are likely to be watches of other manufacturers in the same or similar price category, and these will be taken into account when defining the relevant product market. Cheaper watches, and in particular disposable plastic watches, will be imperfect substitutes, because it is unlikely that a potential purchaser of a ECU 2,000 watch will turn to one costing ECU 20 if the expensive one increased its price by 5%.

account in drawing up this list and in placing the product/ services in their correct order.

Geographic market definition

11.2.3 List all the countries in which the parties are active in the relevant product market(s). Where they are active in all countries within any given groups of countries or trading area (*e.g.* the whole Community or EFTA, the EEA countries, world-wide) it is sufficient to indicate the area in question.

11.2.4 Explain the manner in which the parties produce and sell the goods and/or services in each of these various countries or areas. For example, do they manufacture locally, do they sell through local distribution facilities, or do they distribute through exclusive, or non-exclusive, importers and distributors?

11.2.5 Are there significant trade flows in the goods/services that make up the relevant product market(s) (i) between the EC Member States (please specify which and estimate the percentage of total sales made up by imports in each Member State in which the parties are active), (ii) between all or part of the EC Member States and all or part of the EFTA States (again, please specify and estimate the percentage of total sales made up by imports), (iii) between the EFTA States (please specify which and estimate the percentage of total sales made up by imports in each such State in which the parties are active), and (iv) between all or part of the EEA territory and other countries (again, please specify and estimate the percentage of total sales made up by imports?)

11.2.6 Which producer undertakings based outside the Community or the EEA territory sell within the EEA territory in countries in which the parties are active in the affected products? How do these undertakings market their products? Does this differ between different EC Member States and/or EFTA States?

Section 12

Group members operating on the same markets as the parties to the notified agreement

12.1 For each of the parties to the agreement being notified, provide a list of all undertakings belonging to the same group which are:

    12.1.1 active in the relevant product market(s);

    12.1.2 active in markets neighbouring the relevant product market(s) (*i.e.* active in products/services that represent imperfect and partial substitutes[4] for those included in your definition of the relevant product market(s);

    12.1.3 active in markets upstream and/or downstream from those included in the relevant product market(s).

Such undertakings must be identified even if they sell the product or service in question in other geographic areas than those in which the parties to the notified agreement operate. Please list the name, place of incorporation, exact product manufactured and the geographic scope of operation of each group member.

Section 13

The position of the parties on the relevant product market(s)

Information requested in this section must be provided for the group of the parties as a whole and not in relation to the individual companies directly concerned by the agreement notified.

13.1 In relation to each relevant product market(s), as defined in your reply to question 11.1.2., please provide the following information:

    13.1.1 the market shares of the parties on the relevant geographic market during the previous three years;

    13.1.2 where different, the market shares of the parties in (a) the EEA territory as a whole, (b) the Community, (c) the

---

[4] The following are considered to be partial substitutes: products and services which may replace each other solely in certain geographic areas, solely during part of the year or solely for certain uses.

territory of the EFTA States and (d) each EC Member State and EFTA State during the previous three years.[5] For this section, where market shares are less than 20%, please state simply which of the following bands are relevant: 0 to 5%, 5 to 10%, 10 to 15%, 15 to 20% in terms of value or volume.

For the purpose of answering these questions, market share may be calculated either on the basis of value or volume. Justification for the figures provided must be given. Thus, for each answer, total market value/volume must be stated, together with the sales/turnover of each of the parties in question. The source or sources of the information should also be given, and where possible, copies should be provided of documents from which information has been taken.

13.2 If the market shares in question 13.1 were to be calculated on a basis other than that used by the parties, would the resultant market shares differ by more than 5% in any market (*i.e.* if the parties have calculated market shares on the basis of volume, what would be the relevant figure if it was calculated on the basis of value)? If the figure were to differ by more than 5% please provide the information requested in question 13.1 on the basis of both value and volume.

13.3 Give your best estimate of the current rate of capacity utilization of the parties and in the industry in general in the relevant product and geographic market(s).

Section 14

The position of competitors and customers on the relevant product market(s)

Information requested in this section must be provided for the group of the parties as a whole and not in relation to the individual companies directly concerned by the agreement notified.

---

[5] *i.e.* Where the relevant geographic market has been defined as world wide, these figures must be given regarding the EEA, the Community, the territory of the EFTA States, and each EC Member State and EFTA State. Where the relevant geographic market has been defined as the Community, these figures must be given for the EEA, the territory of the EFTA States, and each EC Member State and EFTA State. Where the market has been defined as national, these figures must be given for the EEA, the Community and the territory of the EFTA States.

For the (all) relevant product market(s) in which the parties have a combined market share exceeding 10% in the EEA as a whole, the Community, the EFTA territory or in any EC Member State or EFTA State, the following questions must be answered.

14.1 Please identify the competitors of the parties on the relevant product market(s) that have a market share exceeding 10% in any EC Member State, EFTA State, in the territory of the EFTA States, in the EEA, or world-wide. Please identify the company and give your best estimate as to their market share in these geographic areas. Please also provide the address, telephone and fax numbers, and, where possible, the name of a contact person at each company identified.

14.2 Please describe the nature of demand on the relevant product market(s). For example, are there few or many purchasers, are there different categories or purchasers, are government agencies or departments important purchasers?

14.3 Please identify the five largest customers of each of the parties for each *relevant product market(s)*. State company name, address, telephone and fax numbers, together with the name of a contact person.

Section 15

Market entry and potential competition

For the (all) relevant product market(s) in which the parties have a combined market share exceeding 10% in the EEA as a whole, the Community, the EFTA territory or in any EC Member State or EFTA State, the following questions must be answered.

15.1 Describe the various factors influencing entry into the relevant product market(s) that exist in the present case. In so doing take account of the following where appropriate:

– to what extent is entry to the markets influenced by the requirements of government authorization or standard setting in any form? Are there any legal or regulatory controls on entry to these markets?

– to what extent is entry to the markets influenced by the availability of raw materials?

- to what extent is entry to the markets influenced by the length of contracts between an undertaking and its suppliers and/or customers?

- what is the importance of research and development and in particular the importance of licensing patents, know-how and other rights in these markets?

15.2 Have any new undertakings entered the relevant product market(s) in geographic areas where the parties sell during the last three years? If so, please identify the undertaking(s) concerned (name, address, telephone and fax numbers, and, where possible, contact person), and provide your best estimate of their market share in each EC Member State and EFTA State that they are active in, and in the Community, the territory of the EFTA States and the EEA territory as a whole.

15.3 Give your best estimate of the minimum viable scale for the entry into the relevant product market(s) in terms of appropriate market share necessary to operate profitably.

15.4 Are there significant barriers to entry preventing companies active on the relevant product market(s):

15.4.1 in one EC Member State or EFTA State selling in other areas of the EEA territory;

15.4.2 outside the EEA territory selling into all or parts of the EEA territory?

Please give reasons for your answers, explaining, where relevant, the importance of the following factors:

- trade barriers imposed by law, such as tariffs, quotas, etc.,

- local specification or technical requirements,

- procurement policies,

- the existence of adequate and available local distribution and retailing facilities,

- transport costs,

- entrenched consumer preferences for local brands or products,

- language.

CHAPTER IV

Final sections

To be completed for all notifications

Section 16

Reasons for the application for negative clearance

If you are applying for negative clearance state:

16.1 why, *i.e.* state which provision or effects of the agreement or behaviour might, in your view, raise questions of compatibility with the Community's and/or the EEA rules of competition. The object of this subheading is to give the Commission the clearest possible idea of the doubts you have about your agreement or behaviour that you wish to have resolved by a negative clearance.

Then, under the following three references, give a statement of the relevant facts and reasons as to why you consider Article 85(1) or 86 of the EC Treaty and/or Article 53(1) or 54 of the EEA Agreement to be inapplicable, *i.e.*:

16.2 why the agreements or behaviour do not have the object or effect of preventing, restricting or distorting competition within the common market or within the territory of the EFTA States to any appreciable extent, or why your undertaking does not have or its behaviour does not abuse a dominant position; and/or

16.3 why the agreements or behaviour do not have the object or effect of preventing, restricting or distorting competition within the EEA territory to any appreciable extent, or why your undertaking does not have or its behaviour does not abuse a dominant position; and/or

16.4 why the agreements or behaviour are not such as may affect trade between Member States or between the Community and one or more EFTA States, or between EFTA States to any appreciable extent.

Section 17

Reasons for the application for exemption

If you are notifying the agreement, even if only as a precaution, in order to obtain an exemption under Article 85(3) of the EC Treaty and/or Article 53(3) of the EEA Agreement, explain how:

17.1 the agreement contributes to improving production or distribution, and/or promoting technical or economic progress. In particular, please explain the reasons why these benefits are expected to result from the collaboration; for example, do the parties to the agreement possess complementary technologies or distribution systems that will produce important synergies? (if, so, please state which). Also please state whether any documents or studies were drawn up by the notifying parties when assessing the feasibility of the operation and the benefits likely to result therefrom, and whether any such documents or studies provided estimates of the savings or efficiencies likely to result. Please provide copies of any such documents or studies;

17.2 a proper share of the benefits arising from such improvement or progress accrues to consumers;

17.3 all restrictive provisions of the agreement are indispensable to the attainment of the aims set out under 17.1. (if you are claiming the benefit of the opposition procedure, it is particularly important that you should identify and justify restrictions that exceed those automatically exempted by the relevant Regulations). In this respect please explain how the benefits resulting from the agreement identified in your reply to question 17.1 could not be achieved, or could not be achieved so quickly or efficiently or only at higher cost or with less certainty of success (i) without the conclusion of the agreement as a whole and (ii) without those particular clauses and provisions of the agreement identified in your reply to question 4.2;

17.4 the agreement does not eliminate competition in respect of a substantial part of the goods or services concerned.

Section 18

Supporting documentation

The completed notification must be drawn up and submitted in one original. It shall contain the last versions of all agreements which are the subject of the notification and be accompanied by the following:

(a) sixteen copies of the notification itself;

(b) three copies of the annual reports and accounts of all the parties to the notified agreement, decision or practice for the last three years;

(c) three copies of the most recent in-house or external long-term market studies or planning documents for the purpose of assessing or analysing the affected market(s) with respect to competitive conditions, competitors (actual and potential), and market conditions. Each document should indicate the name and position of the author;

(d) three copies of reports and analyses which have been prepared by or for any officer(s) or director(s) for the purposes of evaluating or analysing the notified agreement.

Section 19

Declaration

The notification must conclude with the following declaration which is to be signed by or on behalf of all the applicants or notifying parties.[1]

"The undersigned declare that the information given in this notification is correct to the best of their knowledge and belief, that complete copies of all documents requested by form A/B have been supplied to the extent that they are in the possession of the group of undertakings to which the applicant(s) or notifying party(ies) belong(s) and are accessible to the latter, that all estimates are identified as such and are their best

---

[1] Applications and notifications which have not been signed are invalid.

estimates of the underlying facts and that all the opinions expressed are sincere.

They are aware of the provisions of Article 15 (1) (a) of Regulation No 17."

Place and date:

Signatures:

Please add the name(s) of the person(s) signing the application or notification and their function(s).

FORM C*

This form[1] and the supporting documents should be forwarded in 15 copies together with proof in duplicate of the representative's authority to act.

If the space opposite each question is insufficient, please use extra pages, specifying to which item on the form they relate.

To the Commission of the European Communities
Directorate-General for Competition
200 rue de la Loi
B-1049 Brussels.

Application for initiation of procedure to establish the existence of an infringement of Article 85 or 86 of the Treaty, and/or Article 53 or 54 of the Agreement on the European Economic Area[2], submitted by natural or legal persons pursuant to Article 3 of Council Regulation No 17.

I   Information regarding parties concerned

1   Name, forenames and address of person submitting the application. If such person is acting as a representative, state the name and address of his principal; for an undertaking, or association of undertakings or persons, state the name, forenames and address of their legal representatives.

Proof of representatives's authority to act must be supplied.

If the application is submitted by a number of persons or on behalf of a number of persons, the information must be given in respect of each applicant or principal.

2   Name and address of persons to whom the application relates.

---

*OJ 1993 L336/25.
[1] Applications made by using Form C issued by the Commission and Form C issued by the EFTA side are equally valid.
[2] Hereinafter referred to as "the EEA Agreement". Any reference to EFTA States shall be understood to mean those EFTA States which are Contracting Parties to the EEA Agreement.

II   Details of the alleged infringement

Set out in detail, in an Annex, the facts from which, in your opinion, it appears that there is infringement of Article 85 or 86 of the Treaty and/or Article 53 or 54 of the EEA Agreement.

Indicate in particular:

1   the practices of the undertakings or associations of undertakings to which this application relates which have as their object or effect the prevention, restriction or distortion of competition or constitute an abuse of a dominant position within the common market, within the territory of the EFTA States or within the EEA territory;

2   to what extent trade between Member States, between the Community and one or more EFTA States, or between EFTA States may be affected;

3   the nature of the goods affected by the alleged infringements (include the heading number according to the Harmonized Commodity Description and Coding System).

III   Existence of legitimate interest

Set out – if necessary in an Annex – the grounds on which you claim a legitimate interest in the initiation by the Commission of the procedure provided for in Article 3 of Regulation No 17.

IV   Evidence

1   State the names and addresses of persons able to testify to the facts set out, and in particular of persons affected by the alleged infringement.

2   Submit all documentation relating to or directly connected with the facts set out (for example, texts of agreements, minutes of negotiations or meetings, terms of transactions, business documents, circulars).

3   Submit statistics or other data relating to the facts set out (and relating, for example, to price trends, formation of prices, terms of transactions, terms of supply or sale, boycotting, discrimination).

4   Where appropriate, give any necessary technical details to pro-
    duction, sales, etc., or name experts able to do so.
5   Indicate any other evidence of the existence of the alleged
    infringement.

V

Indicate all approaches made, and all steps taken, prior to this
application, by you or any other person affected by the practice
described above, with a view to terminating the alleged infringement
(proceedings commenced before judicial or administrative bodies,
stating in particular the reference numbers of the cases and the
results thereof).

We, the undersigned, declare that the information given in this form
and in the Annexes thereto is given entirely in good faith.

At ....

Signed:

COMMISSION   Brussels,..........
OF THE
EUROPEAN COMMUNITIES
Directorate-General for Competition

To......................

ACKNOWLEDGEMENT OF RECEIPT

(This form will be returned to the address inserted above if the top
half is completed in a single copy by the applicant.)

Your application for a finding of infringement of Article 85 or 86
of the Treaty and/or Article 53 or 54 of the EEA Agreement,
dated ....

(a)   Applicant:

(b)   Infringing parties:

was received on:..............................

and registered under No: IV/.............................

Please quote the above number in all correspondence.

FORM CO*

INTRODUCTION

A   The purpose of this Form

This Form specifies the information that must be provided by an undertaking or undertakings when notifying the Commission of a concentration with a Community dimension. A "concentration" is defined in Article 3 and "Community dimension" by Article 1 of Regulation (EEC) No 4064/89.

Your attention is drawn to Regulation (EEC) No 4064/89 and to Regulation (EC) No. 3384/94, (hereinafter referred to as the "Implementing Regulation") and to the corresponding provisions of the Agreement of the European Economic Area.[1]

Experience has shown that prenotification meetings are extremely valuable to both the notifying party(ies) and the Commission in determining the precise amount of information required in a notification and, in the large majority of cases, will result in a significant reduction of the information required. Accordingly, notifying parties are encouraged to consult the Commission regarding the possibility of dispensing with the obligation to provide certain information (see Section B (b) discussing the possibility of waivers).

B   The need for a correct and complete notification

All information required by this Form must be correct and complete (Article 4 of the Implementing Regulation). In particular you should note that:

---

*OJ 1994 L377/9.

[1] Hereinafter referred to as "the EEA Agreement", in particular Article 57 of the EEA Agreement (point 1 of Annex XIV to the EEA Agreement and Protocol 4 to the Agreement between the EFTA States on the establishment of a Surveillance Authority and a Court of Justice), as well as Protocols 21 and 24 to the EEA Agreement and Article 1, and the Agreed Minutes of the Protocol adjusting the EEA Agreement. In particular, any reference to EFTA States shall be understood to mean those EFTA States which are Contracting Parties to the EEA Agreement.

(a) if the information required by this Form is not reasonably available to you in part or in whole (for example, because of the unavailability of information on a target company during a contested bid), the Commission will accept that the notification is complete and thus valid notwithstanding the failure to provide such information, providing that you give reasons for the unavailability of said information, and provide your best estimates for missing data together with the sources for the estimates. Where possible, indications as to where any of the requested information that is unavailable to you could be obtained by the Commission should also be provided; unless all material information required by this Form is supplied in full or good reasons are given explaining why this has not been possible the notification will be incomplete and will only become effective on the date on which all such information required is received;

(b) the Commission only requires the submission of information relevant and necessary to its inquiry into the notified operation. If you consider that any particular information requested by this Form, in the full- or short-form version, may not be necessary for the Commission's examination of the case, you may explain this in your notification and ask the Commission to dispense with the obligation to provide that information, pursuant to Article 3(2) of the Implementing Regulation;

(c) incorrect or misleading information in the notification will be considered to be incomplete information. In such cases, the Commission will inform the notifying parties or their representatives of this in writing and without delay. The notification will only become effective on the date on which the complete and accurate information is received by the Commission (Article 4 (2) and (4) of the Implementing Regulation). Article 14 (1) (b) of Regulation (EEC) No 4064/89 provides that incorrect or misleading information where supplied intentionally or negligently can make the notifying party or parties liable to fines of up to ECU 50,000. In addition, pursuant to point (a) of Article 8 (5) of Regulation (EEC) No 4064/89 the Commission may also revoke its decision on the compatibility of a notified concentration where it is based on incorrect information for which one of the undertakings is responsible.

C   Notification in short-form

(a) In cases where a joint venture has no, or *de minimis*, actual or foreseen activities within the EEA territory, the Commission intends to allow notification of the operation by means of short-form. Such cases occur where joint control is acquired by two or more undertakings, and where:

  (i) the turnover[1] of the joint venture and/or the turnover of the contributed activities[2], is less than ECU 100 million in the EEA territory; and

  (ii) the total value of assets[3] transferred to the joint venture is less than ECU 100 million in the EEA territory.[4]

(b) If you consider that the operation to be notified meets these qualifications, you may explain this in your notification and ask the Commission to dispense with the obligation to provide the full-form notification, pursuant to Article 3(2) of the Implementing Regulation, and to allow you to notify by means of short-form.

(c) Short-form notification allows the notifying parties to limit the information provided in the notification to the following sections and questions:

---

[1] The turnover of the joint venture should be determined according to the most recent audited accounts of the parent companies, or the joint venture itself, depending upon the availability of separate accounts for the resources combined in the joint venture.

[2] The expression "and/or" refers to the variety of situations covered by the short-form; for example:
  – in the case of the joint acquisition of a target company, the turnover to be taken into account is the turnover of this target (the joint venture),
  – in the case of the creation of a joint venture to which the parent companies contribute their activities, the turnover to be taken into account is that of the contributed activities,
  – in the case of entry of a new controlling party into an existing joint venture, the turnover of the joint venture and the turnover of the activities contributed by the new parent company (if any) must be taken into account.

[3] The total value of assets of the joint venture should be determined according to the last regularly prepared and approved balance sheet of each parent company. The term "assets" includes (1) all tangible and intangible assets that will be transferred to the joint venture (examples of tangible assets include production plants, wholesale or retail outlets, and inventory of goods) and (2) any amount of credit or any obligations of the joint venture which any parent company of the JV has agreed to extend or guarantee.

[4] Where the assets transferred generate turnover, then neither the value of the assets nor that of the turnover may exceed ECU 100 million.

- Section 1,
- Section 2, except questions 2.1(a,b and d), 2.3.4, and 2.3.5,
- Section 3, only question 3.1 and 3.2 (a),
- Section 5, only question 5.1 and 5.3,
- Section 6,
- Section 10, and
- Section 9, only questions 9.5 and 9.6 (optional for the convenience of the parties).

(d) In addition, with respect to the affected markets of the joint venture as defined below in Section 6, indicate the following for the EEA territory, for the Community as a whole, for each Member State and EFTA State, and where different, in the opinion of the notifying parties, for the relevant geographic market:

- the sales in value and volume, as well as the market shares, for the year preceding the operation, and
- the five largest customers and the five largest competitors in the affected markets in which the joint venture will be active. Provide the name, address, telephone number, fax number and appropriate contact person of each such customer and competitor.

(e) The Commission may require full, or where appropriate partial, notification under the Form CO where:

- the notified operation does not meet the short-form thresholds, or
- this appears to be necessary for an adequate investigation with respect to possible competition problems on affected markets.

In such cases, the notification may be considered incomplete in a material respect pursuant to Article 4 (2) of the Implementing Regulation. The Commission will inform the notifying parties or their representatives of this in writing and without delay and will fix a deadline for the submission of a full or, where appropriate partial, notification. The notification will only become effective on the date on which all information required is received.

D Who must notify

In the case of a merger within the meaning of Article 3(1) (a) or the acquisition of joint control in an undertaking within the meaning of Article 3 (1) (b), the notification shall be completed jointly by the parties to the merger or by those acquiring joint control as the case may be.

In case of the acquisition of a controlling interest in an undertaking by another, the acquirer must complete the notification.

In the case of a public bid to acquire an undertaking, the bidder must complete the notification.

Each party completing the notification is responsible for the accuracy of the information which it provides.

E How to notify

The notification must be completed in one of the official languages of the European Community. This language shall thereafter be the language of the proceedings for all notifying parties. Where notifications are made in accordance with Article 12 of Protocol 24 to the EEA Agreement in an official language of an EFTA State which is not an official language of the Community, the notification shall simultaneously be supplemented with a translation into an official language of the Community.

The information requested by this Form is to be set out using the sections and paragraph numbers of the Form, signing a declaration as provided in Section 10, and annexing supporting documentation.

Supporting documents shall be submitted in their original language; where this is not an official language of the Community they shall be translated into the language of the proceeding (Article 2 (4) of the Implementing Regulation).

Requested documents may be originals or copies of the originals. In the latter case the notifying party shall confirm that they are true and complete.

Twenty-four copies of each notification and 19 copies of all supporting documentation must be provided.

The notification should be delivered by registered mail or by hand (or courier service) during normal Commission working hours at the following address:

Commission of the European Communities
Directorate-General for Competition (DG IV)

Merger Task Force
150 avenue de Cortenberg/Kortenberglaan 150
B-1049 Brussels.

F   Confidentiality

Article 214 of the Treaty and Article 17(2) of Regulation (EEC) No
4064/89 as well as the corresponding provisions of the EEA Agreement[5] require the Commission, the Member States, the EFTA Surveillance Authority and the EFTA States, their officials and other
servants not to disclose information they have acquired through the
application of the Regulation of the kind covered by the obligation of
professional secrecy. The same principle must also apply to protect
confidentiality between notifying parties.

If you believe that your interests would be harmed if any of the
information you are asked to supply were to be published or otherwise divulged to other parties, submit this information separately
with each page clearly marked "Business Secrets". You should also
give reasons why this information should not be divulged or
published.

In the case of mergers or joint acquisitions, or in other cases where
the notification is completed by more than one of the parties,
business secrets may be submitted under separate cover, and referred to in the notification as an annex. All such annexes must be
included in the submission in order for a notification to be considered
complete.

G   Definitions and instructions for purposes of this Form

Notifying party or parties: In cases where a notification is submitted
by only one of the undertakings party to an operation, "notifying
parties" is used to refer only to the undertaking actually submitting
the notification.

Party(ies) to the concentration or, parties: these terms relate to both
the acquiring and acquired parties, or to the merging parties, includ-

---

[5] See, in particular, Article 122 of the EEA Agreement, Article 9 of Protocol 24 to
the EEA Agreement and Article 17(2) of chapter XIII of Protocol 4 to the
Agreement between the EFTA States on the establishment of a Surveillance
Authority and a Court of Justice (ESA Agreement).

ing all undertakings in which a controlling interest is being acquired or which is the subject of a public bid.

Except where otherwise specified, the terms "notifying party(ies)" and "party(ies) to the concentration" include all the undertakings which belong to the same groups as those "parties".

Affected markets: Section 6 of this Form requires the notifying parties to define the relevant product and/or service markets, and further to identify which of those relevant markets are likely to be affected by the notified operation. This definition of affected market is used as the basis for requiring information for a number of other questions contained in this Form. The definitions thus submitted by the notifying parties are referred to in this Form as the affected market(s). This term can refer to a relevant market made up either of products or of services.

Year: all references to the word "year" in this Form shall be read as meaning calendar year, unless otherwise stated. All information requested in this Form shall, unless otherwise specified, relate to the year preceding that of the notification.

The financial data requested in Section 2.4 must be provided in ecus at the average conversion rates prevailing for the years or other periods in question.

All references contained in this Form are to the relevant Articles and paragraphs of Council Regulation (EEC) No 4064/89, unless otherwise stated.

SECTION 1

Background information

1.1 *Information on notifying party (or parties)*
Give details of:

    1.1.1   name and address of undertaking;

    1.1.2   nature of the undertaking's business;

    1.1.3   name, address, telephone number, fax number and/or telex of, and position held by, the appropriate contact person.

1.2 *Information on other parties[6] to the concentration*
For each party to the concentration (except the notifying party or parties) give details of:

    1.2.1   name and address of undertaking;

    1.2.2   nature of undertaking's business

    1.2.3   name, address, telephone number, fax number and/or telex of, and position held by the appropriate contact person.

1.3 *Address for service*
Give an address (in Brusscls if available) to which all communications may be made and documents delivered.

1.4 *Appointment of representatives*
Where notifications are signed by representatives of undertakings, such representatives shall produce written proof that they are authorized to act.

    If a joint/notification is being submitted, has a joint representative been appointed?

    If yes, please give the details requested in Sections 1.4.1 to 1.4.4.

    If no, please give details of information of any representatives who have been authorized to act for each of the parties to the concentration, indicating whom they represent;

    1.4.1   name of representative;

    1.4.2   address of representative.

    1.4.3   name of person to be contacted (and address, if different from 1.4.2);

    1.4.4   telephone number, fax number and/or telex.

SECTION 2

Details of the concentration

2.1 *Briefly describe the nature of the concentration being notified. In doing so state*:

---

[6] This includes the target company in the case of a contested bid, in which case the details should be completed as far as is possible.

(a) whether the proposed concentration is a full legal merger, an acquisition of sole or joint control, a concentrative joint venture or a contract or other means of conferring direct or indirect control within the meaning of Article 3(3);

(b) whether the whole or parts of parties are subject to the concentration;

(c) a brief explanation of the economic and financial structure of the concentration;

(d) whether any public offer for the securities of one party by another party has the support of the former's supervisory boards of management or other bodies legally representing that party;

(e) the proposed or expected date of any major events designed to bring about the completion of the concentration;

(f) the proposed structure of ownership and control after the completion of the concentration;

(g) any financial or other support received from whatever source (including public authorities) by any of the parties and the nature and amount of this support.

2.2 *List the economic sectors involved in the concentration.*

2.3 *For each of the undertakings concerned by the concentration[1] provide the following data[2] for the last financial year:*

    2.3.1   world-wide turnover;

    2.3.2   Community-wide turnover;

    2.3.3   EFTA-wide turnover;

    2.3.4   turnover in each Member State;

    2.3.5   turnover in each EFTA State;

---

[1] See Commission notice on the notion of undertakings concerned.
[2] See, generally, the Commission notice on 'Calculation of turnover'. Turnover of the acquiring party or parties to the concentration shall include the aggregated turnover of all undertakings within the sense of Article 5(4). Turnover of the acquired party or parties shall include the turnover relating to the parts subject to the transaction in the sense of Article 5(2). Special provisions are contained in Articles 5(3), (4) and 5(5) for credit, insurance, other financial institutions and joint undertakings.

2.3.6   the Member State, if any, in which more than two-thirds of Community-wide turnover is achieved;[3]

2.3.7   the EFTA State, if any, in which more than two-thirds of EFTA-wide turnover is achieved.[3]

2.4 *Provide the following information with respect to the last financial year:*

2.4.1   does the combined turnover of the undertakings concerned in the territory of the EFTA States equal 25% or more of their total turnover in the EEA territory?

2.4.2   does each of at least two undertakings concerned have a turnover exceeding ECU 250 million in the territory of the EFTA States?

SECTION 3

Ownership and control[4]

For each of the parties to the concentration provide a list of all undertakings to the same group.

This list must include:

3.1 all undertakings or persons controlling these parties, directly or indirectly;

3.2 all undertakings active on any affected market[5] that are controlled, directly or indirectly:

(a) by these parties;

(b) by any other undertaking identified in 3.1.

For each entry listed above, the nature and means of control shall be specified.

The information sought in this section may be illustrated by the use of organization charts or diagrams to show the structure of ownership and control of the undertakings.

---

[3] See guidance note IV for the calculation of turnover in one Member State with respect to Community-wide turnover.
[4] See Articles 3(3) to 3(5) and 5(4).
[5] See section 6 for the definition of affected markets.

SECTION 4

Personal and financial links and previous acquisitions

With respect to the parties to the concentration and each undertaking or person identified in response to Section 3 provide:

4.1 a list of all other undertakings which are active on affected markets (affected markets are defined in Section 6) in which the undertakings, or persons, of the group hold individually or collectively 10% or more of the voting rights, issued share capital or other securities;

in each case identify the holder and state the percentage held;

4.2 a list for each undertaking of the members of their boards of management who are also members of the boards of management or of the supervisory boards of any other undertaking which is active on affected markets; and (where applicable) for each undertaking a list of the members of their supervisory boards who are also members of the boards of management or any other undertaking which is active on affected markets;

in each case identify the name of the other undertaking and the positions held;

4.3 details of acquisitions made during the last three years by the groups identified above (Section 3) of undertakings active in affected markets as defined in Section 6.

Information provided here may be illustrated by the use of organization charts or diagrams to give a better understanding.

SECTION 5

Supporting documentation

Notifying parties shall provide the following:

5.1 copies of the final or most recent versions of all documents bringing about the concentration, whether by agreement between the parties to the concentration, acquisition of a controlling interest or a public bid;

5.2 in a public bid, a copy of the offer document; if unavailable on notification, should be submitted as soon as possible and not later than when it is posted to shareholders;

5.3 copies of the most recent annual reports and accounts of all the parties to the concentration;

5.4 where at least one affected market is identified:

copies of analyses, reports, studies and surveys submitted to or prepared for any member(s) of the board of directors, the supervisory boards, or the shareholders' meeting, for the purpose of assessing or analysing the concentration with respect to competitive conditions, competitors (actual and potential), and market conditions.

SECTION 6

Market definitions

The relevant product and geographic markets determine the scope within which the market power of the new entity resulting from the concentration must be assessed.

The notifying party or parties shall provide the data requested having regard to the following definitions:

I. *Relevant product markets*

A relevant product market comprises all those products and/or services which are regarded as interchangeable or substitutable by the consumer, by reason of the products' characteristics, their prices and their intended use. A relevant product market may in some cases be composed of a number of individual products and/ or services which present largely identical physical or technical characteristics and are interchangeable.

Factors relevant to the assessment of the relevant product market include the analysis of why the products or services in these markets are included and why others are excluded by using the above definition, and having regard to, *e.g.* substitutability, conditions of competition, prices, cross-price elasticity of demand or other factors relevant for the definition of the product markets.

II. *Relevant geographic markets*

The relevant geographic market comprises the area in which the undertakings concerned are involved in the supply of relevant products or services, in which the conditions of competition are sufficiently homogeneous and which can be distinguished from neighbouring geographic areas because, in particular, conditions of competition are appreciably different in those areas.

Factors relevant to the assessment of the relevant geographic market include the nature and characteristics of the products or services concerned, the existence of entry barriers, consumer preferences, appreciable differences of the undertakings' market shares between neighbouring geographic areas or substantial price differences.

III. *Affected markets*

For purposes of information required in this Form, affected markets consist of relevant product markets where in the EEA territory, in the Community, in the territory of the EFTA States, in any Member State or in any EFTA State:

(a)   two or more of the parties to the concentration are engaged in business activities in the same product market and where the concentration will lead to a combined market share of 15% or more. These are horizontal relationships;

(b)   one or more of the parties to the concentration are engaged in business activities in a product market, which is upstream or downstream of a product market in which any other party to the concentration is engaged, and any of their individual or combined market share is 25% or more, regardless of whether there is or is not any existing supplier/customer relationship between the parties to the concentration. These are vertical relationships.

On the basis of the above definitions and market share thresholds, provide the following information:

6.1 Identify each affected market within the meaning of Section III, within the EEA territory, the Community, the territory of the EFTA States, in any Member State or in any EFTA State.

6.2 Briefly describe the relevant product and geographic markets concerned by the notified operation, including those which are closely related to the relevant product market(s) concerned (in upstream, downstream and horizontal neighbouring markets), where two or more of the parties to the concentration are active and which are not affected markets within the meaning of Section III.

SECTION 7

Information on affected markets

For each affected relevant product market, for each of the last three financial years:

(a) for the EEA territory;

(b) for the Community as a whole;

(c) for the territory of the EFTA States as a whole;

(d) individually for each Member State and EFTA State where the parties to the concentration do business;

(e) and, where in the opinion of the notifying parties, the relevant geographic market is different;

provide the following:

7.1 an estimate of the total size of the market in terms of sales value (in ecus) and volume (units)[1]. Indicate the basis and sources for the calculations and provide documents where available to confirm these calculations;

7.2 the sales in value and volume, as well as an estimate of the market shares, of each of the parties to the concentration;

7.3 an estimate of the market share in value (and where appropriate volume) of all competitors (including importers) having at least 10% of the geographic market under consideration. Provide documents where available to confirm the calculation of these market shares and provide the name, address, telephone number, fax number and appropriate contact person, of these competitors.

---

[1] The value and volume of a market should reflect output less exports plus imports for the geographic areas under consideration.

7.4 an estimate of the total value and volume and source of imports from outside the EEA territory and identify:

(a) the proportion of such imports that are derived from the groups to which the parties to the concentration belong:

(b) an estimate of the extent to which any quotas, tariffs or non-tariff barriers to trade, affect these imports, and

(c) an estimate of the extent to which transportation and other costs affect these imports;

7.5 the extent to which trade among States within the EEA territory is affected by:

(a) transportation and other costs; and

(b) other non-tariff barriers to trade;

7.6 the manner in which the parties to the concentration produce and sell the products and/or services; for example, whether they manufacture locally, or sell through local distribution facilities;

7.7 a comparison of price levels in each Member State and EFTA State by each party to the concentration and a similar comparison of price levels between the Community, the EFTA States and other areas where these products are produced (*e.g.* eastern Europe, the United States of America, Japan, or other relevant areas);

7.8 the nature and extent of vertical integration of each of the parties to the concentration compared with their largest competitors.

SECTION 8

General conditions in affected markets

8.1 Identify the five largest suppliers to the notifying parties and their individual shares of purchases from each of these suppliers (or raw materials or goods used for purposes of producing the relevant products). Provide the name, address, telephone number, fax number and appropriate contact person, of these suppliers.

Structure of supply in affected markets

8.2 Explain the distribution channels and service networks that exist on the affected markets. In so doing, take account of the following where appropriate:

(a) the distribution systems prevailing on the market and their importance. To what extent is distribution performed by third parties and/or undertakings belonging to the same group as the parties identified in Section 3?

(b) the service networks (for example, maintenance and repair) prevailing and their importance in these markets. To what extent are such services performed by third parties and/or undertakings belonging to the same group as the parties identified in Section 3?

8.3 Where appropriate, provide an estimate of the total Community-wide and EFTA-wide capacity for the last three years. Over this period what proportion of this capacity is accounted for by each of the parties to the concentration, and what have been their respective rates of capacity utilization?

Structure of demand in affected markets

8.4 Identify the five largest customers of the notifying parties in each affected market and their individual share of total sales for such products accounted for by each of those customers. Provide the name, address, telephone number, fax number and appropriate contact person, of each of these customers.

8.5 Explain the structure of demand in terms of:

(a) the phases of the markets in terms of, for example, take-off, expansion, maturity and decline, and a forecast of the growth rate of demand;

(b) the importance of customer preferences, in terms of brand loyalty, products differentiation and the provision of a full range of products;

(c) the degree of concentration or dispersion of customers;

(d) segmentation of customers into different groups and describe the "typical customer" of each group;

(e) the importance of exclusive distribution contracts and other types of long-term contracts;

(f) the extent to which public authorities, government agencies, state enterprises or similar bodies are important participants as a source of demand.

Market entry

8.6 Over the last five years, has there been any significant entry into any affected markets? If the answer is "yes", where possible provide their name, address, telephone number, fax number and appropriate contact person, and an estimate of their current market shares.

8.7 In the opinion of the notifying parties are there undertakings (including those at present operating only in extra-Community or extra-EEA markets) that are likely to enter the market? If the answer is "yes", please explain why and identify such entrants by name, address, telephone number, fax number and appropriate contact person, and an estimate of the time within which such entry is likely to occur.

8.8 Describe the various factors influencing entry into affected markets that exist in the present case, examining entry from both a geographical and product viewpoint. In so doing, take account of the following where appropriate:

(a) the total costs of entry (R&D, establishing distribution systems, promotion, advertising, servicing, etc.) on a scale equivalent to a significant viable competitor, indicating the market share of such a competitor;

(b) any legal or regulatory barriers to entry, such as government authorization or standard setting in any form;

(c) any restrictions created by the existence of patents, know-how and other intellectual property rights in these markets and any restrictions created by licensing such rights;

(d) the extent to which each of the parties to the concentration are licensees or licensors of patents, know-how and other rights in the relevant markets;

(e) the importance of economies of scale for the production of products in the affected markets;

(f) access to sources of supply, such as availability of raw materials.

Research and development

8.9 Give an account of the importance of research and development in the ability of a firm operating on the relevant market(s) to compete in the long-term. Explain the nature of the research and development in affected markets carried out by the undertakings to the concentration.

In so doing, take account of the following, where appropriate:

(a) the research and development intensities[1] for these markets and the relevant research and development intensities for the parties to the concentration;

(b) the course of technological development for these markets over an appropriate time period (including developments in products and/or services, production processes, distribution systems, etc.);

(c) the major innovations that have been made in these markets and the undertakings responsible for these innovations;

(d) the cycle of innovation in these markets and where the parties are in this cycle of innovation.

Co-operative Agreements

8.10 To what extent do co-operative agreements (horizontal or vertical) exist in the affected markets?

8.11 Give details of the most important co-operative agreements engaged in by the parties to the concentration in the affected markets, such as research and development, licensing, joint production, specialization, distribution, long-term supply and exchange of information agreements.

Trade associations

8.12 With respect to the trade associations in the affected markets:

(a) identify those in which the parties to the concentration are members;

---

[1] Research and development intensity is defined as research and development expenditure as a proportion of turnover.

(b) identify the most important trade associations to which the customers and suppliers of the parties to the concentration belong.

Provide the name, address, telephone number, fax number and appropriate contact person of all trade associations listed above.

SECTION 9

General matters

Market data on conglomerate aspects

Where any of the parties to the concentration hold individually a market share of 25% or more for any product market in which there is no horizontal or vertical relationship as described above, provide the following information:

9.1 a description of each product market and explain why the products and/or services in these markets are included (and why others are excluded) by reasons of their characteristics, prices and their intended use;

9.2 an estimate of the value of the market and the market shares of each of the groups to which the parties belong for each product market identified in 9.1. for the last financial year:

(a) for the EEA territory as a whole;

(b) for the Community as a whole;

(c) for the territory of the EFTA States as a whole;

(d) individually for each Member State and EFTA State where the groups to which the parties belong do business;

(e) and where different, for the relevant geographic market.

Overview of the markets

9.3 Describe the world-wide context of the proposed concentration indicating the position of each of the parties to the concentration outside of the EEA territory in terms of size and competitive strength.

9.4 Describe how the proposed concentration is likely to affect the interests of intermediate and ultimate consumers and the development of technical and economic progress.

Ancillary restraints

9.5 Operations which have as their object or effect the co-ordination of the competitive behaviour of undertakings which remain independent fall, in principle, within Articles 85 and 86 of the Treaty of Rome. However, if the parties to the concentration, and/or other involved parties (including the seller and minority sharcholders), enter into ancillary restrictions directly related and necessary to the implementation of the concentration, these restrictions may be assessed in conjunction with the concentration itself (see in particular the 25th recital to Regulation (EEC) No 4064/89 and Commission notice on restrictions ancillary to concentrations.[1]

(a) Identify each ancillary restriction in the agreements provided with the notification for which you request an assessment in conjunction with the concentration; and

(b) explain why these are directly related and necessary to the implementation of the concentration.

Transfer of notification

9.6 In the event that the Commission finds that the operation notified does not constitute a concentration within the meaning of Article 3 of Regulation (EEC) No 4064/89 do you request that it be treated as an application for negative clearance from, or a notification to obtain an exemption from Article 85 of the Treaty of Rome?

SECTION 10

Declaration

Article 1 (2) of the Implementing Regulation states that where notifications are signed by representatives of undertakings, such

---

[1] OJ No C 203, 14. 8. 1990, p 5.

representatives shall produce written proof that they are authorized to act. Such written authorization must accompany the notification.

The notification must conclude with the following declaration which is to be signed by or on behalf of all the notifying parties.

The undersigned declare that, to the best of their knowledge and belief, the information given in this notification is true, correct, and complete, that complete copies of documents required by Form CO, have been supplied, and that all estimates are identified as such and are their best estimates of the underlying facts and that all the opinions expressed are sincere.

They are aware of the provisions of Article 14 (1)(b) of Regulation (EEC) No 4064/89.

Place and date:

Signatures:

―――――

Guidance notes on calculation of turnover for credit and other financial institutions, for insurance undertakings, for joint under-takings and for the application of the two-thirds rule can be found in the *Official Journal of the European Communities* 1994 L377 pages 22–27.

Form RTP (C)

Restrictive Trade Practices Act 1976

Certificate

---

to accompany documents for registration

IMPORTANT

If you do not submit the details of agreements to the Director General of Fair Trading within the time limits laid down by the Act the restrictions in them will become void. If you are in any doubt about timing you should consult your legal adviser **before** entering into an agreement which might be registrable under the Act.

Notes for guidance

1 The Registration of Restrictive Trading Agreements Regulations 1984 set out more fully how to give the details of agreements for registration.

2 All the parties to a registrable agreement are responsible for giving details of the agreement to the Office of Fair Trading. But it is enough if one of the parties - or someone on their behalf - does so. The person giving details must complete and sign the Certificate (opposite).

3 Two copies of all the documents which together make up the agreement should accompany the Certificate.

4 If the agreement is not in writing you should provide two copies of a memorandum setting out all the terms of the agreement. If part of the agreement is not in writing you should provide two copies of a memorandum setting out the unwritten terms of the agreement together with two copies of the written part of the agreement.

5 You should provide a list of names and addresses of all parties to the agreement. But there is an exception for agreements to which trade associations or service supply associations with more than 100 members are parties. In these cases you can omit names and addresses and list only the number or approximate number of members of the association.

6 Common form agreements are a series of almost identical agreements where one party remains the same. The only differences between the agreements are in the other parties and the dates on which the agreements were made. You need only provide full details of one agreement. For the rest you should provide memoranda giving the dates of other agreements as they are entered into and the names and addresses of the parties to them and stating that otherwise they are the same as the first agreement.

7 Where an agreement is altered or ended you should provide two copies of the document altering or ending the agreement. If the agreement is not altered or ended in writing, you should provide two copies of a memorandum setting out the changes.

8 Please list all the documents provided, including memoranda, on the back of the Certificate.

9 One copy of each document provided, including any memorandum, should be signed by the person who signs the Certificate.

10 When you have completed and signed the Certificate please detach it and send it with your documents to:

Office of Fair Trading
(RTP Registration)
Field House
Bream's Buildings
London EC4 1PR

Form RTP (C)

Restrictive Trade
Practices Act 1976

Certificate

I certify that to the best of my knowledge the documents I enclose with this form give:

tick box(es)

★ All the terms of an agreement subject to registration under the Restrictive Trade Practices Act 1976

★ Full details of the changes to the agreement(s)

Office of Fair Trading reference(s):

_____

★ full details of the ending of the agreement(s)

Office of Fair Trading reference(s):

_____

**The documents are listed on the other side of this form.
I have signed one copy of each document and/or memorandum.**

Signed

_____

Name in BLOCK CAPITALS

_____

on behalf of

_____

_____

_____

_____

(a party to the above agreement)

Status and address of person signing

_____

_____

_____

_____

Dated

Please turn over

List of documents and/or memoranda

Please enclose **two** copies of each document and/or memorandum, **one** of which should be signed.

OFFICE OF FAIR TRADING

Annex to Form RTP(C)

Registrable agreements

For an agreement to be registrable, at least *two* persons who are parties need to be in business in the UK and at least *two* persons need to accept relevant restrictions (see sections 6 and 11 of the Act) or to be subject to information provisions (section 7 of the Act and SI 1969/1842). Reference in the rest of this form to restrictions should be read as including a reference to information provisions.

Sale and purchase and share subscription agreements

If you are submitting a sale and purchase or share subscription agreement, you should refer to statutory instrument numbers 1081 (Goods) and 1082 (Services) of 1989 which exempt many of these agreements from registration.

Time limits

Details of any registrable agreement must be provided before the restrictions in it take effect and, in any case, within three months of the making of the agreement. You can make sure that details of any agreement are provided in time by inserting a clause to provide that any registrable restrictions it contains do not come into effect until the day after it has been received by the Office. The details of an agreement incorporating such a clause must, however, still be provided within three months of the day it was made.

Fail-safe furnishing

If you provide details on a fail-safe basis you should set out your reasons for doubting whether the agreement is registrable.

Duty of the Director General of Fair Trading

The Director General has a duty to refer registered agreements to the Restrictive Practices Court. However, if he decides that the restrictions contained in the agreement are not of such significance as to warrant reference to the court, he can ask the Secretary of State for Trade and Industry to discharge him from his duty (Section 21(2) of the Act).

In order to help us decide whether your agreement is registrable and, if so, whether the agreement will need to be referred to the Restrictive Practices Court would you please provide us with the answers to the questions overleaf. Your answers will also help us to process your agreement much more quickly.

Questionnaire

If the Annex has insufficient space for your answers please use a continuation sheet.

European Community

1 Has specific exemption from Article 85 of the EEC Treaty been sought or received or is the agreement covered by a block exemption? If so please give details.

_____

The agreement

2 Please give a brief description of the arrangement (nature, purpose, date(s) and duration) – fuller details are asked for below.

_____

_____

The parties

3 Please tell us about the parties to the agreement.

Name of each party	Main business of each party	Is the party an individual, (i) partnership (p) or body corporate (c)?	If the party is a body corporate the names of any group to which it belongs
_____	_____	_____	_____
_____	_____	_____	_____
_____	_____	_____	_____
_____	_____	_____	_____
_____	_____	_____	_____
_____	_____	_____	_____

Restrictions

4 In your opinion, what are the relevant restrictions in the agreement and which persons accept them?

Nature of restrictions	Persons accepting the restriction	Clause in agreement containing the restriction
_____	_____	_____
_____	_____	_____

_____   _____   _____
_____   _____   _____
_____   _____   _____
_____   _____   _____

Turnover

5 What is the most recently available total annual turnover in the UK of
each of the parties to the agreement? If any party is a member of a group, the
turnover given should be the turnover of the group.

Names of parties	Annual UK turnover in the goods or service affected	Annual UK turnover in business activities as a whole
_____	£ _____	£ _____
_____	£ _____	£ _____
_____	£ _____	£ _____
_____	£ _____	£ _____
_____	£ _____	£ _____
_____	£ _____	£ _____

The market

6 Please explain the nature of the goods or services affected by the agreement. (Include the 1992
Standard Industrial Classification (SIC) code if possible).

_____

7 Please give a description of the structure of the market for the goods or services concerned, covering
the following points:

• The geographical extent of the market _____

• The main competitors to the parties to the agreement in the relevant market (including any importers)
and their market share

_____

_____

_____

_____

- The total turnover of the market _____

- Ease (or otherwise) of entry for new competitors

_____

_____

- Substitute products for the goods or services affected

_____

- Any other points describing the structure of market

_____

_____

Market share

8 What are the market shares of each of the parties to the agreement in the goods or services affected? If any party is part of a group, the market share should be the market share of the group.

Names of parties   **Market Share (within the
                                                         UK or relevant part of it)
                                                         of the parties in the
                                                         goods or services affected**

_____   _____ %

_____   _____ %

_____   _____ %

_____   _____ %

_____   _____ %

_____   _____ %

Significance

9 Could you please comment on the purpose of the restrictions? If, in your view, the restrictions should not be regarded as having a significant effect on competition please say why (bearing in mind, among any other factors, the answers you have given to questions 5, 6, 7 and 8).

_____

_____

_____

RESTRICTIVE TRADE PRACTICES ACT 1976
REQUEST FOR "FAST TRACK" REGISTRATION PROCEDURE

1.   In accordance with the principles of the Code for Enforcement Agencies the Office of Fair Trading has undertaken within two months of the date of their furnishing an agreement which meets the criteria detailed below to inform the parties:

- Whether, in the Office's view, the agreement is registrable or not; and

- That a representation has been made to the Secretary of State under section 21(2); or

- That the Director General will refrain from taking proceedings before the court under section 21(1)(s); or

- That the Director General has in mind to refer the agreement to the court.

The criteria

2.   The criteria are:

(a)   The aggregate turnover of the parties to the agreement in their business activities as a whole is less than £5m or the market share of the parties in the goods or services subject of the agreement is less than 5 per cent; or

The agreement has specific exemption from Article 85 of the EEC Treaty or is covered by a block exemption (excluding opposition procedure cases) and a copy of any specific exemption is attached;

and

(b)   The agreement contains no price fixing restrictions or information provisions on the prices of goods; and

(c)   The parties have made no application to the Secretary of State for all or part of the agreement to be placed on the special section of the register under section 23(3); and

(d)   The parties consider the agreement to be registrable and are not furnishing it on a fail-safe basis; and

(e)   An annex to form RTP(C) has been completed; and

(f)   The declaration below has been made.

Declaration

3.   I request "fast track" procedure and declare that the criteria detailed at paragraph 2 above are met.

_____ (Signature)   _____ Date

Name   _____

Address   _____

          _____

Footnote: The Office may not be able to keep to the fast track procedure if it is necessary to refer back to the parties on any question of the registrability of the agreement.
C:\WPDATA\F\R-FT-TG.FMP

OFFICE OF FAIR TRADING

MERGER NOTICE

Office of Fair Trading
Mergers Secretariat
Room F406
Field House
15-25 Breams Buildings
London, England EC4A 1PR

Telephone No: 0171 269 8918/8917/8915
      Fax No: 0171 269 8916
    Telex No: 269009 OFTRIN G

Ref No:
(Office use only)

Note: Use this Merger Notice only for notifying the Director General of *proposed* mergers which will *not* be completed before expiry of the consideration period. Do not use it for notifying *completed* mergers or for submitting requests for *confidential guidance.* If you need any help or further information contact the Mergers Secretariat at the above address.

The Guidance Notes form part of the Notice. Read them in full before answering any of the questions.

Please complete Parts One and Three of the notice in typescript or block letters. Give your answers to Part Two in typescript on separate sheets.

Part One - General Information

See *Guidance Note 1.1*   1 Who is the *authorised person* giving this Notice?

                              Name:

                              Position:

                              Company/firm:

                                                                          Yes   No
                                                                          ☐   ☐
See *Guidance Note 1.2*   2 Have you authorised any representative to act on
                                your behalf?

                              Name:

                              Position:

                              Company/firm:

See *Guidance Note 1.3*   3 To which person and address should the Director General send any correspondence?

Name:

UK Address:

Postcode:

Telephone No:

Telex No:

Fax No:

See *Guidance Note 1.4*   4 *Briefly* describe the merger proposal being notified.

See *Guidance Note 1.5*   5 Briefly describe the steps taken to *publicise* the proposal.

Now go to Part Two

Part Two - Merger Details

Now give a full description of the merger proposal, on separate sheets, by replying to the following questions. Some of the questions are complex, and they may not all be relevant in every case. If in doubt, seek legal advice.

The Merger Situation
See *Guidance Note 2.1*

1 Give details of the proposed arrangements by which the main enterprises *will* cease to be distinct ('the merging enterprises'). Include share acquisitions, changes of directorships etc, and any factors upon which completion of the merger is conditional.

2 Give details of the ownership and control of the merging enterprises:

(a) before the merger; and
(b) following the merger.

3 What other enterprises *may* cease to be distinct as a result of the notified arrangements? Give details of the proposed change in shareholdings or in other relationships by which they might cease to be distinct.

Financial Information
See *Guidance Note 2.2*

4 Supply, for each of the merging enterprises, two copies of the latest *annual report and accounts.*

If annual reports are not available, give, for each of the merging enterprises, the most recent annual figures for: total turnover (excluding VAT); profit before tax; and worldwide gross assets.

See *Guidance Note 2.3*

5 What is the *book value of the worldwide gross and net assets* to be acquired?

Where you believe the *net replacement cost of net assets* to be significantly different from their book value, give your best estimate of the difference.

6 What is the *value* of the *consideration* being offered? What *form* will it take?

See *Guidance Note 2.4*

7 If the proposed merger is to be financed by borrowing, consider the effect on the *gearing* of the merged company. If this is significant, provide a pro-forma balance sheet and estimate the interest cover of the new group in the year following the merger.

Timing
See *Guidance Note 2.5*

8 What is the expected *timescale* for:

(a) *exchange of contracts;* and
(b) *completion* of the merger?

City Code On Takeovers
And Mergers
See *Guidance Note 2.6*

9 If the offer is subject to the City Code on Takeovers and Mergers, please supply two copies of the *Offer Document* and *Listing Particulars*. If these are not yet available, provide copies of the latest drafts and supply the final versions as soon as they are issued.

10 What is the *effective closing date* likely to be?

11 Has the offer been *recommended* by the Board of the target company?

Plans and Motives

12 What are the *reasons* for the merger and the *plans* for the merged businesses?

What *benefits* are expected to arise?

Comment on any other aspects of the merger which may affect the *public* interest, rather than the private interests of shareholders and other parties.

Include in your reply details of any significant effects on employment and any changes in the locations in which the merged businesses will operate.

Markets
See *Guidance Note 2.7*

13 *Briefly* describe the *main products and services* supplied by each of the main enterprises. Give an estimate of market share for any product or service of any description where any of the merging businesses has a market share in the UK, by value or volume, of 25 per cent or more.

Horizontal Links

See *Guidance Note 2.8*

14 Where the merger will *create or increase a market share* for the merged businesses of *10 per cent or more*, by value or volume, in any product or service of any description, in the UK as a whole, *or in any regional market*, give the following information. Refer to industry data where available. Use the most recent figures available and specify the period they cover:

(a) *a brief description of each product or service market*, including the extent to which it is served at regional or national level. Use SIC codes where appropriate, and refer to any independent sources of information (eg MINTEL, trade publications, independent commissioned research etc);

(b) an *estimate* of the merged companies' *market share;*

(c) an *estimate* of the *value and volume* of the UK market as a whole (ie UK output less exports, plus imports);

(d) an *estimate* of the *value and volume of imports and exports* for the UK market as a whole;

(e) an *estimate* of the *value and volume of UK sales* in this market for each business;

(f) the names and market shares of your *competitors* (including overseas companies/importers) with over five per cent of the market;

(g) the names of your five largest UK *customers;*

(h) a brief description, in terms of characteristics/price differences, of any product(s) or service(s) which might be considered close *substitutes;*

(i) an estimate of the *capital expenditure* required to *enter the market* on a scale necessary to gain a five per cent market share, both as a new entrant, and as a company which already has the necessary technology and expertise (eg a company located overseas);

(j) an estimate of the scale of *annual expenditure on advertising/promotion* relative to sales required to enter the market on a scale equivalent to your main competitor(s);

(k) an indication of any other factors affecting *market entry* , eg planning restraints, technology or R&D requirements, availability of raw materials, length of contract;

(l) an assessment of the extent to which *imports* provide actual competition in the UK market, and the extent of potential competition from imports. (Cover factors such as transport costs, tariffs, quotas, standards, government regulations etc);

(m) an assessment of the ease of *exit* from the market. Indicate any trends in both market entry and exit over the past five years;

See *Guidance Note 2.9*   (n) an assessment of any effects the merger may have at *local* level. Describe the nature of local competition and give details of any localities where competition may be reduced as a result of the merger;

(o) a brief assessment of *any other features of the market* that the Director General should take into account in considering the effect of the merger.

Combined Purchases

15 Identify any product(s) (including raw materials) or service(s) for which the *combined purchases* of the merged businesses will account for more than 10 per cent of the total UK sales of that product or service.

Vertical Links

See *Guidance Note 2.10* 16 Give details of the nature and extent of any *vertical links* between the merging businesses.

Guidance Notes to Merger Notice

Guidance Note 1.1
Only an *authorised person* can give a Merger Notice. An authorised person is defined by Regulations as any person carrying on an enterprise to which the notified arrangements relate.

Guidance Note 1.2
An authorised person can appoint a representative, eg a firm of solicitors, to complete the Notice on his behalf and to act for him in further correspondence with the Director General. If you do authorise someone to act in this way you must sign the authorisation at Part Three of the Notice.

You can withdraw or change the authorisation at any time but if you do so you must give immediate notice to the Director General in writing.

Guidance Note 1.3
You must give a full address to which the Director General can send all correspondence. If you have appointed a representative and wish correspondence to be sent to him, give his address here. Otherwise give details of the person within your company who will deal with correspondence, and the address to which the Director General should write.

Wherever possible, give a UK address and a fax number and ensure that the Office can make contact between 9.00am and 5.00pm on weekdays. If your address changes, you must notify the Director General immediately in writing.

Guidance Note 1.4
Part Two of the Notice seeks a full description of the proposed merger. Give a short description here on the following lines:

> *AB Holdings Limited announced on 3 June that it was to acquire the whole of the assets and business of CD Co plc (which is a wholly owned subsidiary of XY Group plc) by share issue, for a consideration of £25 million. The overlap of products/services is in business computers and office equipment.*

If there are any changes in the circumstances of the merger after you have submitted the Notice, tell the Director General immediately.

Guidance Note 1.5
Use this Notice only to notify the Director General of proposals which have already been made *public*. You are asked to enclose a copy of any press release or report, (including those in specialist or trade journals) and details of any notifications to listing authorities, eg the Stock Exchange. The Director General will consider whether any further publicity is needed. If you have already issued a press release, he may decide that no action is required. In other cases he may issue a statement on the lines that: 'the proposed acquisition by A of B was notified to the Director General of Fair Trading on [x date]. The period for considering the merger will end on [y date]'.

The Merger Situation

Guidance Note 2.1
Questions 1-3 will enable the Office to identify each of the merger situations which may arise from the single transaction being notified. This is important because if the period for considering the Notice expires without the notified merger being referred to the Monopolies and Mergers Commission (MMC), there are restrictions on the Secretary of State referring any of the qualifying merger situations which might arise from completion of the notified merger. (This does not affect the Secretary of State's powers to make a reference where material information was withheld or where the information given was false or misleading.)

The Fair Trading Act definition of a merger situation requires two or more enterprises to 'cease to be distinct'.

Section 63(2) of the Fair Trading Act defines an *enterprise* as the 'activities or part of the activities of a business'.

Under section 65(1) enterprises can *cease to be distinct* in two ways:

two or more enterprises are brought under common ownership or control; or

there is an arrangement or transaction whereby one or more enterprises ceases to be carried on in order to prevent competition between those enterprises.

Sections 65(3) and (4) of the Fair Trading Act define the three ways in which enterprises can be brought under common control:

where A acquires the ability *materially to influence* the policy of B;

where A acquires the ability to *control* the policy of B;

where A acquires a *controlling interest* in B.

The concepts of material influence and control are not defined according to objective criteria such as percentage shareholdings. In the case of a minority shareholding, the Office will consider other factors which will affect the degree of influence the holding confers, eg the balance of other shareholdings, board representation or any special provisions in the Articles, including restrictions on voting rights.

For the purposes of deciding whether enterprises have been brought under common ownership or control, section 77 of the Fair Trading Act provides that associated persons and any bodies corporate which any of them control should be treated as a single person. This means, for instance, that separate acquisitions by relations, or by persons or companies acting together to acquire control of an undertaking, may be aggregated and treated as a single holding.

There are thus several sets of circumstances in which enterprises can cease to be distinct and which may give rise to a qualifying merger situation. There will usually be little doubt that the main parties to a merger situation *will* cease to be distinct. However, the merger situation being notified *may* give rise to a number of other changes in shareholdings or relationships by which other enterprises *may* cease to be distinct. If in any doubt, disclose details of all such changes. The Secretary of State has discretion to make a reference where it appears to him that it is or *may be* the fact that arrangements are in progress or contemplation which will result in the creation of a qualifying merger situation. It is thus for him to determine whether a merger situation may arise.

The most common merger situation is where one company (A) takes over another company (B). In those circumstances A and B will cease to be distinct from each other and any subsidiaries of A will cease to be distinct from subsidiaries of B.

A or B may also own minority shareholdings in other companies which may or may not be associates for accounting purposes. B may, for example, own 25 per cent of the voting shares in X. This may give A the ability materially to influence the policy of X and its subsidiaries, which will cease to be distinct from the enterprises carried on by A.

A minority shareholding may lead to enterprises ceasing to be distinct by a less direct route. For example, if B owns 25 per cent of X, which owns 25 per cent of Y, the acquisition by A of B will mean that enterprises carried on by A may cease to be distinct from those carried on by Y. Another

example is where another company (M) has a minority holding in A. The acquisition by A of B may mean that M and B cease to be distinct as do M and subsidiaries of B.

Acquisitions of shareholdings by individuals or partnerships may also lead to enterprises ceasing to be distinct. In particular, an individual (I) may own a large shareholding in A. If I acquires a significant holding in X this may lead to X ceasing to be distinct from A.

Finally, relationships other than shareholdings may give rise to qualifying mergers. If A depends on N for the supply of certain goods or finance, this could mean that N may be able materially to influence the policy of A and thus of B.

Financial Information

Guidance Note 2.2
The Office will usually need only the *report and accounts* of the main parties to the merger. However, where the acquiring company is part of a larger group, the Office will normally also need the group report and accounts. It will not need them where the target is a subsidiary or associate company and separate accounts are prepared for that company.

If no annual report or accounts are available, provide separate figures (audited if possible) on turnover, profits and assets. On *turnover*, the Office needs details of sales before VAT and duty. On *profits*, it requires details of operating profit before tax and interest.

If a merger gives rise to a significant increase in market share, the Office may subsequently wish to review profits, sales and capital employed in the relevant market. Ensure that this information is available, or could be estimated if required, for both the acquiring and target company.

Guidance Note 2.3
Asset values are determined in accordance with section 67 of the Fair Trading Act. The *gross* book value of a company's worldwide assets is calculated by adding together the tangible and intangible fixed assets, investments and current assets. Deductions are made for provisions for depreciation, renewals or diminution in value. The figures in the latest published accounts will normally suffice, except where there have since been substantial changes.

The *book* value of net assets is the gross value less any liabilities and provisions taken over. When considering the difference between book value and net replacement cost, give your best estimates, using market values for property and any other assets for which market prices can be estimated.

Guidance Note 2.4
The Secretary of State does not normally regard
gearing on its own as a ground for reference.
However, he may consider a reference where a high
degree of gearing, combined with other features of
the bid, may pose a threat to the public interest.
What is considered a high degree of gearing
depends on the circumstances. These include the
target's existing level of gearing; the speed with
which the acquiror plans to reduce the gearing; the
volatility of future cash flows; and the current levels
of gearing of competing companies and companies
generally. It is unlikely that a capital gearing ratio of
less than 150 per cent would be considered high.
The capital gearing ratio is defined as the ratio of
borrowing, including overdrafts, and net of cash on
deposit, to the total of share capital, reserves and
minority interests, less goodwill.

Timing

Guidance Note 2.5
Section 75C (1) (b) of the Fair Trading Act provides
that if *any* of the enterprises to which the Notice
relates cease to be distinct from each other at any
time during the consideration period, the pre-notified
merger could remain liable for reference to the MMC
for six months from the date of its completion. You
should bear this in mind when considering the timing
of completion of a merger or submission of a Notice.

City Code on Takeovers and Mergers

Guidance Note 2.6
To allow for submission of a Notice before the
posting of an offer, you can supply the *Offer
Document and Listing Particulars* in draft form. The
consideration period will run from submission of the
drafts, although the Office will still need copies of the
final versions as soon as these are published.

The Office does not envisage that the
pre-notification timetable will raise significant
difficulties in relation to the *timing of public offers.*
You should however bear in mind the need to
reconcile submission of the Notice with the
requirements of the City Code on Takeovers and
Mergers. If you are seeking a decision by the first
closing date of an offer, the Director General will
need to receive the Notice before the posting of the
Offer Document. This will enable the Secretary of
State to reach a decision by the first closing date.
The Secretary of State cannot be bound by the first
closing date however, and where he is not in a
position to reach a decision by then, the Director
General will need to extend the consideration period.

Markets

Guidance Note 2.7
Even where there is little or no overlap at horizontal
level, the Office will wish to know whether the
merging businesses have high market shares in any
product or service. These could, for example, allow
the merged company to tie-in sales, or to exclude its
competitors' products.

In answering questions 13 and 14, bear in mind that
some products and services are capable of different
descriptions. They can be defined narrowly (gin) or
widely (spirits). If you are in doubt about the product
or service description, use that which gives rise to
the highest market share (or, in reply to question 14,
the highest *combined* market share). If any of the
merging businesses supply the market at distinct
levels, for example wholesale and retail, these must
be treated as separate markets.

Guidance Note 2.8
In considering the effect of a merger on competition,
the Office will primarily be interested in those
markets where the merged businesses overlap. This
will be the case even where the merger does not
meet the so-called 'market share test'. (This is met
where, as a result of the merger, the merged
businesses will account for at least one quarter of
the supply or consumption of products or services of
a particular description in the UK as a whole, or in a
substantial part of it.)

The 10 per cent threshold is not a statutory barrier.
The aim of question 14 is to provide the Office with
information on any market where the merger may
affect competition. Not all the information sought will
be relevant to every area of overlap. If, for example,
the merger will add only one per cent to A's existing
share of nine per cent or more of a market where
there are three larger competitors, the Office is
unlikely to need all the details sought in question 14.

A merger may only give rise to a minimal increment
to market share at national level, but to a substantial
increase at regional level. The Office will want
details of any regional overlaps, where the overlap is
significantly greater than the overlap at national level
and/or the market is primarily served at regional
level. A region may encompass parts of, or the
whole of, more than one county, eg the South West
or the Anglia region. In some instances it may be the
area served by one of the regional television
franchises. Possible examples of regional markets
are the wholesale distribution, bus services and
brewing (beer) industries.

Guidance Note 2.9
Even where a market is mainly supplied at national
or regional level, competition may take place
primarily at *local* level. There is no statutory

definition of a local market. The Office will want to discover whether the merger will reduce the choice for consumers in the area within which they would normally purchase the products or services being supplied. In its report on the acquisition by Grand Metropolitan plc of the William Hill Organisation Ltd (Cmnd 776) the MMC found that competition in the betting industry was limited to a quarter mile radius of a particular betting office. In other industries the local market may be larger.

Guidance Note 2.10

The Office may be interested in *vertical links* between the merging enterprises even where there is no, or little, overlap at horizontal level. For example, where a *supplier* company (A) takes over one of its *customers* (B), the Office may need to investigate whether A will be in a position after the merger to require B to make all its purchases from within the group. In these circumstances, competing suppliers might find themselves excluded from part of their actual or potential market.

Part Three - Declaration

Guidance Note 3.1

The Declaration *must* be signed by the authorised person. It draws your attention to two important provisions of the Fair Trading Act. The first relates to the *provision of false or misleading information.* New section 93B of the Fair Trading Act introduces an offence of intentionally or recklessly giving false or misleading information. In relation to pre-notification, it is an offence:

+ knowingly or recklessly to give false or misleading information to the Director General, either in response to the Notice, or in reply to any additional questions raised by the Director General during the consideration period; or

+ knowingly or recklessly to furnish false or misleading information to a third party, for example your authorised representative or legal adviser, in the knowledge that they will then supply it to the Director General.

The *penalties* for breach of this provision are severe: a fine of up to the current maximum of £2,000, or a maximum of two years imprisonment, or both.

The Director General also has powers to reject the Notice, at any time before the period for considering it expires, where he *suspects* that any *information* given in the Notice, or in response to further enquiries, is *false or misleading.* The effect of rejection is that the proposal which has been notified will remain liable for reference to the MMC for a period of six months after the date of its completion.

Secondly, the Declaration reminds you that the Director General will publicise the existence of the merger proposal as notified. He may also draw it to the attention of third parties in order to seek their views (Guidance Note 1.5). The Director General will not of course reveal any commercially confidential information supplied in response to the Notice. His aim is solely to ensure that those with an interest in the merger are given an opportunity to comment.

Guidance Note 3.2

The Declaration also confirms the authorisation of any representative named in reply to question 1.2. If you are authorising a representative to act on behalf of a *company* the Declaration must be signed by a director or other officer of that company.

Office of Fair Trading

August 1994

Part Three - Declaration

Declaration

Please return Parts One and Three of the Notice, with your answers to Part Two, to:

Office of Fair Trading
Mergers Secretariat
Room F406
Field House
15-25 Breams Buildings
LONDON EC4A 1PR

The Director General will not accept a Merger Notice unless the Declaration has been signed by the authorised person. (See *Guidance Notes 3.1 and 3.2*).

I understand that:

✦ It is a criminal offence for a person to supply information in a Merger Notice which he knows to be false or misleading in any material respect.

✦ The Director General may reject any Merger Notice if he suspects that it contains information which is false or misleading in any material respect.

✦ The Director General may bring the existence of the merger proposal described in this Notice, and the fact that the Notice has been given, to the attention of interested parties.

Signed:

Name: *(Block Letters)*

Position: *(Block Letters)*

Date:

I confirm that the person named in reply to question 1.2 (if any) is authorised to act on my behalf for the purposes of this Notice.

Signed:

Have you attached *(as appropriate):-*

☐ Press Release

☐ Two copies of the latest Annual Report and Accounts

☐ Pro-forma balance sheet

☐ Two copies of the Offer Document and Listing Particulars

INDEX